THREE VARIATIONS ON

Jenny, Natalie & Misty's
Favorite Classic Quilt Blocks

by MISSOURI STAR QUILT CO.

EXECUTIVE EDITOR
Natalie Earnheart

CREATIVE TEAM
Jenny Doan, Natalie Earnheart, Misty Doan, Christine Ricks, Gunnar Forstrom, Mike Brunner, Lauren Dorton, Jennifer Dowling, Dustin Weant, Jessica Toye, Kimberly Forman, Denise Lane

EDITOR & COPYWRITER
Nichole Spravzoff

SEWIST TEAM
Jenny Doan, Natalie Earnheart, Misty Doan, Courtenay Hughes, Carol Henderson, Janice Richardson, Aislinn Earnheart, Cathleen Tripp

ADDITIONAL PHOTOGRAPY
Derek Israelsen Studio, Salt Lake City, UT
Story School, Kansas City, MO

PRINTING COORDINATOR
Rob Stoebener

PRINTING SERVICES
Walsworth Print Group
803 South Missouri
Marceline, MO 64658

CONTACT US
Missouri Star Quilt Company
114 N Davis
Hamilton, MO 64644
888-571-1122
info@missouriquiltco.com

TRIPLE PLAY: Three Variations on Jenny, Natalie and Misty's Favorite Classic Quilt Blocks ©2021. All Rights Reserved by Missouri Star Quilt Company. Reproduction in whole or in part in any language without written permission from Missouri Star Quilt Company or TRIPLE PLAY: Three Variations on Jenny, Natalie and Misty's Favorite Classic Quilt Blocks is prohibited. No one may copy, reprint, or distribute any of the patterns or materials in this book for commercial use without written permission of Missouri Star Quilt Company. Anything you make using our patterns or ideas, it's yours!

8	What's a Triple Play?
10	Quilting Guide
14	Precuts

WONKY STAR TRIPLE PLAY

20	Cottage Stars
26	Evening Stars
32	Luminary

38	**Jenny Doan:** Enjoying the Journey One Stitch at a Time

DRUNKARD'S PATH TRIPLE PLAY

50	Tropical Paradise
56	River Path
62	Morning Glory

TULIP FIELDS TRIPLE PLAY

Tulip Time — **72**

Tulip Fields — **78**

Tulip Garden — **84**

Home Run: Mini Tulip Crossbody Bag — **90**

Natalie Earnheart: Finding Inspiration in Unlikely Places — **94**

FLYING GEESE TRIPLE PLAY

Every Which Way But Goose — **104**

West Wind — **110**

Gaggle of Geese — **116**

Home Run: Finished is Better Than Perfect — **122**

HALF-HEXAGON TRIPLE PLAY

130 Half-Hexagon Boats and Braids

136 Half-Hexi Links

142 Half-Hexi Whirligigs

148 Home Run: Half-Hexi Denim Apron

DOUBLE SQUARE STARS TRIPLE PLAY

156 Double Square Star Four-Patch

162 Double Square Star Table Runner

168 Sashed Double Square Star

174 **Misty Doan:** Imperfection is Beautiful

OHIO STAR TRIPLE PLAY

Ohio Star Celebration Table Runner **184**

Blue Ribbon Ohio Star **190**

Ohio Starlight Mini **196**

3D PINWHEELS TRIPLE PLAY

Pinwheel Toss **206**

Pinwheel Patch **212**

Pinwheel Dance **218**

Home Run: 3D Pinwheel Market Tote **224**

REFERENCE

Quilts and Projects **230**

Templates **235**

Construction Basics **238**

Inspiration–Times Three
TRIPLE THE WAYS TO EXPLORE YOUR CREATIVITY

This book contains the very best of our Triple Play tutorials and we hope you enjoy making these projects just as much as we did. In baseball, a triple play is a rare event where three outs take place during the same play, but we like to think of these tutorials more like three home runs! As Babe Ruth once said, "It's hard to beat a person who never gives up."

There's no way you can go wrong, no matter which pattern you tend to like the best—or maybe you can't decide and you want to try all three variations! Among this array of patterns you'll find pretty wall hangings, lovely table toppers, gorgeous quilts, and even a few new bonus projects like a cute tote, mini bag, and an apron.

The Triple Play tutorial gives us the opportunity to be inspired by each other. We would definitely say that we have great synergy when we work together! The result of our combined efforts is much greater than what we might create on our own. That's the beauty of Triple Play. We literally get to play, we find ourselves feeling more creative as we collaborate, and it's so interesting to see what unique quilts we all make from one traditional quilt block. From flying geese to drunkard's path blocks, we all use our imaginations to dream up new variations on tried and true designs.

Triple Play has quickly become one of our favorite tutorials to do because, first of all, we all get to collaborate. They say two heads is better than one, and three is even better! We agree that we bring out the best in each other and we have so much fun sewing together. Triple Play tutorials are different from our typical weekly quilting tutorials because they are literally three in one. Instead of releasing only one quilting project that week, we all take our cues from a well-known quilt block and we each make a different version of it in a brand new project—for a total of three projects in one tutorial. Those projects might include a full-sized quilt, but they also might be wall hangings, pillows, table runners, and much more. We don't feel constrained to quilts alone because individual blocks can be used in so many different ways! There's so much you can do with these fabulous quilt blocks; we have a feeling you'll find even more ways to explore your creativity.

Creating a Quilt

Making a quilt from start to finish is a wonderful creative journey. I like to savor each step, from measuring and cutting to quilting and binding. There are learning opportunities throughout and while it can be a challenge for a first-time quilter to see how it all comes together, I assure you, it's entirely doable. Here are a few tips to help you on your way as you stitch up your beautiful quilted creation. I can't wait to see what you make! Share your projects with us at **#msqcshowandtell** on social media.

Cutting Fabric

To get started, gather up your rotary cutter, ruler, and cutting mat. Remember your rotary cutter has a razor-sharp blade, so be careful and protect your fingers. Every time you're done cutting, make sure you close it up! And when the blade gets dull, change it right away so you can keep cutting smoothly.

Before you cut any fabric with a rotary cutter, put your cutting mat down to protect the table. It has a handy grid on it to help you line up your fabric as you cut. The ruler will help you as you cut your fabric. Line up your fabric with the ruler to get a nice straight line instead of using the grid on the cutting mat. Always cut away from yourself and keep your fingers far away from the blade using smooth, steady pressure.

Press to the Dark Side
As you press your seams, when possible, press to the dark side. That way your darker seams will not show through underneath lighter fabrics.

Sewing
Once you have your fabrics cut, it's a good idea to change out your needle before you begin sewing. Use an 80/12 size universal needle. It's good for medium weight fabrics like quilting cotton. Also make sure you're using quality thread; 50wt cotton thread is great for piecing. Be sure to change your needle after about 8 hours of sewing.

If your machine has a foot with a ¼" seam guide, attach it to your machine to help you keep a consistent seam allowance. If you don't have one, use a piece of tape or a seam guide to stay on track, but don't be obsessed with perfection. It's more important to have a consistent seam allowance than a perfect ¼" seam. It will all work out in the end.

Pressing Seams
As you sew blocks together, take care to keep your seams at a consistent ¼". Trim your blocks before you sew them together into rows. As you press your seam, when possible, press to the dark side. That way your darker seams will not show through lighter fabrics. As you create your rows of blocks, pay attention to which direction you are pressing the seams so that your seams will nest. Press one row of blocks one direction and then press the next row the opposite direction. As you sew the rows together, match up the seams, pin them, and then you'll find that they nest together neatly, creating less bulk.

When you're finished piecing your blocks together and it's time to add borders, please refer to the individual pattern for instructions to attach borders as placement may vary. Give your quilt top a good pressing with some starch or flattening spray. It's so much easier to work with a quilt top that isn't wonky and seams that lay nice and flat.

Backing
Once you've pieced your beautiful quilt top, it's time to choose your backing! Using 108" wide backing does make things easier, but if you are using standard 42" wide fabric, you may need to piece your fabric together to cover the entire back of your quilt.

Measure the length and width of your quilt top. Add an extra 8" to both the length and width of your quilt if it's going to be machine quilted. Trim off all selvages and use a ½" seam allowance when piecing the backing. Sew the pieces together along the longest edge. Press the seam allowance to the side. Use horizontal seams for smaller quilts (under 60" wide) and vertical seams for larger quilts. It's a good idea to choose a backing layout that best suits your quilt. Think about the direction of the pattern and pattern matching. If the print is directional, try to orient it so it makes sense with the front of your quilt.

As for quilting thread color, white, gray, or beige thread blends well with just about anything. Be sure to match your bobbin thread to your top thread. If you have any tension issues, using two different colored threads might result in a mess!

Binding

The last step in creating your quilt is binding. Call me crazy, but I savor this part. I could easily stitch my binding on with a machine, but I love hand tacking my binding while I watch one of my favorite shows on the couch. It's just so cozy. You can create your own binding or you can buy it, but I often make binding from a jelly roll as it's already 2½" and ready to go.

To make your binding, cut fabric straight across from edge to edge or width of the fabric. You can cut it on a 45° angle into 2½" strips to create bias binding, which is recommended for curved or scalloped quilt edges. Sew your binding strips together with diagonal seams using the plus sign method. Press your joined binding strips in half and you're ready to sew your binding onto your quilt.

Finishing your very own quilt can be a pleasure. Taking the time to enjoy each step makes it even better. Instead of rushing through, find joy in your journey to the finished product. I often speak of quick and easy, and while that's true for many patterns, quilting is still a creative process to be enjoyed. It really does make a difference to thoughtfully finish a quilt. It takes your project to the next level and helps your quilt last longer as the years go by. I hope these tips help you create even more beautiful quilts that will be treasured for a lifetime. Now, let's get quilting!

Using Precuts

Here at Missouri Star Quilt Company, we're all about making quilting and sewing easier and more accessible than ever before and precuts are the best thing since sliced bread! Precut fabrics are packages of fabric that are cut to size in advance. There's no need to cut fabrics for hours; they help you get right to the good part without all the fuss. Almost every single Missouri Star pattern is made to be used with precut fabrics so all you need to know is how many precuts to choose of each size and you're good to go!

Triple Play projects are handpicked especially for precuts, along with a few tips and tricks to make sewing them together fast and fun. When you begin quilting with precut fabrics, it really couldn't be any easier. Keep on reading and learn how to make the most of each type of featured precut.

10" PRECUT
LAYER CAKE

Layer cakes sound so delicious, don't they? These lovely stacks of fabric help big, beautiful quilts come together in a snap! Whenever we get our hands on one, they don't last long. We can't help but cut into them and get right to the good part—sewing! These fantastic 10" squares are perfect for quilters who are just starting out because of their versatility. You can do so much with a simple square. For example, you can make a quick set of eight half-square triangles with just two 10" squares. It's absolutely magical.

5" PRECUT
CHARM PACK

Prepare to be charmed! Charm packs are so cute and so easy to use. We like to keep them on hand for quick projects. Gather up a whole bunch of them and before you know it, they're quickly used right up without a single regret. These wonderful stacks of 5" squares can be used as-is for easy patchwork quilts or you cut them up into neat little quilt blocks that couldn't be simpler to create. Some of our favorite 5" square quilts include Falling Charms, anything made with the Half-Hexi Template and sweet little Periwinkle blocks.

2½" PRECUT
JELLY ROLL

This is how we roll! Jelly rolls or 2½" strips are one of the most popular precuts out there for a reason. They look so cute all rolled up and they are incredibly useful. It's almost a shame to open them up for a project, but it's totally worth it. If you've ever spent a good amount of time trying to cut perfect strips, you know how valuable these rolls are! From log cabin quilts to sashing and binding, 2½" strips get the job done. You can even slice them up into mini charms and use them to snowball corners and add cornerstones. There are just so many uses for these simple strips!

Wonky Star

TRIPLE PLAY

Twinkle, twinkle, wonky star, you're our favorite block by far! These spunky little wonky stars are filled with personality and they're so much fun to piece. They have just the right amount of freedom, so you can stop scrutinizing measurements and sew to your heart's content. It's the perfect relaxing project that's sure to pull you out of a quilting rut. Because we all enjoy wonky stars so much, it was one of the first Triple Play tutorials we wanted to do. We each love them for different reasons and had fun ideas to share, so we decided to shoot for the stars!

When you make a wonky star, you get to play around a little with the cute star legs. That's where the wonky part comes in. How they turn out is all up to you; some star legs might be shorter, some longer, some wider, and some narrower. The overall effect of these unique star points is that they seem to twinkle just a bit. And we all interpreted the color of these stars differently as well. Some stars shine bright and nearly white against the night sky, while others radiate in a variety of colors. The fun thing about this block is that it's based around a square, so really any size square will work, from tiny 2½" squares to large 10" squares. You get to decide how big and bright you want your stars to be!

Cottage Stars
Jenny's Play

For this Triple Play tutorial, Jenny created quaint rows of houses featuring a line of wonky stars running right down the center, resulting in her Cottage Stars table runner. This sweet table runner features miniature houses accented with twinkling wonky stars. It's the perfect tiny neighborhood on your kitchen table.

materials

QUILT SIZE
36" x 17"

HOUSE BLOCK SIZE
4½" x 6" unfinished,
4" x 5½" finished

WONKY STAR BLOCK SIZE
6½" unfinished, 6" finished

QUILT TOP
1 package 5" print squares
½ yard background fabric

BINDING
¼ yard

BACKING
¾ yard

SAMPLE PROJECT
Seasons by Jason Yenter for In the Beginning Fabrics

1 sort & cut

Select (18) 5" print squares to use for the houses. Cut a 1½" strip across the width of a square. Subcut (1) 1½" x 4½" rectangle for the top of a house. Trim the remainder of the fabric left from the square to measure 3" x 5", then subcut into (2) 2" x 3" rectangles. Keep the 3 rectangles together. Repeat to cut the additional 17 selected 5" print squares.

Select (6) 5" print squares to use for the doors of the houses. Cut a 3" strip across the width of each 5" square. Subcut the strip into (3) 1½" x 3" rectangles. A **total of 18** door rectangles are needed.

Select (9) 5" print squares to use for the roofs of the houses. Cut each square in half to yield 2 rectangles. Trim each rectangle to measure 2½" x 4½".

Select (8) 5" print squares to use for the wonky stars and set the remaining square aside for another project. Cut each 5" square in half vertically and horizontally to yield (4) 2½" squares. **A total of (30)** 2½" squares are needed for the wonky stars.

From the background fabric, cut (6) 2½" strips across the width of the fabric—subcut each strip into 2½" squares. Each full strip will yield 16 squares and a **total of 84** are needed.

2 make tiny houses

Mark a diagonal line on the reverse side of (36) 2½" background squares. **2A**

Select a set of 3 matching rectangles, 1 door rectangle, 1 roof rectangle, and 2 background squares. Be sure the rectangles you select are cut from different fabrics for the house, the door, and the roof. Sew the (2) 2" x 3" rectangles to either side of the 1½" x 3" door rectangle. Press the seam allowances away from the door rectangle. **2B**

Sew the 1½" x 4½" rectangle to the top of the unit. Press the seam towards the top and set this house unit aside for the moment. **2C**

Lay a marked background square on the left side of the roof rectangle with right sides facing as shown. Sew on the marked line. Trim away the excess fabric ¼" from the sewn seam. Open and press towards the corner. **2D**

Lay the other marked background square on the right side of the roof rectangle with right sides facing as shown. Sew on the marked line and trim away the excess fabric ¼" from the sewn seam. Open and press towards the corner to complete the roof unit. **2E**

Pick up the house unit you set aside earlier. Sew it to the bottom of the roof unit you just made. Press the seam towards the bottom to complete the block. **Make 18** blocks. **2F**

Block Size: 4½" x 6" unfinished, 4" x 5½" finished

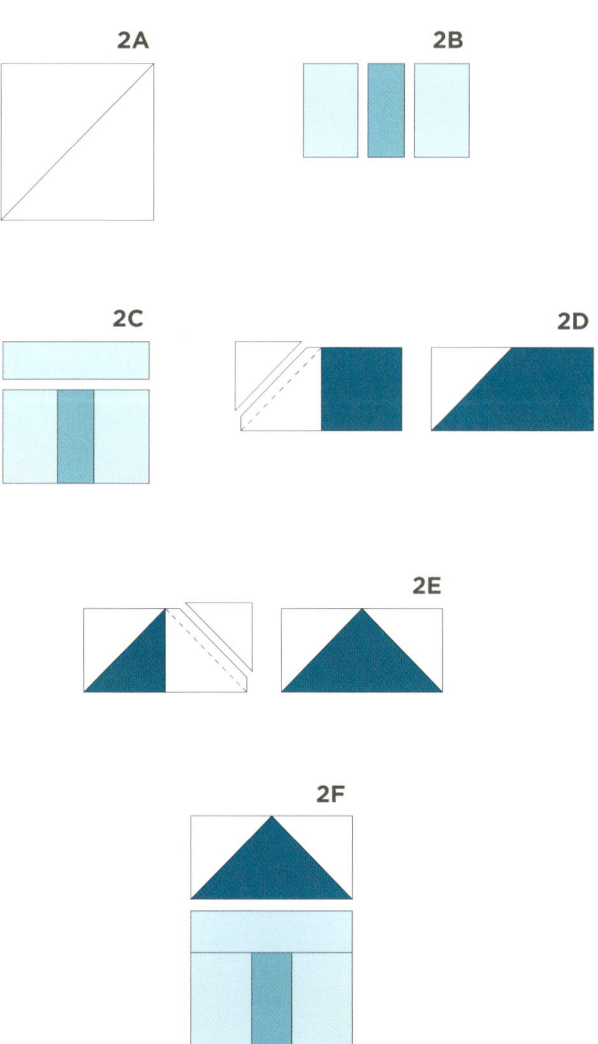

3 make wonky stars

Select (6) 2½" print squares to use in the center of the stars and (24) 2½" background squares and set them aside for the moment. Use the remaining 2½" print squares and 2½" background squares to make the star legs.

Place a 2½" print square on an angle (any angle) atop a 2½" background square with right sides facing. Make sure your print square is placed a little past the halfway point. Sew ¼" in from the angled edge of the print square. **3A**

Press the piece flat to set the seam, then press the print piece over the seam allowance. **3B**

Turn the unit over and use the background square as a guide to trim the print fabric so that all of the edges are even. Save the trimmed scrap to use for another leg of the star. (You should be able to make at least 2 star legs from each print square.) **3C**

Turn the unit back over so that the right side of the fabric is facing up. Fold the print fabric of the star leg back to reveal the seam allowance and trim the excess background fabric ¼" away from the sewn seam. Fold the star leg back so the right side of the fabric is facing up and press. **3D**

Place another print square or a trimmed print scrap on the adjacent side of the square. Make sure the edge of the second print piece crosses over the first star leg by at least ¼". Stitch ¼" in from the edge of the print piece. **3E**

Press the print piece over the seam allowance. Turn the unit over and use the background square as a guide to trim the print fabric so all of the edges are even. Notice your square is still 2½". **3F**

Turn the unit back over so that the right side of the fabric is facing up. Fold the print fabric of the star leg back to reveal the seam allowance and trim the excess fabric ¼" away from the sewn seam. **3G**

Fold the star leg back so the right side of the fabric is facing up and press. **Make 24** star leg squares. **3H**

Note: Have fun with this and don't try to make all of the star legs alike!

1. Sew a door rectangle between a pair of matching 2" x 3" rectangles. Press the seams outward. Sew the matching 1½" x 4½" rectangle to the top of the unit and press the seam upwards to create a house unit.

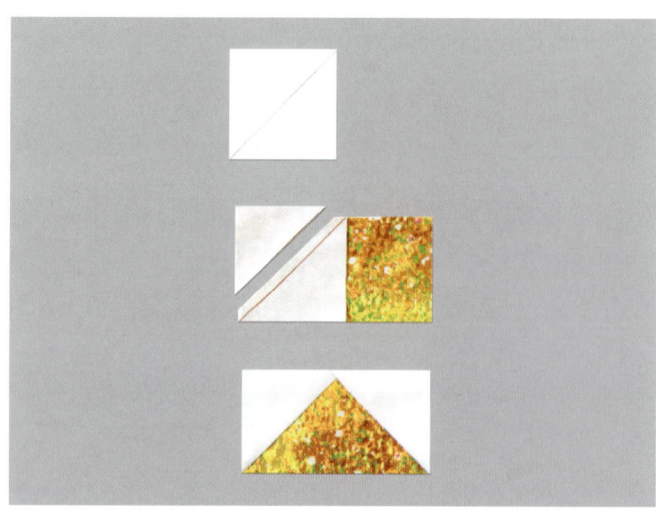

2. Mark a diagonal line on the reverse side of a background square. Place the square on the left corner of a roof rectangle and sew along the marked line. Trim away the excess fabric and press towards the corner. Repeat to snowball the other side of the rectangle to make a roof unit.

3. Sew the roof unit to the top of the house unit. Press the seam towards the bottom to complete the block.

4. Place a 2½" print square on top of a 2½" background square at an angle with right sides facing. The print square should cross over the center of the bottom edge of the background square. Fold the print square over the seam and press.

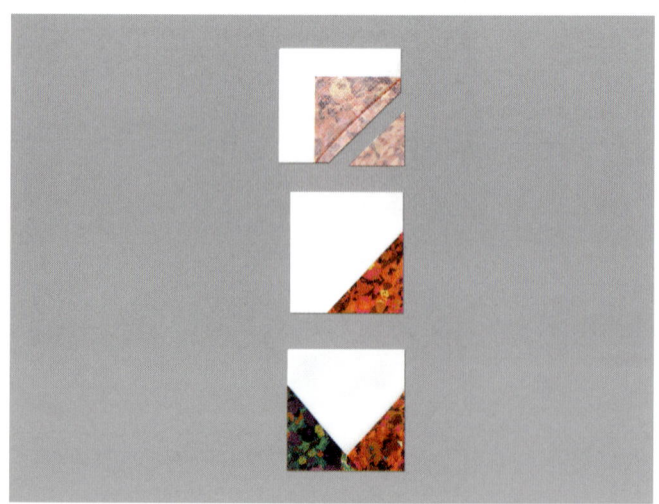

5. Turn the piece over and use the background square as a guide to trim the excess print fabric away. Fold the print fabric back and trim ¼" away from the seam. Add another star leg just like before using another print square.

6. Arrange 4 star leg squares, 4 background squares, and 1 print square in 3 rows of 3 units as shown and sew together in rows. Press the seams of the top and bottom row towards the background squares. Press the seams of the middle row towards the print square.

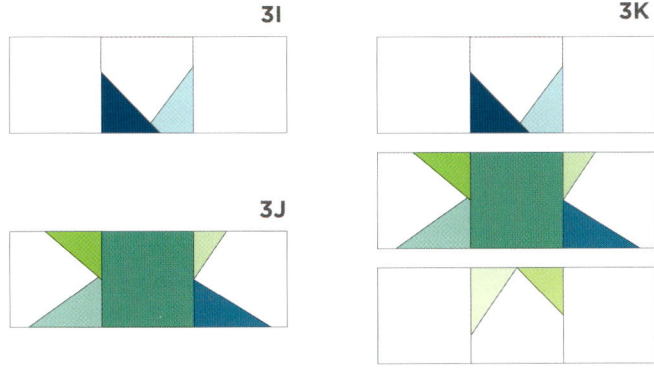

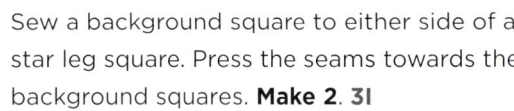

Sew a background square to either side of a star leg square. Press the seams towards the background squares. **Make 2**. **3I**

Sew a star leg square to either side of each print square you set aside earlier. Make sure the star legs point away from the center square. Press the seams toward the center square. **3J**

Nest the seams and sew the rows together to complete the block. **Make 6** blocks. **3K**

Block Size: 6½" unfinished, 6" finished

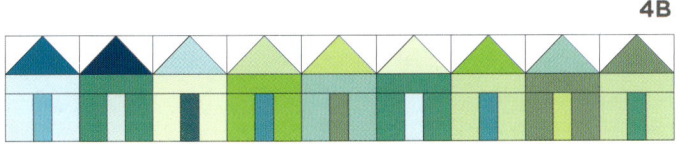

4 arrange & sew

Arrange the 6 wonky star blocks into a row. Sew the blocks together and press the seams to 1 side. **4A**

Select 9 tiny house blocks and arrange them into a single row. Sew the blocks together and press the seams towards the right. Make a second row, but press the seams of this row towards the left. **4B**

Arrange the 3 rows together as shown in the diagram on your left. Be sure to make note of the orientation of the tiny house blocks. Nest the seams and sew the rows together. Press to complete the table runner top.

5 quilt & bind

Layer the table runner top with batting and backing, then quilt. See Construction Basics (pg. 238) to finish your project.

Evening Stars
Natalie's Play

Natalie tried something new and played around with the layout of the wonky stars in her Evening Star quilt. By offsetting the stars and allowing the star legs to intersect at key points, it really gave the design added interest. These lovely evening stars shine brightly in cool hues of blue and violet. Start stitching on a dark night and get ready to see stars!

materials

QUILT SIZE
54" x 58½"

QUILT TOP
1 package 10" print squares
2 packages 5" background squares
½ yard background fabric

BORDER
1 yard

BINDING
½ yard

BACKING
3½ yards - horizontal seam(s)

SAMPLE QUILT
Violet Twilight by Kanvas Studio for Benartex

1 sort & cut

Sort the 10" print squares into 15 pairs of matching prints and set the remaining 10" squares aside for another project.

From your chosen 10" print squares, cut 1 square from each pair in half vertically and horizontally to create 4 matching 5" print squares. Cut each of the remaining 10" print squares in half vertically creating (2) 5" x 10" rectangles. Set 1 rectangle of each print aside for another project. Cut the remaining rectangles in half, creating (2) 5" squares from each. Keep 1 print square in a set with the previous matching 4 print squares and set the remaining 5" print squares aside for another project. You should have 15 sets of 5 matching 5" print squares.

From the background fabric, cut (2) 5" strips across the width of the fabric. Subcut 1 strip into (8) 5" squares. From the second strip, cut (3) 5" squares and set the rest of the strip aside for another project. Add these 11 squares to your 2 packages of background squares for a **total of 95** background squares.

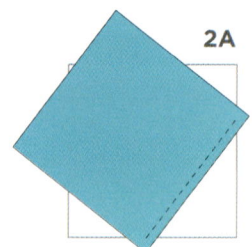

2A

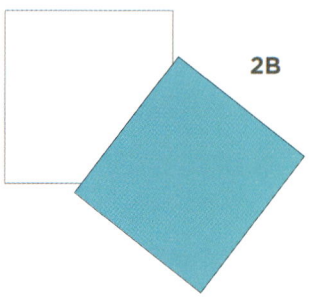

2B

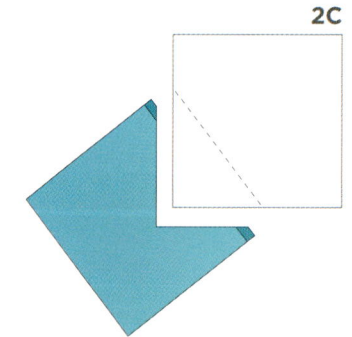

2C

2 make star legs

Select 1 set of print squares and 4 background squares. Choose 1 of the print squares from the set to use in the center of the star and lay it aside for the moment. Use the remaining print squares and background squares to make the star legs.

Place a print square on an angle (any angle) atop a background square with right sides facing. Make sure your print square is placed a little past the halfway point. Sew ¼" in from the angled edge of the print square. **2A**

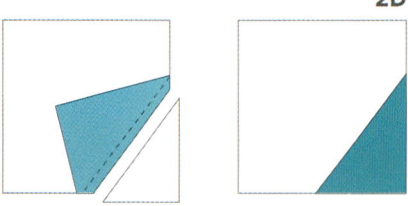

2D

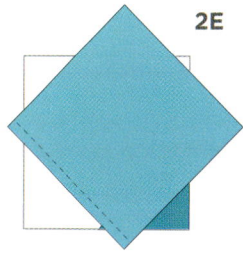

Press the piece flat to set the seam, then press the print piece over the seam allowance. **2B**

Turn the unit over and use the background square as a guide to trim the print fabric so that all of the edges are even. Save the trimmed scrap to use for another leg of the star. (You should be able to make at least 2 star legs from each print square.) **2C**

Turn the unit over so that the right side of the fabric is facing up. Fold the print fabric of the star leg back to reveal the seam allowance and trim the excess background fabric ¼" away from the sewn seam. Fold the star leg back so the right side of the fabric is facing up and press. **2D**

Place another print square or a trimmed print scrap on the adjacent side of the square. Make sure the edge of the second print piece crosses over the first star leg by at least ¼". Stitch ¼" in from the edge of the print piece. **2E**

Press the print piece over the seam allowance. Turn the unit over and use the background square as a guide to trim the print fabric so all of the edges are even. Notice your square is still 5". **2F**

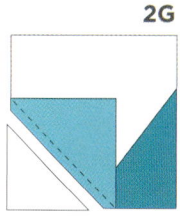

Turn the unit over so that the right side of the fabric is facing up. Fold the print fabric of the star leg back to reveal the seam allowance and trim the excess fabric ¼" away from the sewn seam. **2G**

Fold the star leg back so the right side of the fabric is facing up and press. **Make 60** star leg units. Have fun with this and don't try to make all of the star legs alike! Keep matching sets of 4 star leg units and 1 print square for the center together. The remaining (35) 5" background squares will be used in the quilt center. **2H**

1. Sew a 5" print square on an angle atop a 4½" background square with right sides facing. Press the print piece over the seam allowance.

2. Use the background square as a guide to trim the print fabric so that all of the edges are even.

3. Repeat using the trimmed print scrap to add another star leg to the adjacent side.

4. Repeat to trim the print piece even with the background square edges. Make 80 star leg squares.

3 arrange & sew

Referring to the diagram on your left, lay out your background squares, print squares, and matching sets of star legs in **11 rows of 10** each, being sure to arrange each of the star leg units around the matching 5" print squares. Sew the units together in rows. Press the rows in opposite directions. Nest the seams and sew the rows together. Press.

4 border

Cut (6) 5" strips across the width of the fabric. Sew the strips together to make 1 long strip. Trim the borders from this strip. Refer to Borders (pg. 238) in the Construction Basics to measure, cut, and attach the borders. The lengths are approximately 50" for the sides and 54" for the top and bottom.

5 quilt & bind

Layer the quilt with batting and backing, then quilt. See Construction Basics (pg. 238) to finish your quilt.

Luminary
Misty's Play

Misty's Luminary quilt takes wonky stars and adds a fun four-patch center along with sashing to give the design a nice scrappy, homemade feel. Put together a truly luminescent version of this quilt in a cheerful palette to let the pattern shine through. The result will leave you starstruck!

materials

QUILT SIZE
58" x 72"

BLOCK SIZE
12½" unfinished, 12" finished

QUILT TOP
3 packages 5" print squares
 - includes cornerstones
3¾ yards background fabric
 - includes sashing

BINDING
¾ yard

BACKING
3¾ yards - horizontal seam(s)

SAMPLE QUILT
Kaffe Fassett 2021 Cool Collection by Kaffe Fassett for FreeSpirit Fabrics

1 sort & cut

From the background fabric, cut (18) 4½" strips across the width of the fabric. Subcut (9) 4½" squares from each strip for a **total of (160)** 4½" background squares. Set the background squares aside for now.

Select (80) 5" print squares and set them aside for the star legs.

Select (8) 5" print squares and cut each in half vertically and horizontally to create (4) 2½" squares from each. Set 30 of these 2½" print squares aside for your cornerstones.

2 make 4-patches

Select (20) 5" print squares for your 4-patch star centers. Set the rest of the 5" print squares aside for another project.

Layer a 5" print square atop a differing 5" print square right sides together. Sew down the 2 sides of the square with a ¼" seam allowance. **2A**

Cut the sewn squares in half vertically. **2B**

Open to reveal 2 strip units. Repeat pairing, sewing, and cutting the remaining 5" print squares you selected. Press the seam allowances of each strip unit toward the darker fabric. **2C**

Select 2 differing strip units. With seams running horizontally and right sides together, layer 1 unit on top of the other. Sew down 2 sides of the strip units. **2D**

Cut the sewn strip units in half vertically. **2E**

Open to reveal (2) 4-patch units. Press. **Make 20. 2F**

Set the 4-patches aside for the moment.

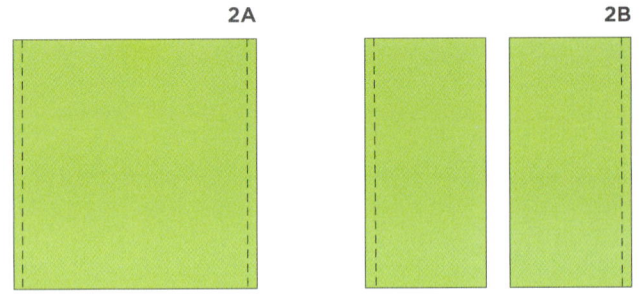

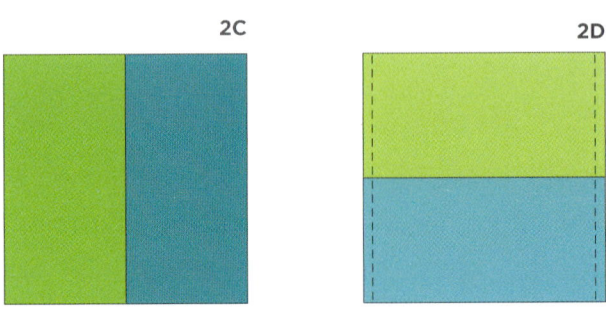

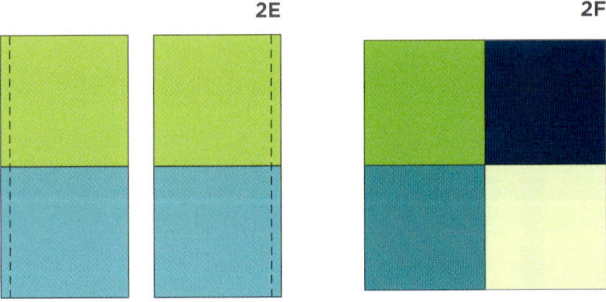

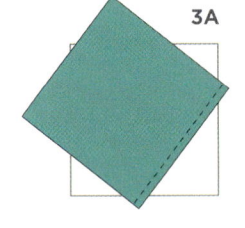

3 make star legs

Place a 5" print square on an angle (any angle) atop a 4½" background square with right sides facing. Make sure your print square is placed a little past the halfway point. Sew ¼" in from the angled edge of the print square. **3A**

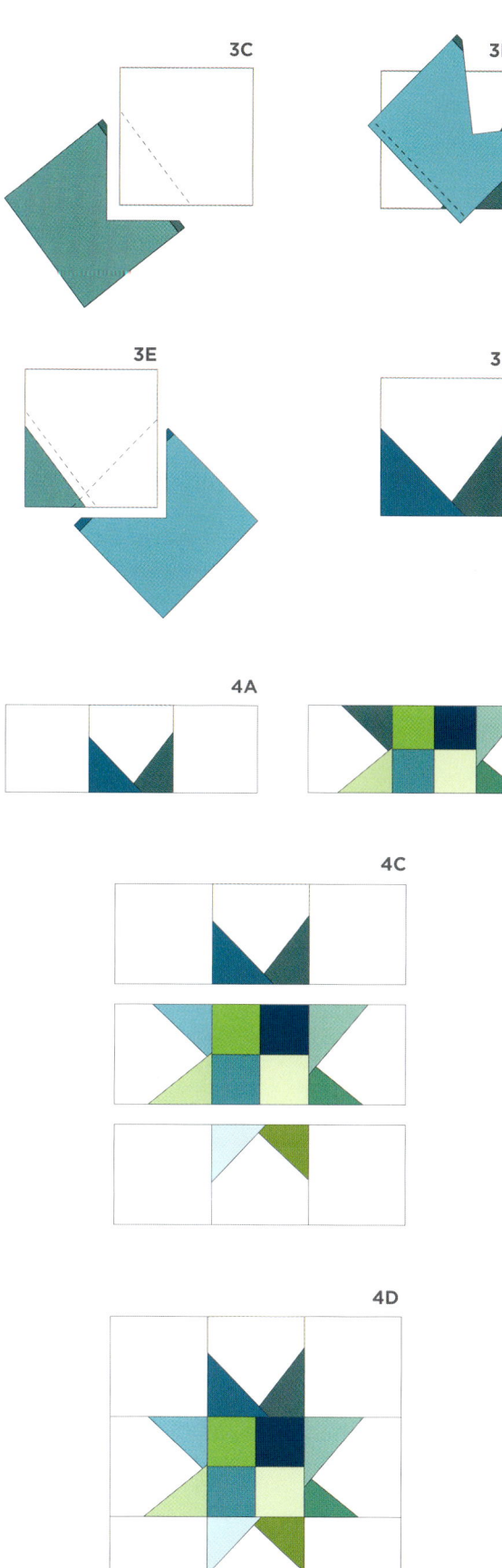

Press the piece flat to set the seam, then press the print piece over the seam allowance. **3B**

Turn the unit over and use the background square as a guide to trim the print fabric so that all of the edges are even. Save the trimmed scrap to use for another star leg. (You should be able to make at least 2 star legs from each print square.) **3C**

Place the trimmed print scrap on the adjacent side of the square. Make sure the edge of the print piece crosses over the first star leg by at least ¼". Stitch ¼" in from the edge of the print piece. **3D**

Press the print piece over the seam allowance. Turn the unit over and use the background square as a guide to trim the print fabric so all of the edges are even. Notice your square is still 4½". **3E**

Fold the star leg back so the right side of the fabric is facing up and press. **Make 80** star leg squares. **Tip:** Have fun with this and don't try to make all of the star legs alike! **3F**

Note: Turn the unit back over so that the right side of the fabric is facing up. Fold the print fabric of the star leg back to reveal the seam allowance and trim the excess background fabric ¼" away from the sewn seam. Fold the star leg back so the right side of the fabric is facing up and press.

4 block construction

Sew a background square to either side of a star leg square. Press the seams towards the background squares. **Make 2. 4A**

Sew a star leg square to either side of a 4-patch you set aside earlier, making sure the star legs point away from the 4-patch. Press the seams toward the 4-patch. **4B**

Lay out the star units in 3 rows as shown. **4C**

Nest the seams and sew the rows together to complete the block. **Make 20. 4D**

Block Size: 12½" unfinished, 12" finished

35

1. Sew down 2 opposite sides of 2 layered 5" print squares. Cut the sewn squares in half vertically and open to reveal 2 strip units. Press toward the darker fabric.

2. With seams running horizontally and right sides together, layer 1 strip unit on top of a differing strip unit. Sew down 2 opposite sides. Cut the sewn strip units in half vertically. Open to reveal (2) 4-patch units. Press. Make 20.

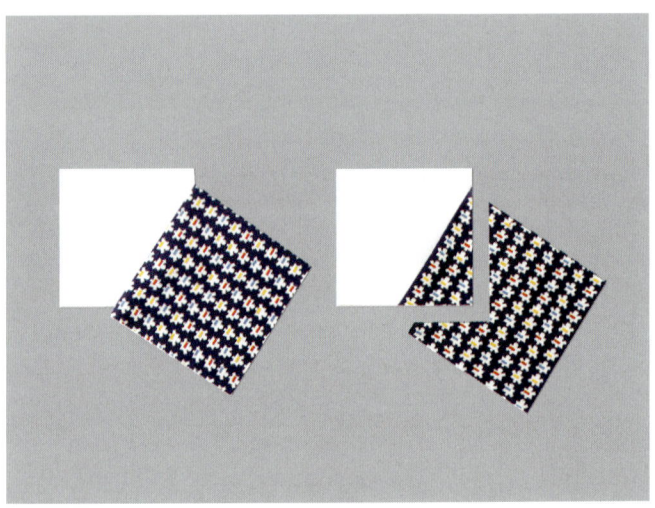 

3. Sew a 5" print square on an angle atop a 4½" background square with right sides facing. Press the print piece over the seam allowance. Use the background square as a guide to trim the print fabric so that all of the edges are even.

4. Repeat using the trimmed print scrap to add another star leg to the adjacent edge. Make 80 star leg squares.

5. Sew the squares in 3 rows as shown. Match the seams and sew the rows together to complete the block. Make 20.

5A

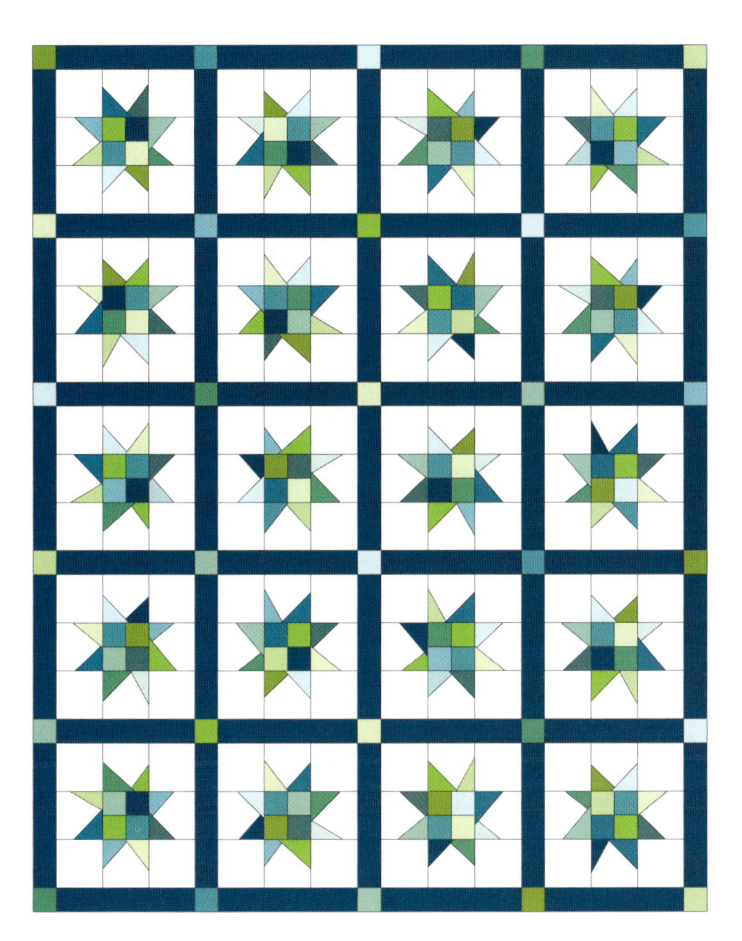

5 make horizontal sashing strips

From the background fabric, cut (17) 2½" strips across the width of the fabric. Subcut (3) 2½" x 12½" sashing rectangles from each strip. A **total of (49)** 2½" x 12½" sashing rectangles are needed.

Sew a 2½" print square to the end of (4) 2½" x 12½" rectangles. Sew another 2½" print square to the opposite end of 1 of the units. Sew all the units together to form a row, making sure to alternate between squares and rectangles. Press all of the seams toward the rectangles. **Make 6. 5A**

6 arrange & sew

Lay out the blocks in **5 rows** with each row being made up of **4 blocks**. As you make each row, sew a 2½" x 12½" sashing rectangle between each block and to the beginning and end of the row. Press toward the sashing rectangles. Sew the rows together adding a horizontal sashing strip between each row. Sew a horizontal sashing strip to the top and bottom of the quilt center. Refer to the diagram to your left, if necessary.

7 quilt & bind

Layer the quilt with batting and backing, then quilt. See Construction Basics (pg. 238) for binding instructions.

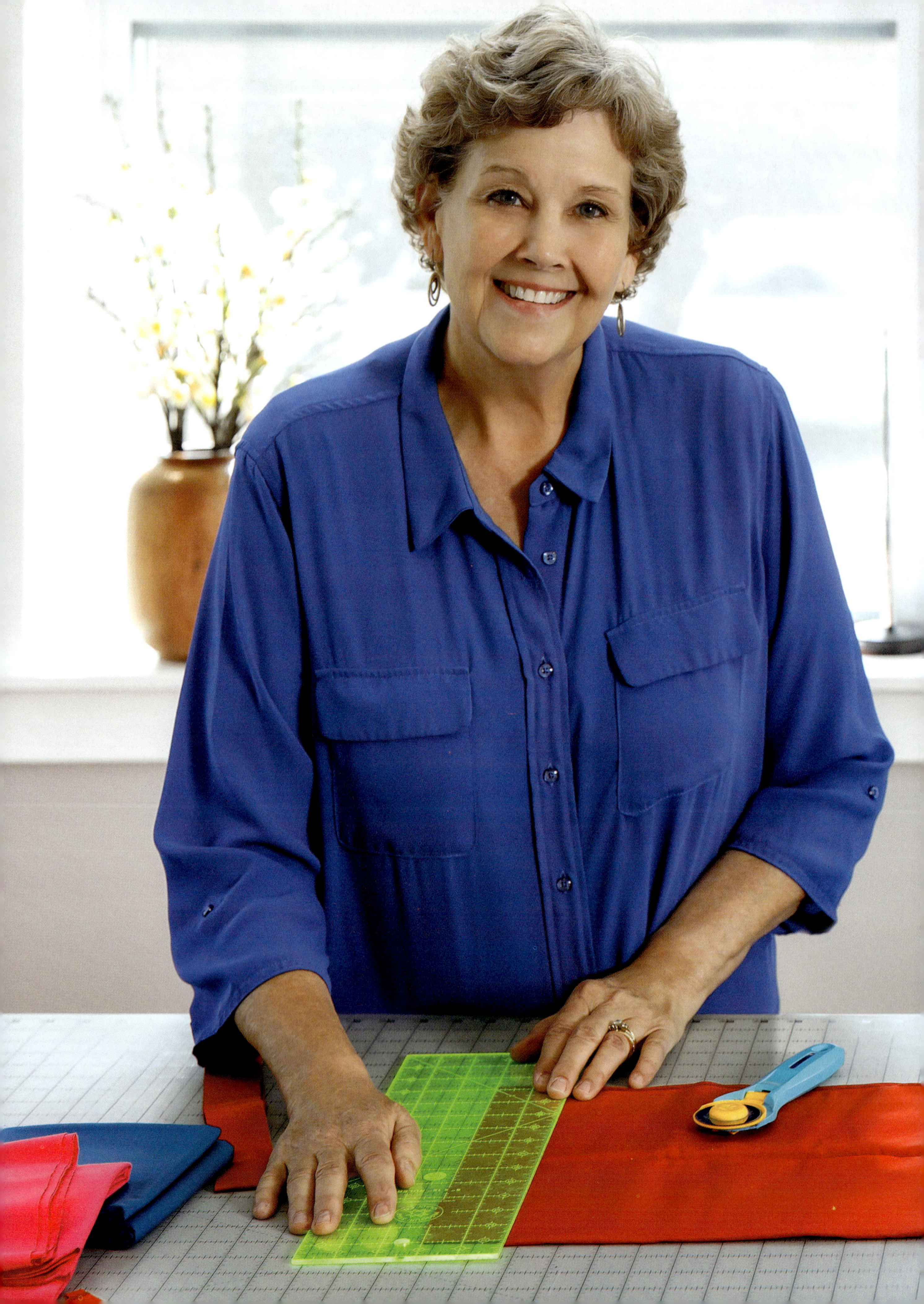

Jenny Doan

Enjoying the Journey, One Stitch at a Time

Jenny Doan doesn't need much of an introduction nowadays, but before she was one of the most popular quilting teachers online, she first began sewing quilts when she moved to Missouri. As a sewist and a costumer for the theater, she enjoyed making clothing for her family, but soon found her way to quilting and has been hooked ever since. At first, she says, "I didn't think quilting was something I could do." But after she took a log cabin quilting class at the Vo-tech school in nearby Chillicothe, she was captivated. She continues, "I knew about quilting, but I was a clothing sewer. Quilting seemed too hard. When we came to Hamilton, somebody suggested that I take a quilting class. I was really curious about the whole process, so I actually called the teacher and talked to her about it. We were making a log cabin, and the idea of choosing seven lights and seven darks that would all go together was so overwhelming to me that she even took me shopping." Everyone starts somewhere and after completing her first log cabin quilts, Jenny realized that she enjoyed discovering the endless possibilities for new quilt patterns.

> "All my creativity is trial and error. I try it and if it works, it works. And if it doesn't, it doesn't."

When asked what she loves the most about quilting she says, "My favorite thing about quilting is when you make a block and you see that secondary design. It's the creative part. It's the 'ooh aah' factor, when you put those blocks together and something new appears! It's totally unexpected. You're expecting to make the block. You're expecting to finish the quilt, but when you slide those two blocks together or you turn them, and something new appears, that's my favorite part. It's that serendipitous moment."

One of Jenny's greatest strengths in quilting is finding those opportunities to create something out of nothing, as she likes to say. She says that creativity is "making something that hasn't been there before." All her life she has enjoyed the creative process. She explains, "When I was a young girl, if I could have chosen an occupation, it probably would have been a builder because I love creating something from nothing. You can be creative at dinnertime. Well, I have tomatoes, and onions, and macaroni, so what can we do?" We don't always get to choose the ingredients, but we can choose what we'll make out of them. Jenny has shown this in her life time and time again. She's become a master at finding ingenious solutions to challenges that come her way.

Creativity poses its own questions as we seek to find opportunities to express ourselves. How is it possible to stay creative on a deadline? What can we create within constraints? Despite the challenge of needing to be creative on demand, week after week, as she films her quilting tutorials, Jenny does her best to stay inspired and communicate her love of quilting to you. She says, "I want people to feel the creativity and the love I have for what

I'm making. And you have to feel it to actually do it." To maintain her creative energy, she has a daily practice that helps to keep her fresh. She says, "I do something for myself and it's fairly random. I have crumb blocks that I work on. And I have birds that I work on. And little houses that I work on. I can't make a mistake with those. I never make an ugly house. I never make an ugly crumb block." Being free to explore fabric combinations and sew without restrictions is key to keeping her creativity flowing.

Jenny is mindful about the time she spends quilting and works exclusively from her sewing studio. She explains, "I only work here at the studio now unless it's snowing and I make Ron go and get my machine for me. I'm very protective of my space. I have to feel safe and creative here. I can't let a lot of the business interfere with my creative process. It's not an option for me to not be creative." Setting a boundary between her personal and professional life has been important for her to remain present wherever she happens to be. But inspiration weaves its way throughout her life and she is always on the lookout for new quilt designs.

So, how does Jenny go about creating a new quilt design? How does she plan and make so many quilts? She says, "I get ideas all the time. I take pictures with my phone. I love perusing the *Encyclopedia of Pieced Quilt Patterns* by Barbara Brackman. Nobody's really inventing new shapes; all the shapes have been invented. Those books are really a wealth of information for me." But those familiar shapes are a jumping off point for Jenny to make quilting magic happen. She enjoys taking a well-known quilt block, cutting it up, and rearranging the pieces to see "what happens if." She says, "The only thing I've really done that nobody else has really done a lot of is cutting blocks up. All of my creativity is trial and error. I try it and if it works, it works. And if it doesn't, it doesn't. The creative process happens as I go along. I add and take away. I have a project at the end that makes sense to my brain."

> "My favorite thing about quilting is when you make a block and you see that secondary design ... when something new appears!"

We asked Jenny, what's the most unusual source of inspiration you've ever found? and she responded, "Floors! I was really surprised at how many carpets and how many floors have intricate patterns. I never saw them that way before until I was a quilter. I remember walking down the hall in a hotel, stopping in the middle of the hall, and taking a picture of the floor." Throughout her travels across the U.S. and around the world, you can bet that Jenny has her eye trained to seek out inspiration, from her hotel's carpet to the tile in the bathroom, it's all inspiration to a seasoned quilter. And it goes far beyond carpets. She says, "You really do see the world through different eyes once you start noticing." A typical walk through your neighborhood can reveal sources of untapped inspiration once you go looking for them. Jenny would tell you that inspiration is everywhere.

Tile inspiration taken on Jenny's cellphone

Jenny, Natalie, and Misty taking a pottery class

> "I have to create in a different area to get my creative flow going again. I paint watercolor. I have to forgive myself for being imperfect. I preach that in quilting; it's the same with painting."

But what if inspiration remains elusive? Jenny has a great solution for those moments when you lose your "sew-jo," as she puts it. She says, "I have to create in a different area to get my creative flow going again. I paint watercolor. I have to forgive myself for being imperfect. I preach that in quilting; it's the same with painting. It's just practice, you get better and better. If I'm outside, I'm walking. I try to see things differently. Maybe I'll do handwork. Maybe I'll pick up my knitting." Exploring other areas of her creativity helps her to feel rejuvenated. And if you're interested in branching out yourself, go check out two of our sister companies One Big Happy Yarn Co. and Let's Make Art. Jenny loves following along with LMA's weekly watercolor tutorials and learning more about knitting with One Big Happy.

The Triple Play tutorials are another great way for Jenny to explore new creative avenues, stitching up fresh ideas alongside her daughter, Natalie, and her daughter-in-law, Misty. Just working in the same studio as these two brilliant women helps her to feel inspired. Together, they are able to bounce ideas off of each other and make even more beautiful quilts than ever before. She says, "Natalie is one who is a wealth of information and I can build my ideas from there." They are always there to help each other. Out of all the Triple Play projects they've created together so far, Jenny says that, hands down, her favorite is the wonky stars. She explains, "The reason I love them is that it lets me be free in a safe environment. I have a square, I'm safe in that square. I can make that leg go anywhere I want it to. I feel free because it's not a have-to. I like the freedom. I like that every star is different." It's the perfect metaphor for how Jenny works. In any project, she's able to find her own creative wiggle room and make that quilt truly shine. Her ability to see possibilities is her trademark.

"I want people to feel the creativity and the love I have for what I'm making."

Jenny's first quilt.

If you're just starting out quilting, Jenny has some words of encouragement for you: "Just start and practice. It's a learned skill. And if you sew a little today, tomorrow you'll be better." Each block is just one small part of a quilt and it's important to focus on one block at a time to avoid feeling overwhelmed. She continues, "You're only sewing straight from here to here. It doesn't matter how hard that block looks, when you break it down it's just one seam at a time. This is your journey. Enjoy the journey, right where you begin. Because tomorrow you won't be in that place. You're going to be even better." We couldn't have said it any better than Jenny.

"Just start and practice. It's a learned skill. And if you sew a little today, tomorrow you will be better. It doesn't matter how hard that block looks, when you break it down it's just one seam at a time."

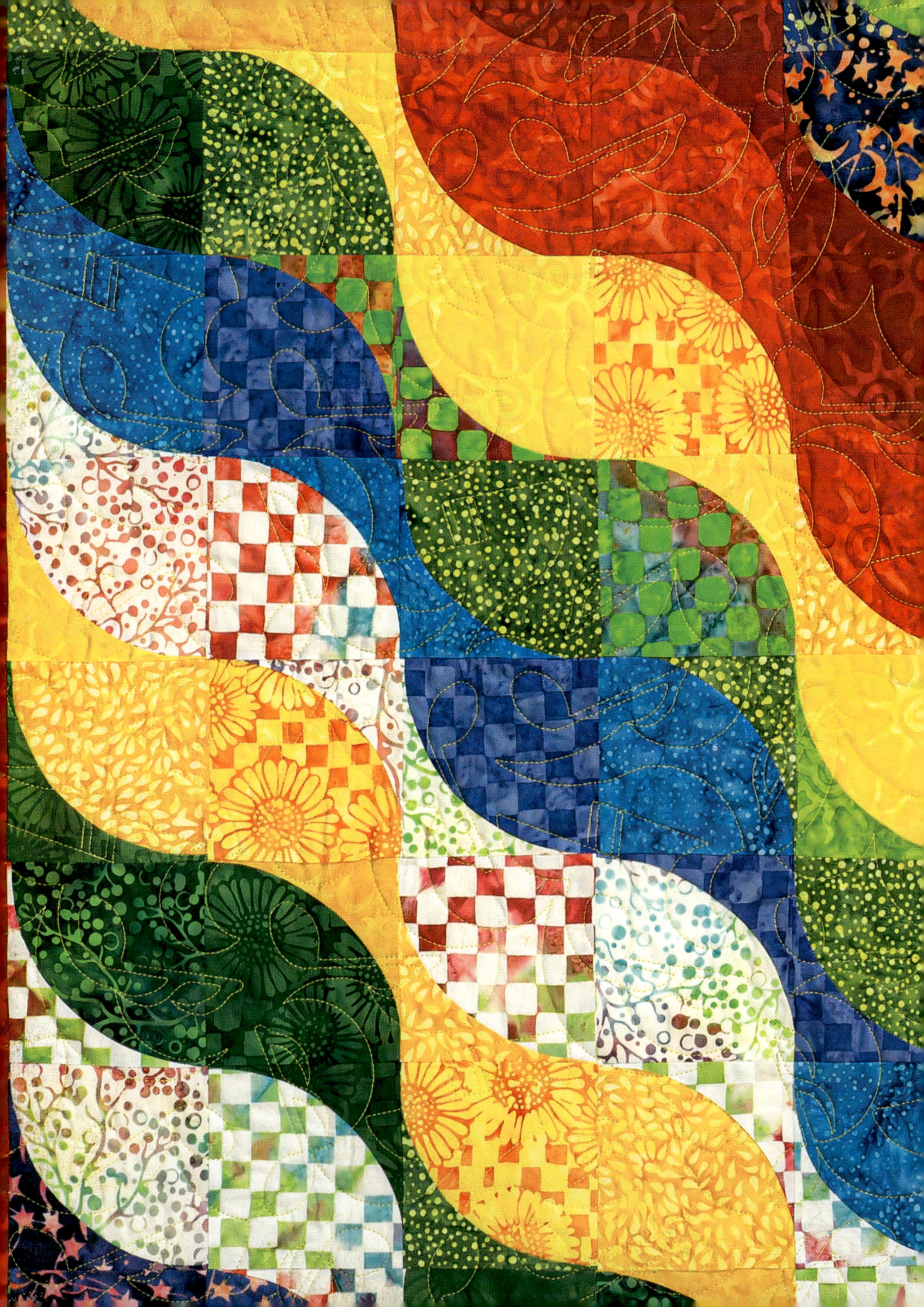

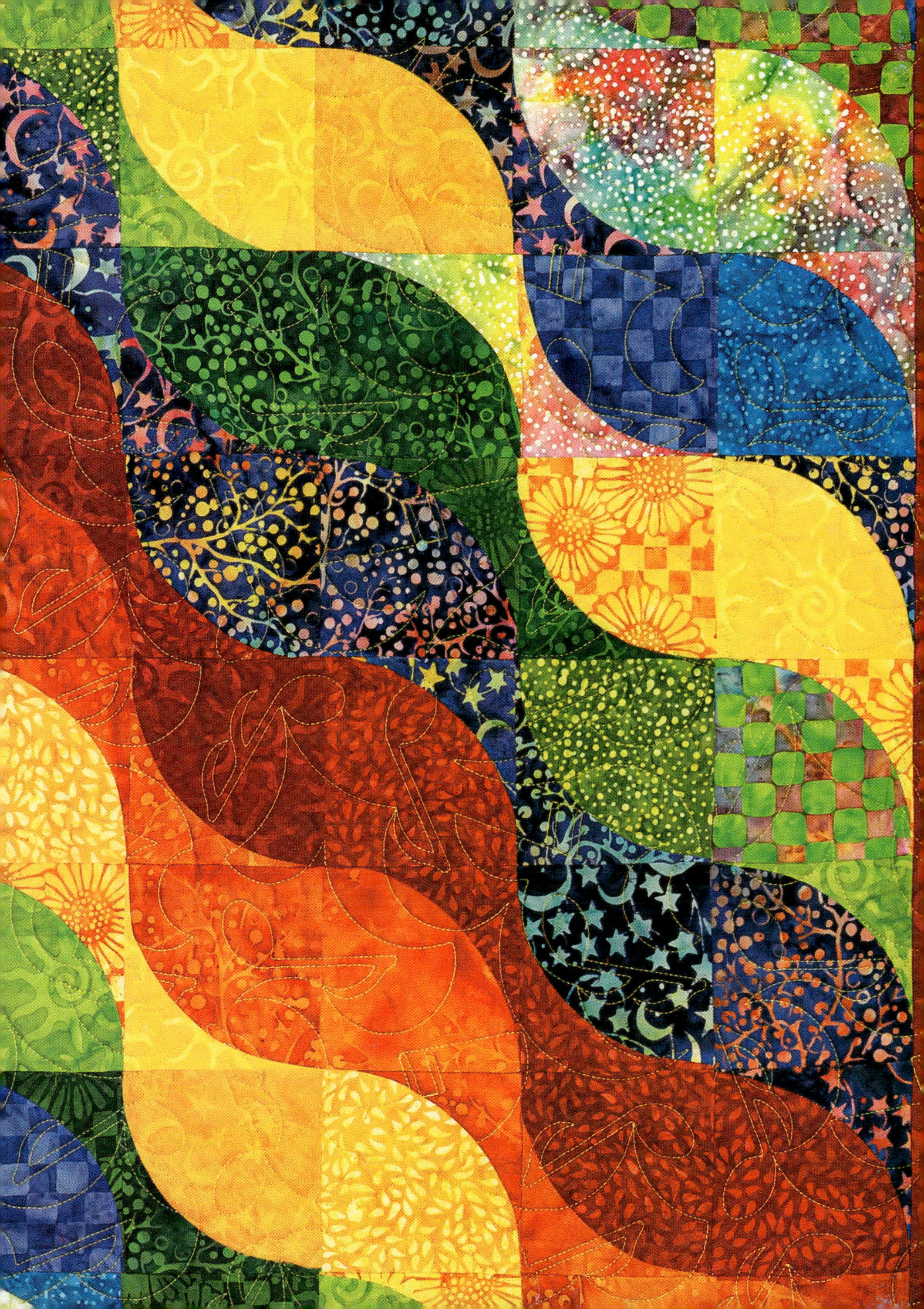

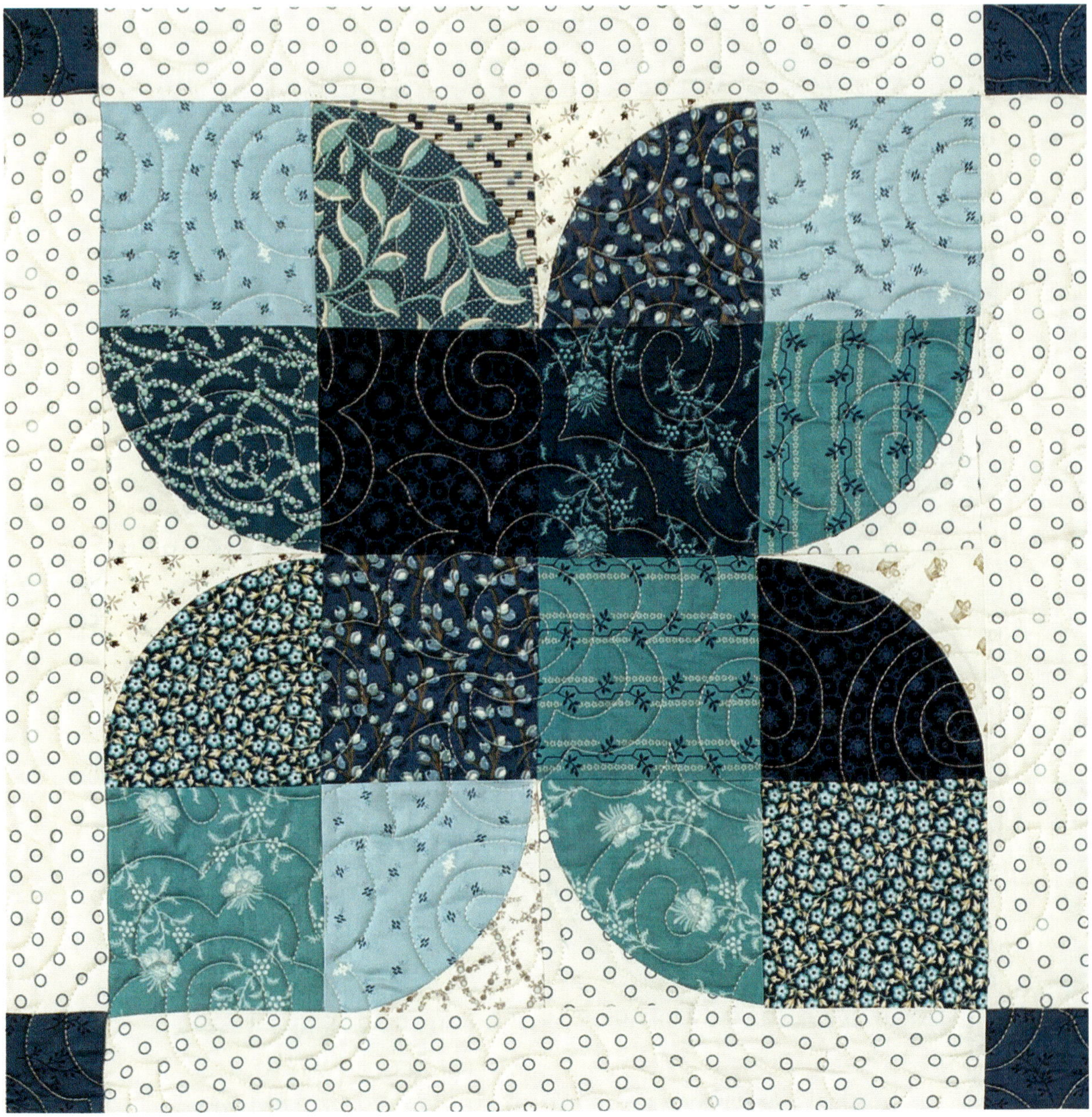

Drunkard's Path

TRIPLE PLAY

If you've ever heard the phrase "walking like a drunken sailor" a tipsy, sideways walk comes to mind. Likewise, the Drunkard's Path quilt block has a meandering diagonal pattern that is reminiscent of a tipsy path, sewn together from curved pieces of fabric. It's a familiar motif we know and love that actually began with the Temperance Movement in the 1900s. Since then, it has remained a popular quilt pattern and there are endless variations.

The Drunkard's Path quilt block is a wonderful introduction to curved piecing as well and that's one of the reasons we chose it for a Triple Play tutorial. If you've never tried conquering this intermediate quilting technique, have no fear. It's simpler than you might imagine and our Missouri Star templates in two sizes help it come together effortlessly. It's really incredible all the things you can create with this simple quarter-circle block.

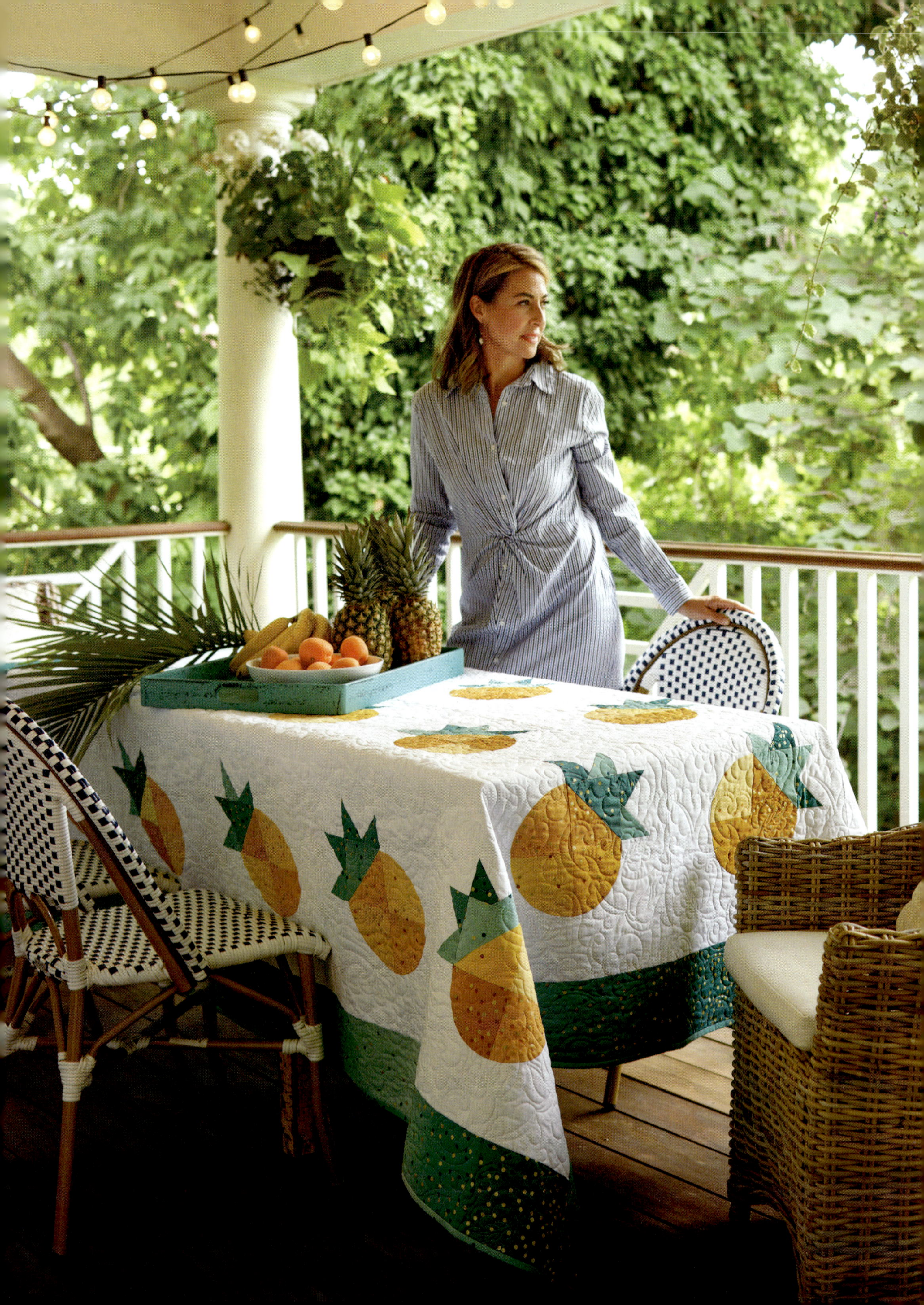

Tropical Paradise
Jenny's Play

Jenny started by taking three Drunkard's Path units and combining them with one wonky star leg unit to create a fabulous pineapple block design. Find yourself in paradise with this spectacular pineapple quilt pattern!

materials

QUILT SIZE
75" x 91"

BLOCK SIZE
16½" unfinished, 16" finished

QUILT TOP
¾ yard each of 2 yellow ombre fabrics
1¼ yards green ombre fabric
4½ yards background fabric

BORDER
1½ yards

BINDING
¾ yard

BACKING
5½ yards - vertical seam(s) or 2¾ yards 108" wide

OTHER
Missouri Star Drunkard's Path Circle Template Set - Small
Clearly Perfect Slotted Trimmer A - optional

SAMPLE QUILT
Ombre Fairy Dust and Ombre Confetti Metallic by V & Co. for Moda Fabrics

1 cut

From each yellow ombre fabric, cut (5) 5" strips across the width of the fabric. Subcut a **total of (70)** 5" squares from the strips.

From the green ombre fabric, cut (7) 5" strips across the width of the fabric. Subcut a **total of (50)** 5" squares from the strips.

Set 10 yellow ombre squares and 10 green ombre squares aside for the half-square triangles.

From the background fabric, cut:
- (15) 8½" strips across the width of the fabric. Subcut a **total of (60)** 8½" squares.

- (7) 4½" strips across the width of the fabric. Subcut a **total of (60)** 4½" squares.

2 make the pineapple bodies
Cut
Lay an 8½" background square on your cutting surface. Line up the 8½" marks on the Drunkard's Path template A with your square and carefully cut along the curve. Repeat to cut a **total of 60** background A pieces. Set the quarter-circle pieces aside for another project. **2A**

Lay a 5" yellow ombre square on your cutting surface. Place the Drunkard's Path template B in the corner of your square as shown. Cut along the curve. Repeat to cut a **total of 60** yellow ombre B pieces. **2B**

Unit Assembly
Pair an A piece with a B piece. Fold each piece in half on the diagonal and finger press to mark the midway point of each curved edge. Place the B piece on top of the A piece, right sides facing, and finger pressed centers aligned. Pin at the midway point and at both ends of the seam allowance. **2C**

Stitch the 2 pieces together along the curve. Use your fingers to ease in the fullness around the curve and avoid stretching the fabric as you sew. Press towards the A piece to complete the unit. **Make 60**. **2D**

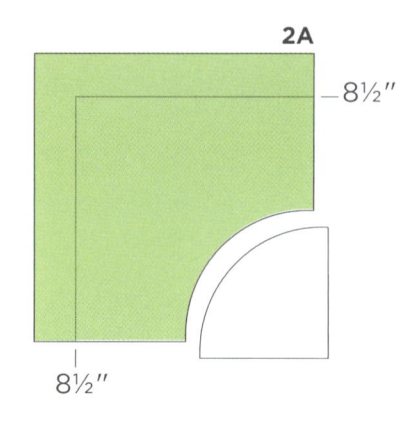

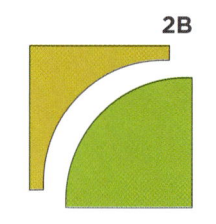

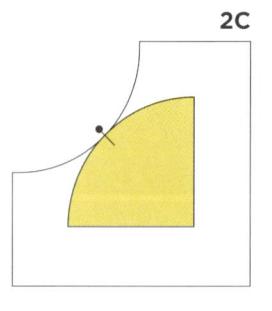

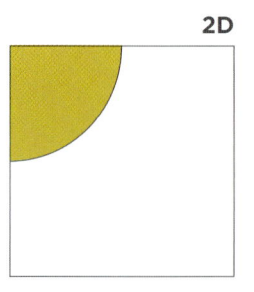

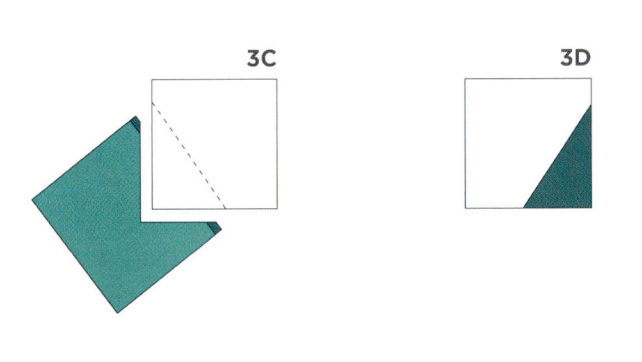

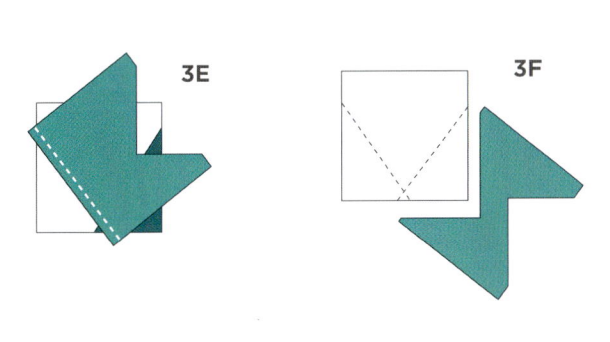

3 make the pineapple crowns

Wonky Points

Place a 5″ green ombre square on an angle (any angle) atop a 4½″ background square, right sides facing. Make sure your ombre square is placed a little past the halfway point. Sew ¼″ in from the angled edge of the ombre square. **3A**

Press the piece flat to set the seam, then press the ombre piece over the seam allowance. **3B**

Turn the unit over and use the background square as a guide to trim the green ombre fabric so that all of the edges are even. Save the trimmed scrap for the next wonky point. (You should be able to make at least 2 wonky points from each ombre square.) **3C 3D**

Note: If you wish to trim the excess background fabric from the back of the unit, you can turn the unit right side up, fold the ombre fabric of the wonky points back, and trim the excess background fabric ¼″ away from the sewn seam. Fold the wonky points back so the right side of the fabric is facing up and press.

Place the trimmed green ombre scrap on the adjacent side of the square. Make sure the edge of the ombre piece crosses over the first wonky point by at least ¼″. Stitch ¼″ in from the edge of the ombre piece. **3E**

Press to set the seam, then press the ombre piece over the seam allowance. Turn the unit over and use the background square as a guide to trim the green ombre fabric so all of the edges are even. Notice your square is still 4½″. **Make 40** wonky point units. **3F 3G**

Tip: Have fun with this and don't try to make all of the units alike!

Half-Square Triangles

Mark a line from corner to corner on the reverse side of each remaining 5″ yellow ombre square. **3H**

1. Lay an 8½″ background square on your cutting surface. Line up the 8½″ marks on the Drunkard's Path template A with your square and cut along the curve. Lay a 5″ yellow square on your cutting surface. Place the Drunkard's Path template B in the corner of your square as shown. Cut along the curve.

2. Fold an A piece and B piece in half on the diagonal and finger press to mark the midway point of each curved edge. Place the B piece on top of the A piece, right sides facing, and centers aligned. Pin at the midway point and at both ends of the seam allowance. Stitch the 2 pieces together along the curve. Press.

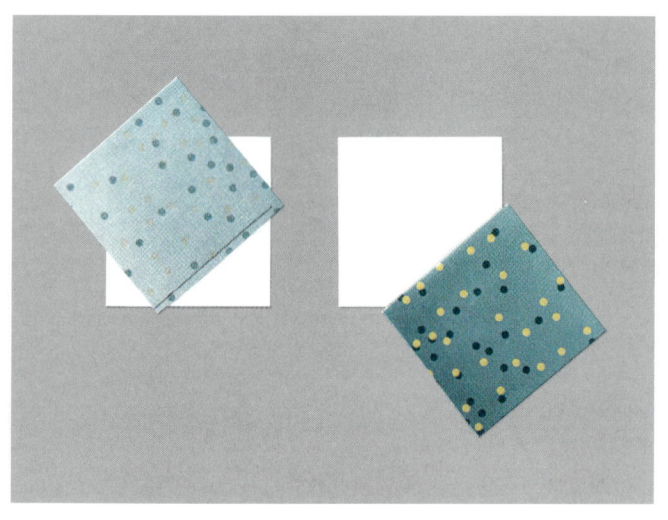

3. Place a 5″ green square on an angle atop a 4½″ background square, right sides facing. Sew ¼″ in from the angled edge of the green square. Press.

4. Turn the unit over and use the background square as a guide to trim the green fabric. Repeat to add another pineapple leaf to an adjoining side of the background square.

5. Mark a line from corner to corner on the reverse side of each remaining 5″ yellow square. Place a marked square atop a 5″ green square with right sides facing. Sew on both sides of the marked line using a ¼″ seam allowance. Cut on the marked line. Square each unit to 4½″.

6. Arrange 3 pineapple body units and 1 pineapple crown unit as shown. Sew the block together in 2 rows. Press the rows in opposite directions. Nest the seams and sew the rows together. Press.

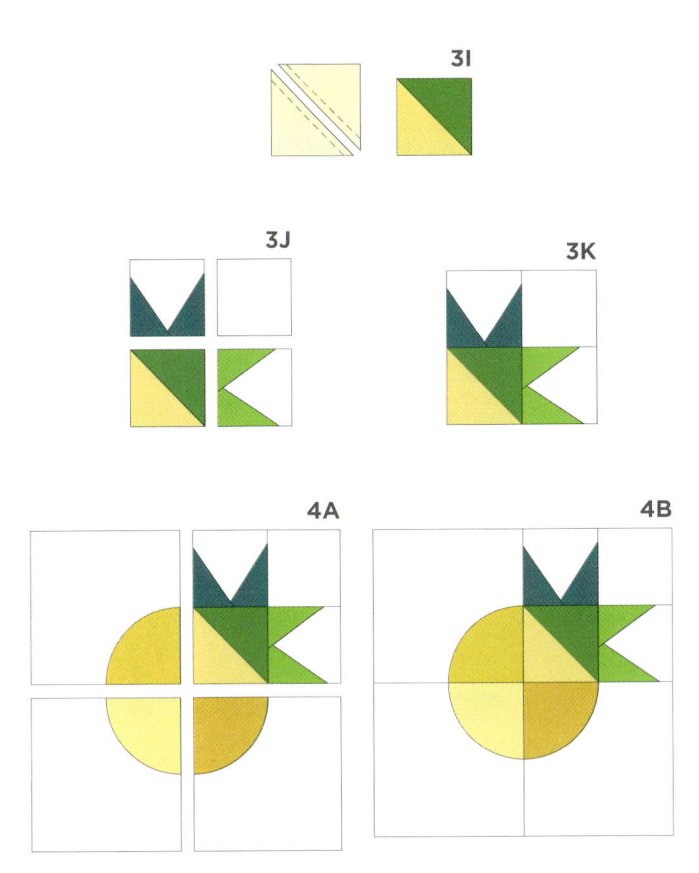

Place a marked square atop a 5" green ombre square with right sides facing. Sew on both sides of the marked line using a ¼" seam allowance. Cut on the marked line. Use the slotted trimmer to square each unit to 4½" then press open—or press, then square to 4½" if you're not using the trimmer. **Make 20**. **3I**

Unit Assembly
Arrange 2 wonky point units, 1 half-square triangle, and (1) 4½" background square as shown. Sew the unit together in 2 rows. Press the rows in opposite directions. Nest the seams and sew the rows together to complete the unit. **Make 20**. **3J 3K**

4 block construction
Arrange 3 pineapple body units and 1 pineapple crown unit as shown. Sew the block together in 2 rows. Press the rows in opposite directions. Nest the seams and sew the rows together. Press. **Make 20**. **4A 4B**

Block Size: 16½" unfinished, 16" finished

5 arrange & sew
Arrange the blocks into **5 rows of 4 blocks** as shown in the diagram on the left. Sew the blocks together to form rows and press in opposite directions. Nest the seams and sew the rows together. Press.

6 border
From the border fabric, cut (8) 6" strips across the width of the fabric. Sew the strips together to create 1 long strip. Trim the borders from this strip. Refer to Borders (pg. 238) in the Construction Basics to measure, cut, and attach the borders. The strip lengths are approximately 80½" for the sides and 75½" for the top and bottom.

7 quilt & bind
Layer the quilt with batting and backing, then quilt. After the quilting is complete, see Construction Basics (pg. 238) to finish your quilt.

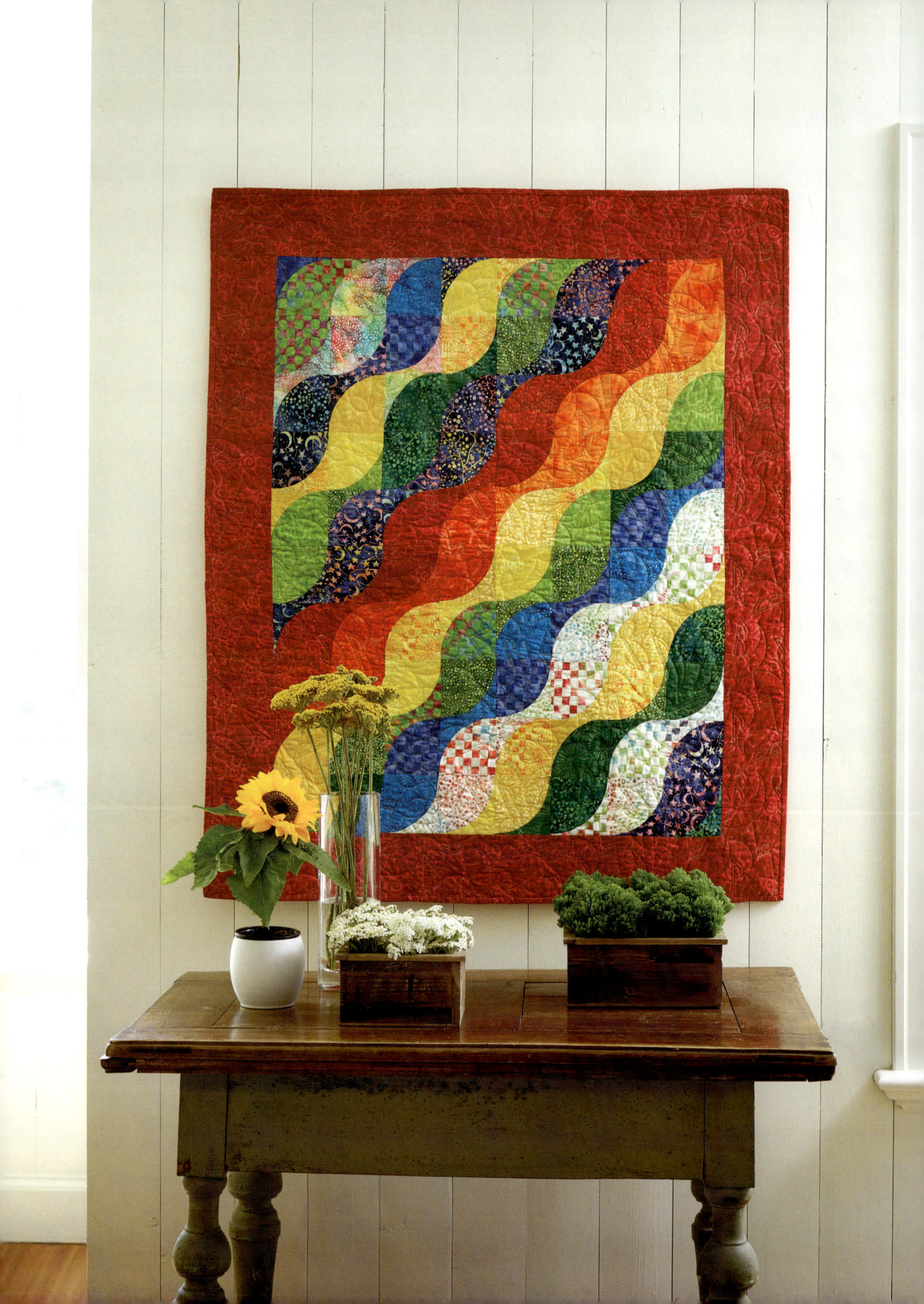

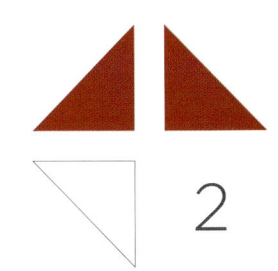

River Path
Natalie's Play

Natalie's lovely River Path quilt ripples with gorgeous color. With clever fabric placement, she creates a rainbow effect that flows diagonally across the entire quilt from corner to corner. Rivers aren't in any hurry. They're bound to get there someday! Relax and make a quilt you'll enjoy with every stitch. It's a brand new way of looking at Drunkard's Path blocks and the result is absolutely mesmerizing.

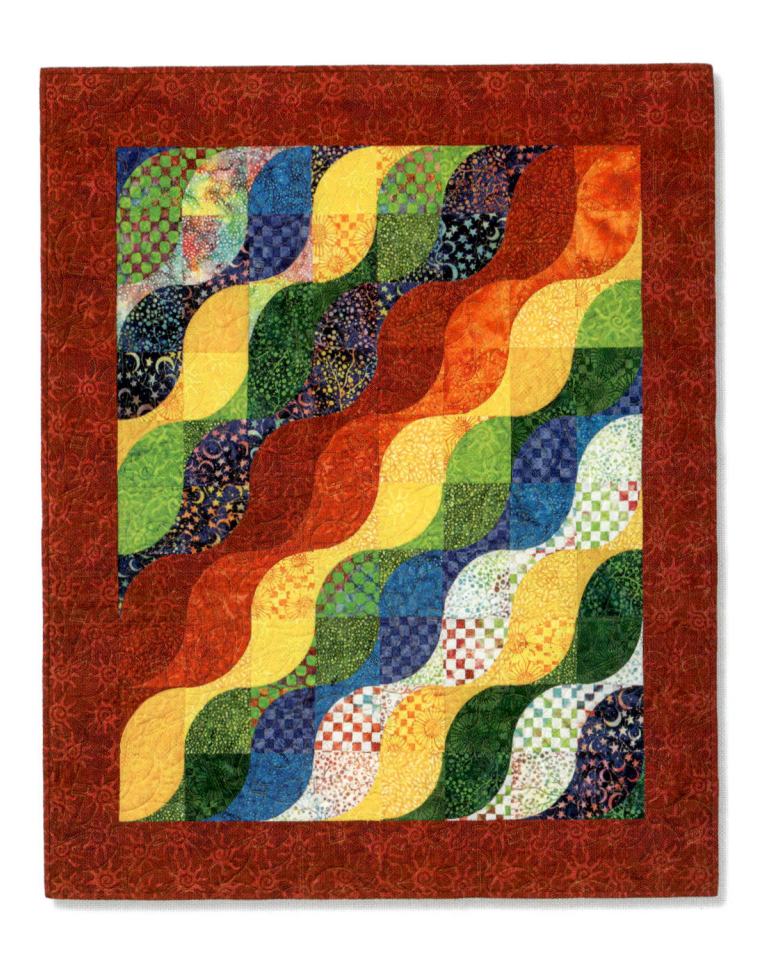

materials

QUILT SIZE
41" x 49"

BLOCK SIZE
4½" unfinished, 4" finished

QUILT TOP
2 packages 5" print squares

BORDER
¾ yard

BINDING
½ yard

BACKING
2¾ yards - horizontal seam(s)

OTHER
Missouri Star Drunkard's Path Circle Template Set - Small

SAMPLE QUILT
Colorpop Batiks Stamps by Kathy Engle for Island Batiks

1 sort & cut

Select (4) 5" print squares and set them aside for another project.

Place 1 square on your cutting surface. Lay template A on top of your square with the 4½" marks at the top and left edges of the square. Carefully cut around the curve to create an A piece. Set the quarter-circle piece aside for the B piece. Trim and discard the small ends of the A piece. Repeat cutting the template A curve from each 5" print square for a **total of 80** A pieces. **1A**

Lay a quarter-circle on your cutting surface. Lay template B on top of your quarter-circle, aligning the 2 straight edges of the template with the square edges, and trim away the excess fabric along the curve to create a B piece. Repeat cutting the template B curve from each quarter-circle for a **total of 80** B pieces. **1B**

2 block construction

Pair an A piece with a B piece.

Note: To make your quilt like ours, refer to the diagram on page 61 to assign your colors within the quilt. You will need to pair the A and B pieces using the diagram.

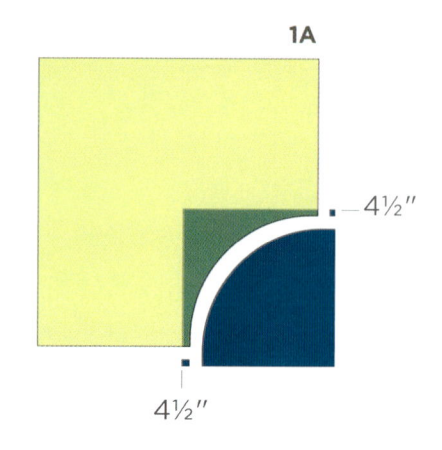

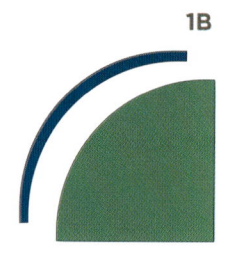

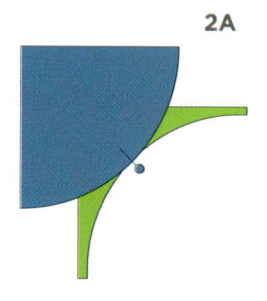

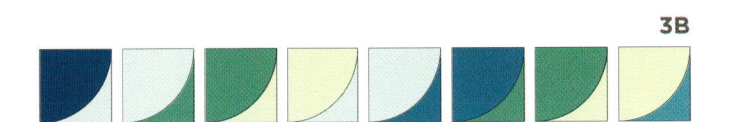

Fold each piece in half on the diagonal and finger press to mark the midway point of each curved edge. Place a B piece on top of the A piece with right sides facing and finger pressed centers aligned. Pin at the midway point and at both ends of the seam allowance. **2A**

Stitch the 2 pieces together along the curve. Use your fingers to ease in the fullness around the curve and avoid stretching the fabric as you sew. Press the seam allowance towards the A piece to complete the unit. **Make 80**. **2B**

Block Size: 4½″ unfinished, 4″ finished

3 arrange & sew

Referring to the diagram on page 61, lay out your blocks in **10 rows** of **8 blocks** each.

All odd-numbered rows will have the quarter-circle in the bottom right corner of each block. **3A**

All even-numbered rows will have the quarter-circle in the top left corner of each block. **3B**

Sew the blocks together in rows. Press the rows in opposite directions. Nest the seams and sew the rows together. Press.

1. Lay template A on top of your square with the 4½" marks at the top and left edges of the square. Carefully cut around the curve to create an A piece. Set the quarter-circle piece aside for the B piece. Trim and discard the small ends of the A piece. Cut 80 A pieces.

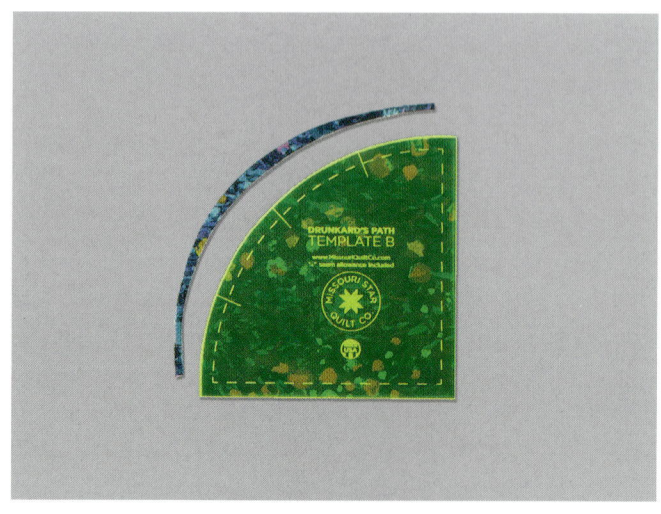

2. Lay a quarter-circle on your cutting surface. Lay template B on top of your quarter-circle, aligning the 2 straight edges of the template with the square edges, and trim away the excess fabric along the curve to create a B piece. Cut 80 B pieces.

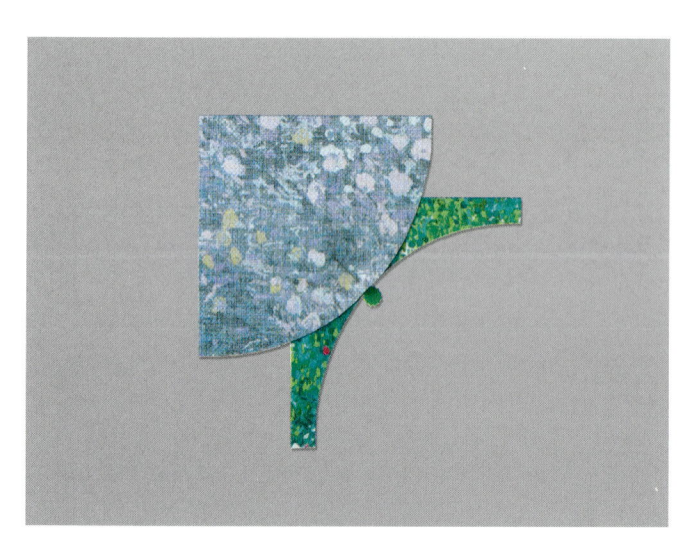

3. Fold each piece in half and finger press to mark the midway point of each curved edge. Place a B piece on top of an A piece with right sides facing and finger pressed centers aligned. Pin as desired.

4. Stitch the 2 pieces together along the curve. Use your fingers to ease in the fullness around the curve and avoid stretching the fabric as you sew. Press the seam allowance towards the A piece to complete the unit. Make 80.

4 border

Cut (5) 5″ strips across the width of the fabric. Sew the strips together to make 1 long strip. Trim the borders from this strip. Refer to Borders (pg. 238) in the Construction Basics to measure, cut, and attach the borders. The lengths are approximately 40½″ for the sides and 41½″ for the top and bottom.

5 quilt & bind

Layer the quilt with batting and backing, then quilt. See Construction Basics (pg. 238) to finish your quilt.

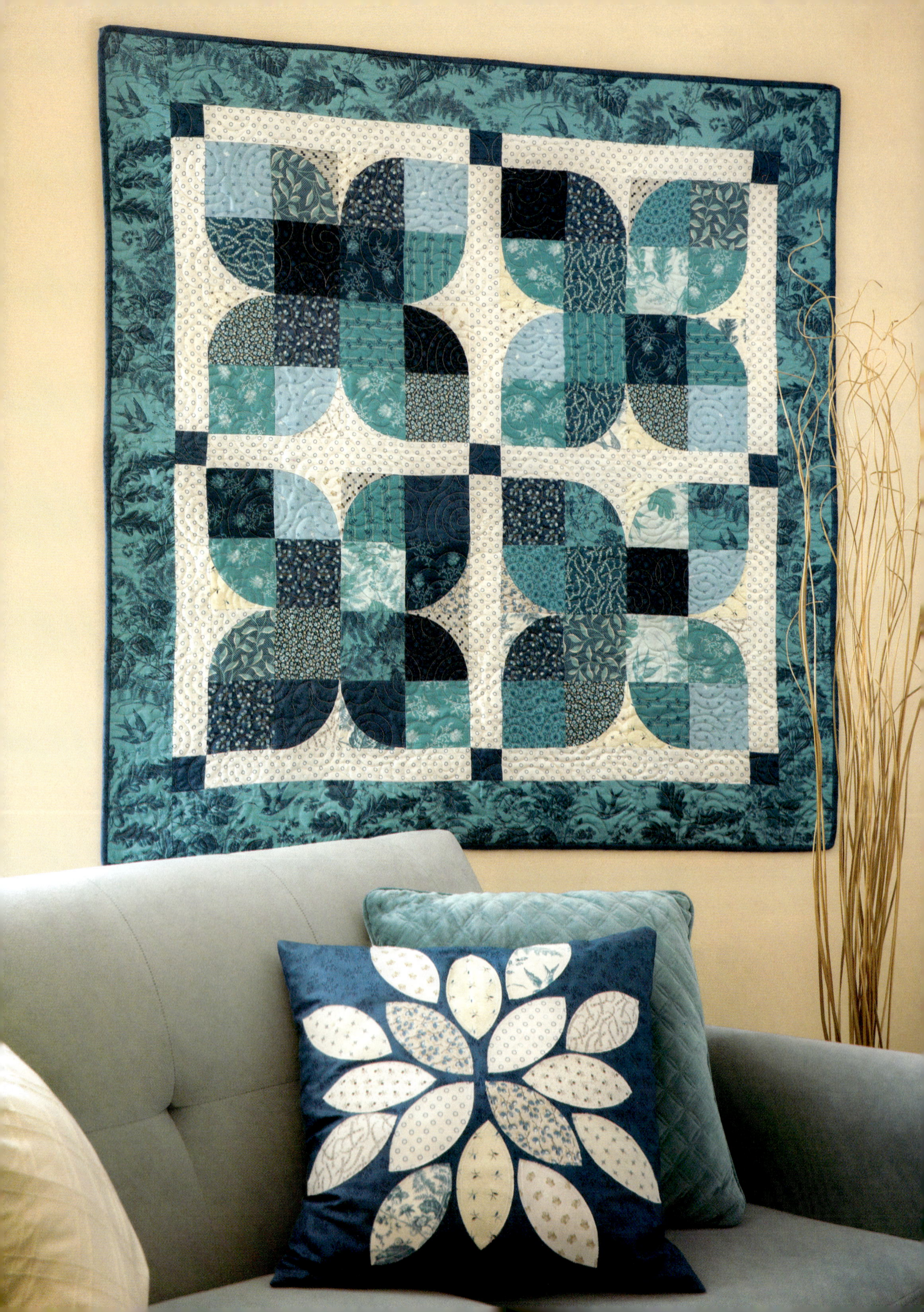

Morning Glory
Misty's Play

Oh what a beautiful morning! That's what you'll be singing when you catch a glimpse of this pretty little quilt in cool blue fabrics. Misty made her Morning Glory quilt by stitching together two Drunkard's Path units with two simple squares to form one flower petal. By making four of these petal units, they combine to create a big, beautiful scrappy flower. The result is sure to be glorious.

materials

QUILT SIZE
47" x 47"

BLOCK SIZE
16½" unfinished, 16" finished

QUILT TOP
2 packages 5" print squares
 - includes cornerstones

SASHING
½ yard

BORDER
¾ yard

BINDING
½ yard

BACKING
3 yards - horizontal seam(s)

OTHER
Missouri Star Drunkard's Path Circle Template Set - Small

SAMPLE QUILT
Anna by Edyta Sitar of Laundry Basket Quilts for Andover Fabric

1 sort & cut

Sort the 5" squares into 16 light prints and 67 dark prints. Set the remaining square aside for another project.

Place 1 light print square on your cutting surface. Lay template A on top of your square with the 4½" marks at the top and left edges of the square. Carefully cut around the curve. Save the quarter-circle piece. Trim and discard the small ends of the A piece. **1A**

Turn the quarter-circle piece 180°. Lay template A on top of your quarter-circle with the 4½" marks at the top and left edges. Carefully cut around the curve to create another A piece. Set the remaining piece aside for another project. **1B**

Repeat to cut 2 A pieces from each light print square for a **total of 32** A pieces. **1C**

Select (32) 5" dark print squares and trim them to 4½". Set these aside for now.

From your remaining dark squares, choose 3 matching squares for cornerstones. Cut these squares in half vertically and horizontally. Each square will yield (4) 2½" squares and a **total of 9** are needed. Set these aside for the cornerstones.

Lay a 5" dark print square on your cutting surface. Lay template B on top of your square, aligning the 2 straight edges of the template with the corner of the square, and trim along the curve. Repeat to cut a **total of 32** dark print B pieces. **1D**

2 drunkard's path units

Pair an A piece with a B piece.

Fold each piece in half on the diagonal and finger press to mark the midway point of each curved edge. Place a B piece on top of the A piece with right sides facing and finger pressed centers aligned. Pin at the midway point and at both ends of the seam allowance. **2A**

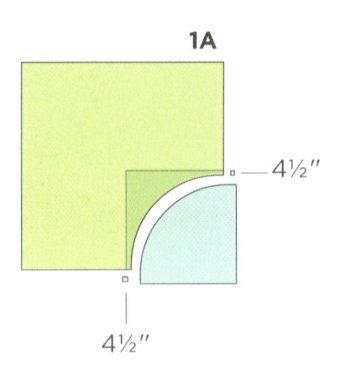

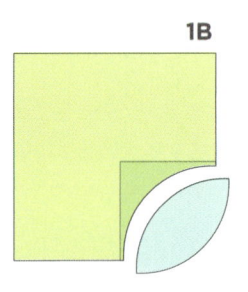

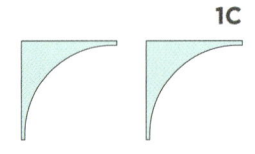

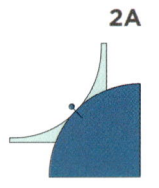

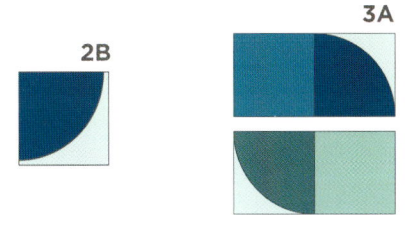

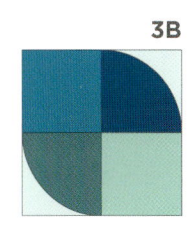

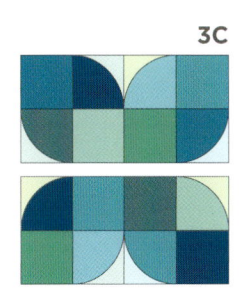

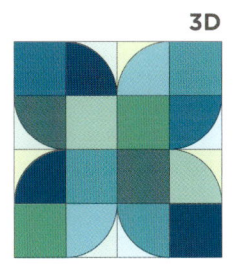

Stitch the 2 pieces together along the curve. Use your fingers to ease in the fullness around the curve and avoid stretching the fabric as you sew. Press the seam allowance towards the A piece to complete the unit. **Make 32**. **2B**

3 block construction

Select 2 drunkard's path units and (2) 4½" dark squares and arrange them as shown. Sew the units together in rows. Press the seam of the top row to the left and the seam of the bottom row to the right. **3A**

Sew the rows together to complete 1 quadrant. **Make 16**. **3B**

Arrange 4 quadrants as shown. Sew the quadrants together in rows. **3C**

Press the seam of the top row to the left and the seam of the bottom row to the right. Nest the seams and sew the rows together to complete the block. **Make 4**. **3D**

Block Size: 16½" unfinished, 16" finished

4 sashing

From the sashing fabric, cut (6) 2½" strips across the width of the fabric. Subcut (2) 2½" x 16½" sashing rectangles from each strip for a **total of 12** rectangles.

Sew a sashing rectangle to the opposite sides of a 2½" dark square. Sew a 2½" dark square to both ends of the unit. Press all of the seams toward the rectangles to complete the horizontal sashing strip. **Make 3**. **4A**

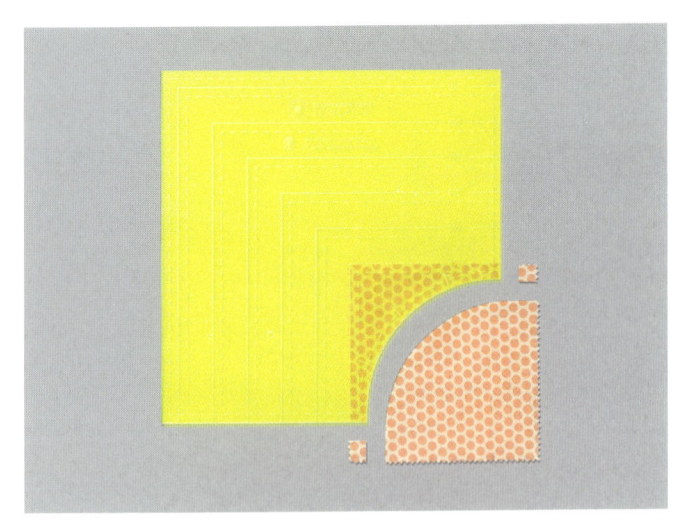

1. Place 1 light print square on your cutting surface. Lay template A on top of your square with the 4½" marks at the top and left edges of the square. Carefully cut around the curve. Save the quarter-circle piece. Trim and discard the small ends of the A piece.

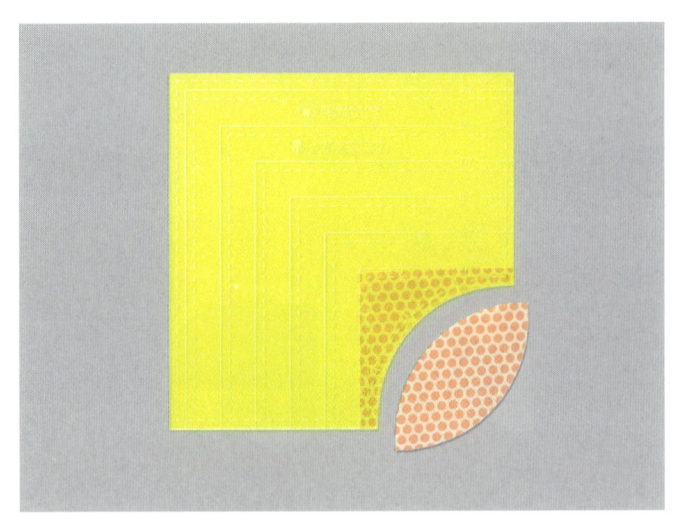

2. Turn the quarter-circle piece 180°. Lay template A on top of your quarter-circle with the 4½" marks at the top and left edges. Carefully cut around the curve to create another A piece. Set the remaining piece aside for another project. Repeat to cut 2 A pieces from each light print square for a total of 32 A pieces.

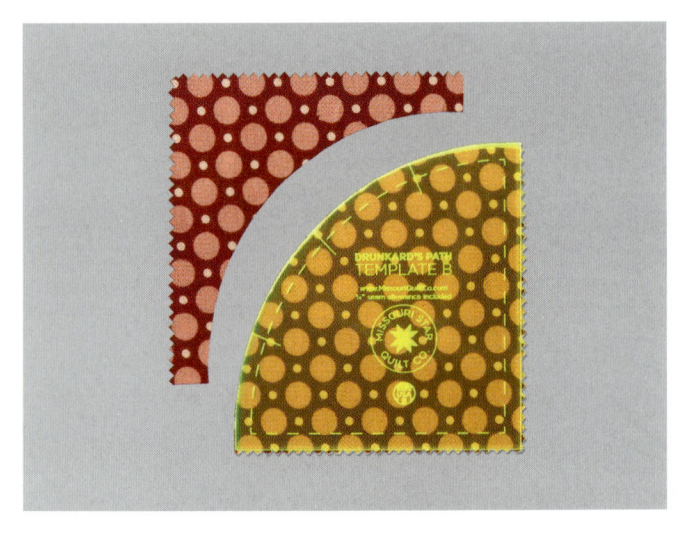

3. Lay template B on top of your dark 5" square, aligning the 2 straight edges of the template with the corner of the square, and trim along the curve. Repeat to cut a total of 32 dark print B pieces.

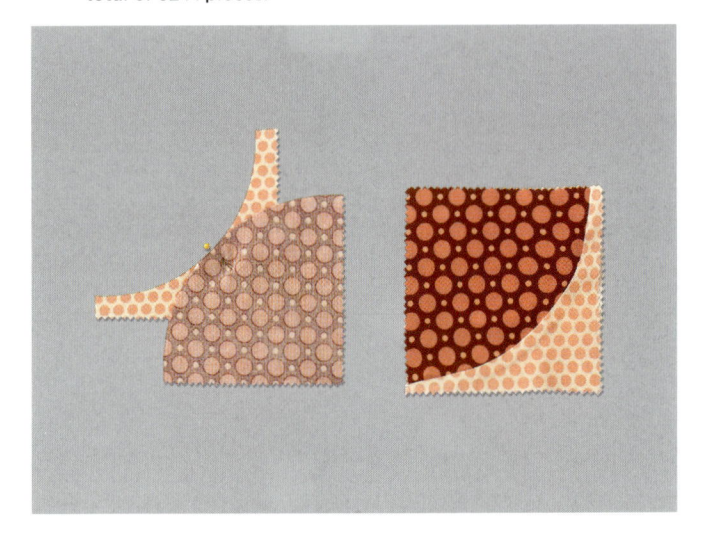

4. Fold each piece in half and crease to mark the midway point each curve. Place a B piece on top of an A piece with right sides facing and creases aligned. Pin as desired. Sew together along the curve and press toward the A piece. Make 32.

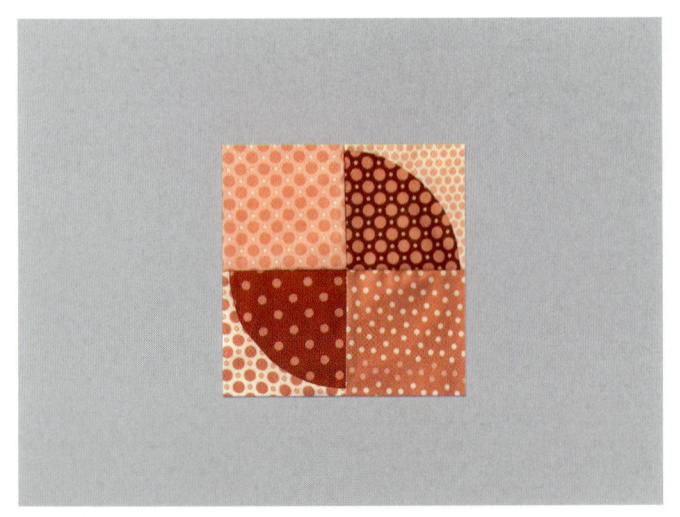

5. Select 2 drunkard's path units and (2) 4½" dark squares and arrange them as shown. Sew the units together in rows. Nest the seams and sew the rows together to complete 1 quadrant. Make 16.

6. Arrange 4 quadrants as shown. Sew the quadrants together in rows. Nest the seams and sew the rows together to complete the block. Make 4.

5A

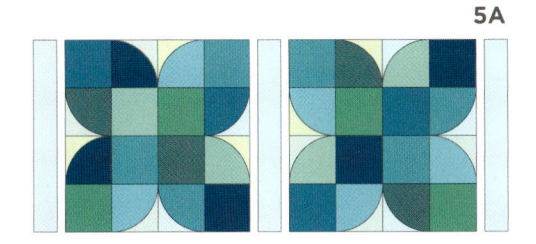

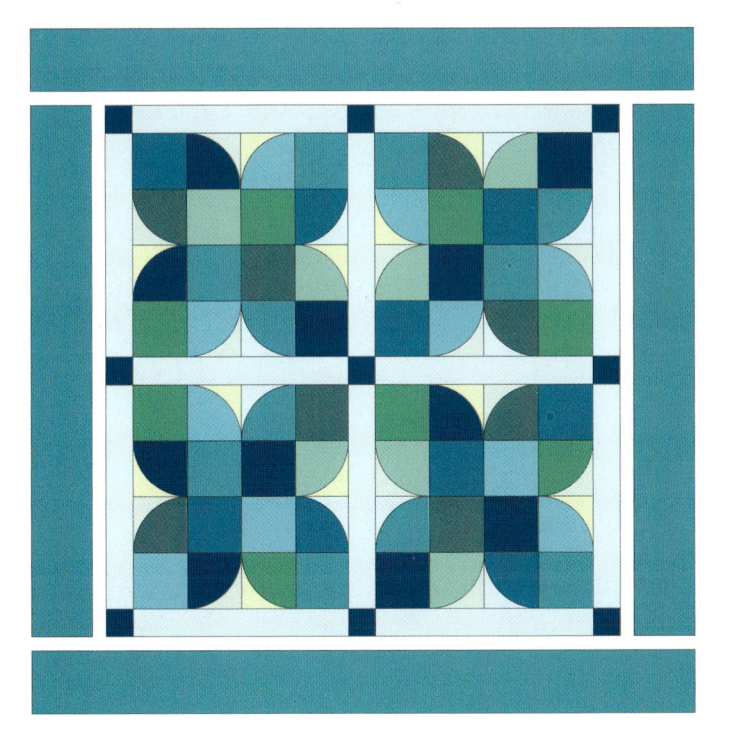

5 arrange & sew

Referring to the diagram on your left, lay out your blocks in **2 rows** of **2 blocks** each. Sew the blocks together with a sashing rectangle between each block and to both ends to create the rows. Press the seams toward the rectangles. **5A**

Nest the seams and sew the rows together with a sashing strip between the rows, on the top, and on the bottom to complete the quilt center.

6 border

Cut (5) 5" strips across the width of the fabric. Sew the strips together to make 1 long strip. Trim the borders from this strip. Refer to Borders (pg. 238) in the Construction Basics to measure, cut, and attach the borders. The lengths are approximately 38½" for the sides and 47½" for the top and bottom.

7 quilt & bind

Layer the quilt with batting and backing, then quilt. See Construction Basics (pg. 238) to finish your quilt.

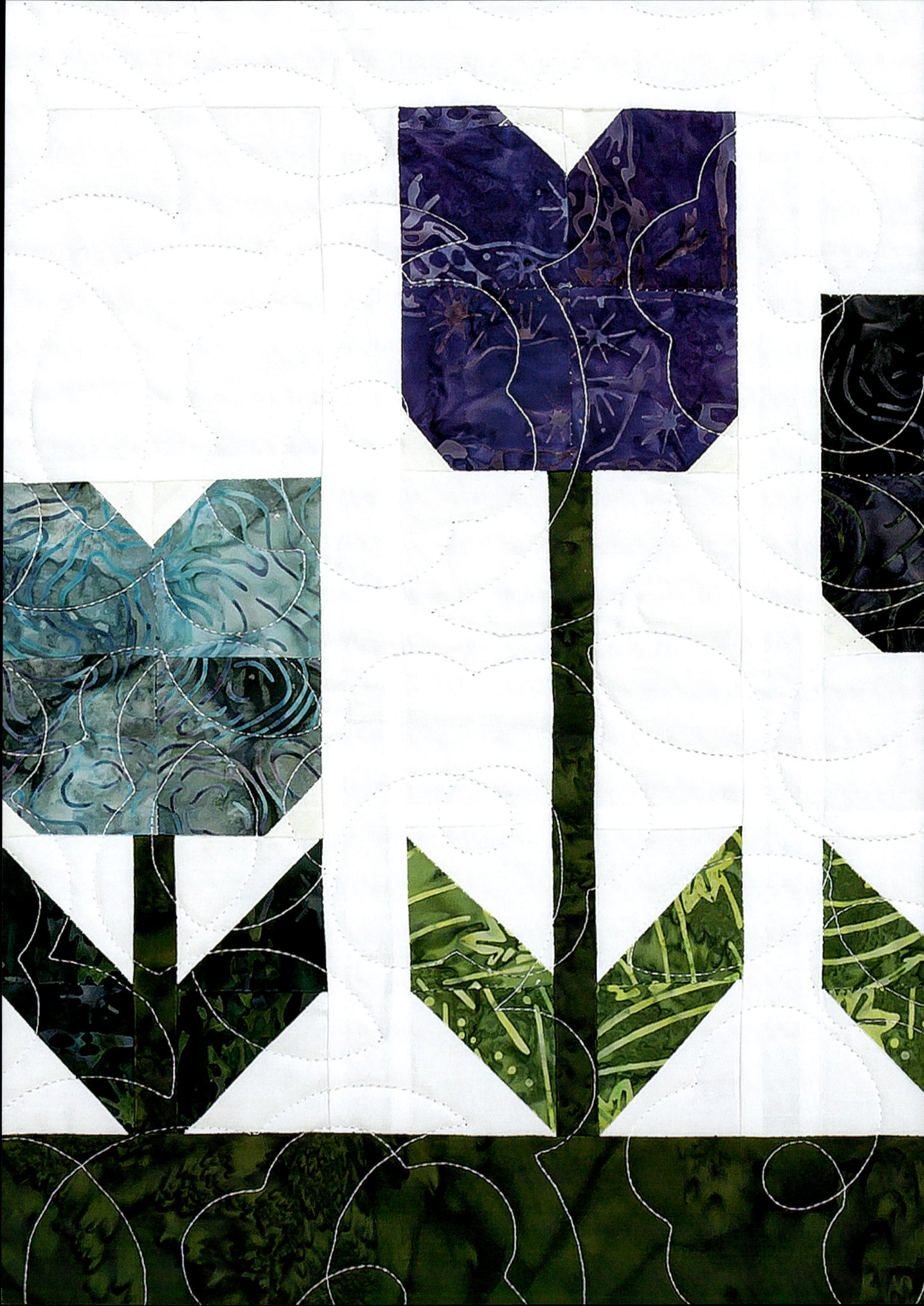

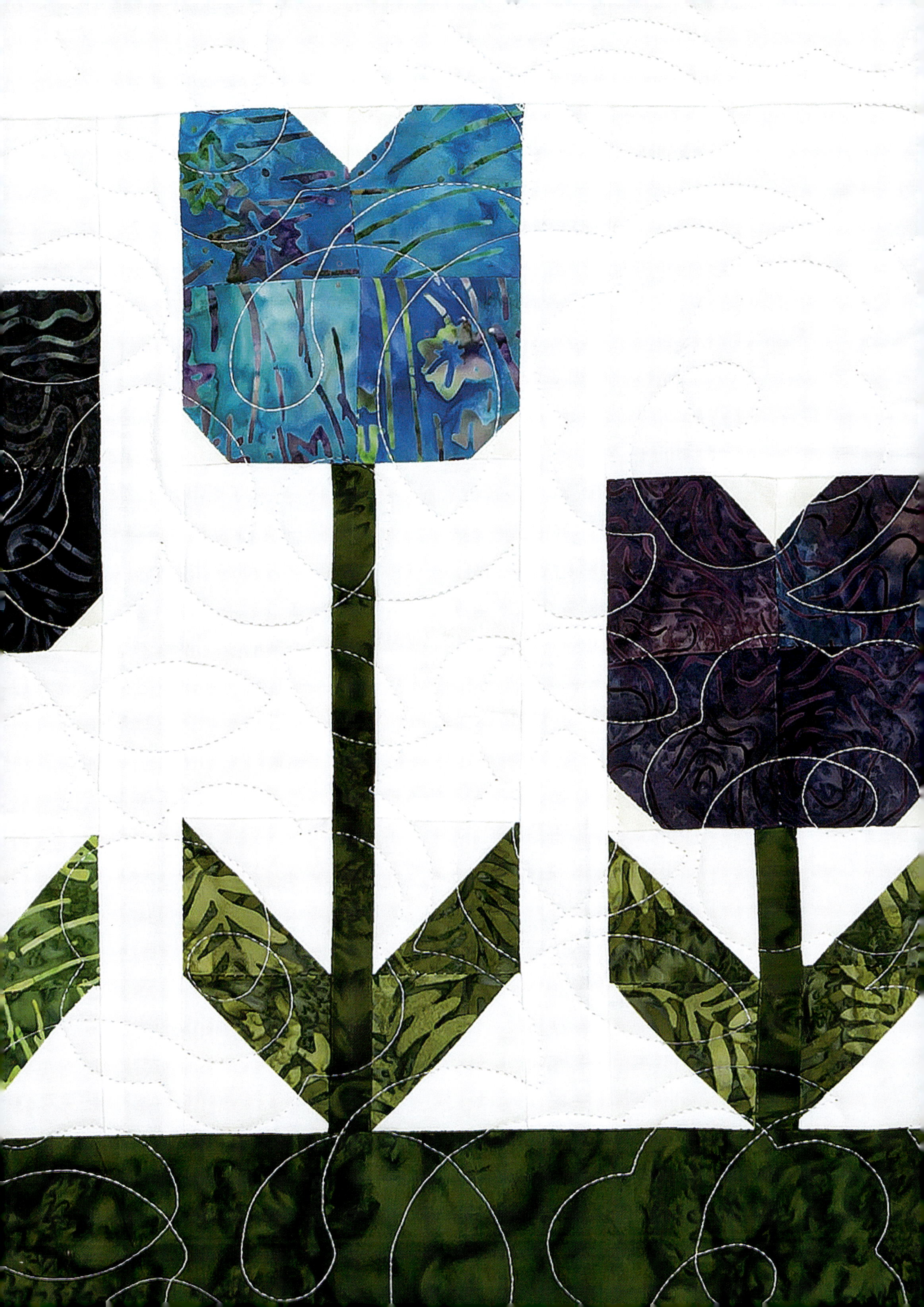

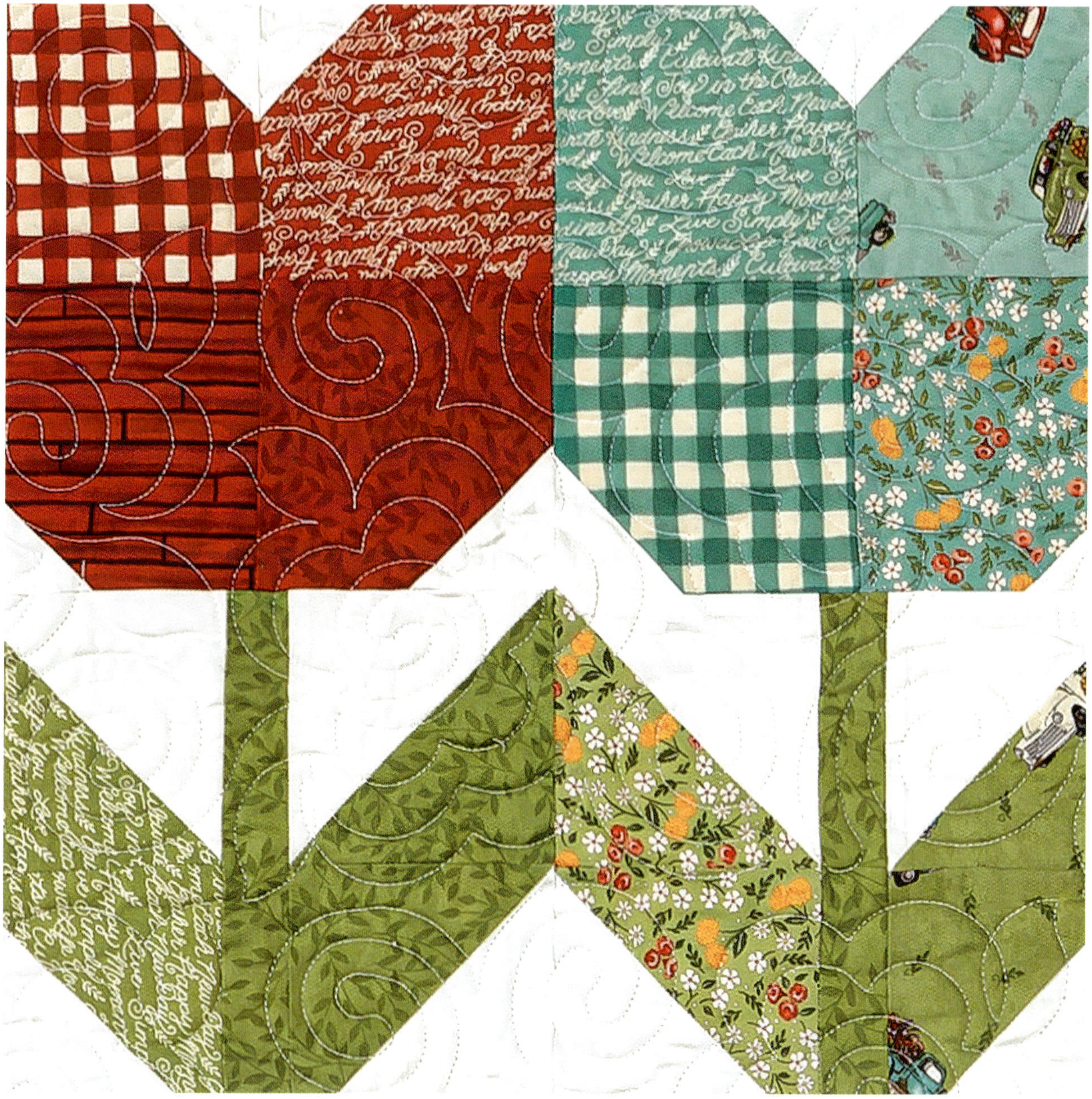

Tulip Fields

TRIPLE PLAY

What do you get when you plant kisses? Tulips! This darling quilt block may look complicated, but it couldn't be simpler. These sweet tulips are created with snowballed squares and half-square triangles for a fresh, springtime look you'll enjoy all year long. These cute tulips can be made in many different sizes and colors, you can bunch them up or let them stand alone, but no matter how you make them, they're bound to liven up any quilt design.

Choosing tulip blocks for our Triple Play tutorial was a no-brainer. It was early spring at the time, we had all been cooped up indoors for far too long, and seeing bright, beautiful tulips opening up after all the snow had finally melted gave us so much hope. We needed the color in our lives! If you're looking for an excuse to use your favorite colorful fabrics, tulip quilt blocks are a fun project for quilters of all levels. Although the individual pieces are incredibly simple to create, they combine into designs that look absolutely stunning. We hope you enjoy stitching along!

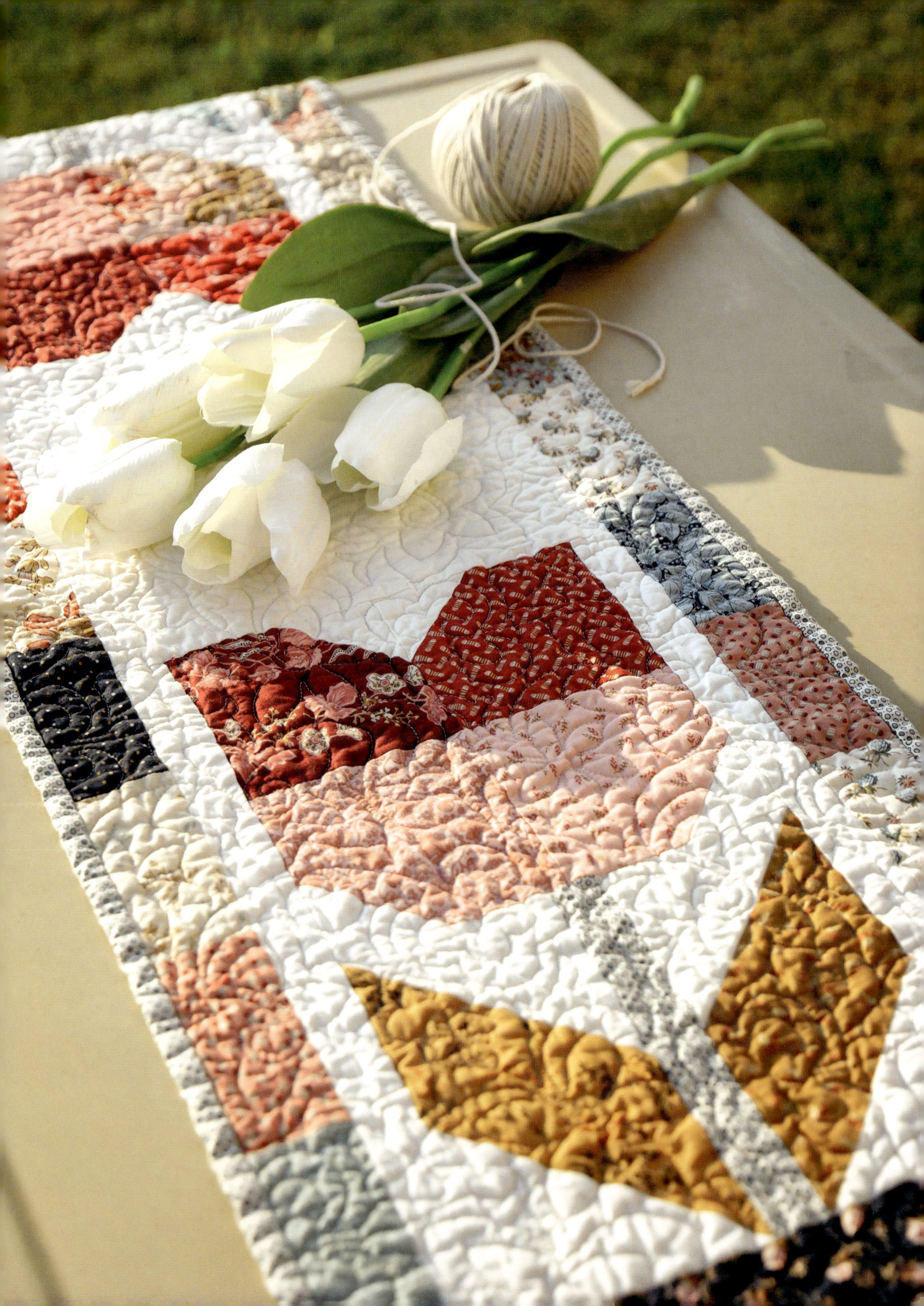

Tulip Time
Jenny's Play

What time is it? It's tulip time! Right at the start of the season, tulips peek out from the cold earth, ready to welcome sunny spring days. Stitch along with Jenny as she makes a lovely table runner featuring two large tulip blooms. It's sure to create a welcoming atmosphere in your home.

materials

TABLE RUNNER SIZE
15" x 49"

BLOCK SIZE
11½" x 17½" unfinished, 11" x 17" finished

PROJECT TOP
1 package 5" print squares
¼ yard light print*
¼ yard dark print*
½ yard background

BINDING
½ yard

BACKING
¾ yard - cut parallel to the selvages and sewn together along the short ends

SAMPLE PROJECT
Super Bloom by Edyta Sitar of Laundry Basket Quilts

*Note: You could substitute the fabric listed above for scraps if available. You'll need at least a 1½" wide strip of the light print and a 2½" wide strip of the dark print.

1 cut

Select (10) 5" print squares from your package and cut each in half once. Each square will yield (2) 2½" x 5" rectangles and a **total of 20** are needed. Set the rectangles and the rest of the squares aside for now.

From the light print, cut (1) 1½" strip across the width of the fabric. Subcut (2) 1½" x 8½" rectangles from the strip and set the remainder of the fabric aside for another project.

From the background fabric, cut (1) 11½" strip along the **length** of the fabric. Subcut (1) 11½" square. From the remainder of the fabric, cut:

- (1) 5" strip across the **width** of the fabric. Subcut (4) 5" squares from the strip.

- (1) 2½" strip across the **width** of the fabric. Subcut (8) 2½" squares from the strip.

- (4) 1½" strips across the **width** of the fabric. Subcut a 1½" x 17½" rectangle from each strip for a **total of 4** rectangles.

2 tulip blossoms

On the reverse side of the 2½" background squares, mark a line from corner to corner once on the diagonal either by folding the square and pressing in a crease or by marking it with a pencil. **2A**

Place a marked background square atop a 5" print square with right sides facing. Sew on the marked line. Trim the excess fabric away ¼" from the sewn seam. **Make 8** snowballed squares. **2B**

Arrange 4 snowballed squares in a 4-patch formation as shown. Sew the squares together in pairs to form rows. Press. Nest the seams and sew the rows together. Press. **Make 2** units and set them aside for the moment. These will be used as the tulip blossoms. **2C**

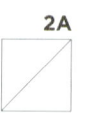

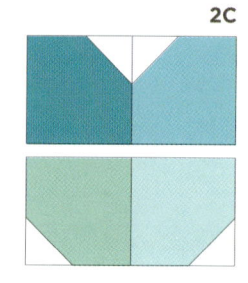

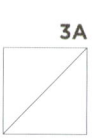

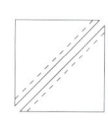

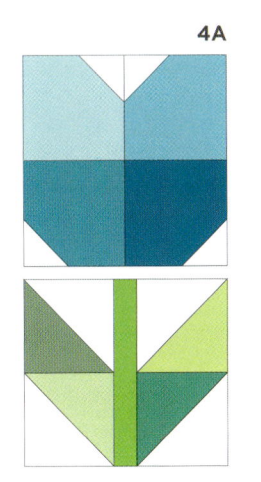

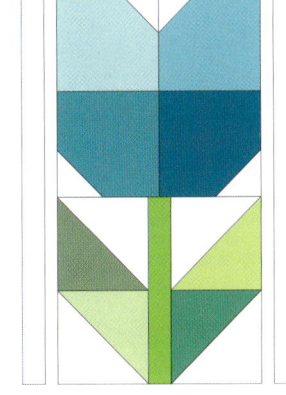

3 leaf units

On the reverse side of the 5" background squares, mark a line from corner to corner once on the diagonal. **3A**

Place a marked background square atop a 5" print square with right sides facing. Sew on both sides of the marked line with a ¼" seam allowance. Cut on the marked line. Open each unit and press. Trim the units to 4½". **Make 8** half-square triangles. **3B**

Arrange 4 half-square triangles in 2 rows of 2, as shown. Sew the squares together in pairs to form vertical rows. Press. **3C**

Sew the vertical rows to both long edges of a 1½" x 8½" print rectangle. Press. **Make 2** units and set them aside for the moment. These will be used as the leaf units. **3D**

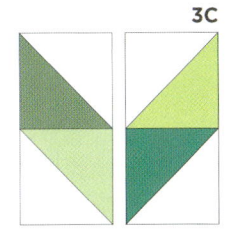

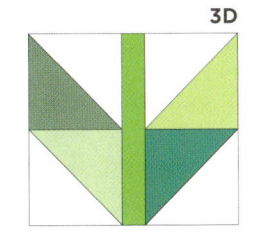

4 block construction

Sew a blossom unit to a leaf unit as shown. Press. **4A**

Sew a 1½" x 17½" background rectangle to both sides of the unit. Press to complete the block. **Make 2** blocks. **4B**

Block Size: 11½" x 17½" unfinished, 11" x 17" finished

5 make side borders

Note: You may like to measure the length of your project at this point. If your project measures differently than ours, you can make adjustments to the seam allowances in the border strips if necessary. See the instructions for measuring a quilt for borders in the Construction Basics (pg. 238) if you need additional guidance.

Sew (10) 2½" x 5" print rectangles together end-to-end to form a row. **Make 2** side border strips. **5A**

1. Place a marked background square atop a 5" print square with right sides facing. Sew on the marked line, then trim ¼" away from the sewn seam. Press the seam allowance of the snowballed square toward the print fabric. Make 4.

2. Sew 4 snowballed 5" squares together in a 4-patch formation as shown.

3. Make leaf units by stitching 2 half-square triangles together vertically. Notice the 2 leaf units are mirror images of each other.

4. Sew a leaf unit to either side of a 1½" x 8½" solid rectangle. Press.

5. Sew a tulip top to a tulip stem unit as shown.

6. Sew a 1½" x 17½" background rectangle to both sides of the unit. Make 2 blocks.

6 arrange & sew

Sew the blocks to 2 opposite sides of the 11½" background square. Press. **6A**

7 borders

Sew a side border strip to each long edge of the table runner as shown in the diagram on your left. Press.

From the dark print, cut a 2½" strip across the width of the fabric. Set the remainder of the fabric aside for another project.

Measure the width of your project in 3 places. See the instructions for measuring a quilt for borders in the Construction Basics (pg. 238) if you need additional guidance. Your project should be approximately 15½" wide. Trim 2 rectangles from the 2½" strip to the same width as your project.

Sew the dark print rectangle to each end of the table runner. Press.

8 quilt & bind

Layer the table runner with batting and backing, then quilt. See Construction Basics (pg. 238) to finish your table runner.

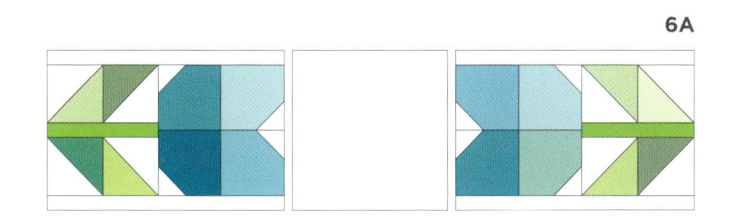

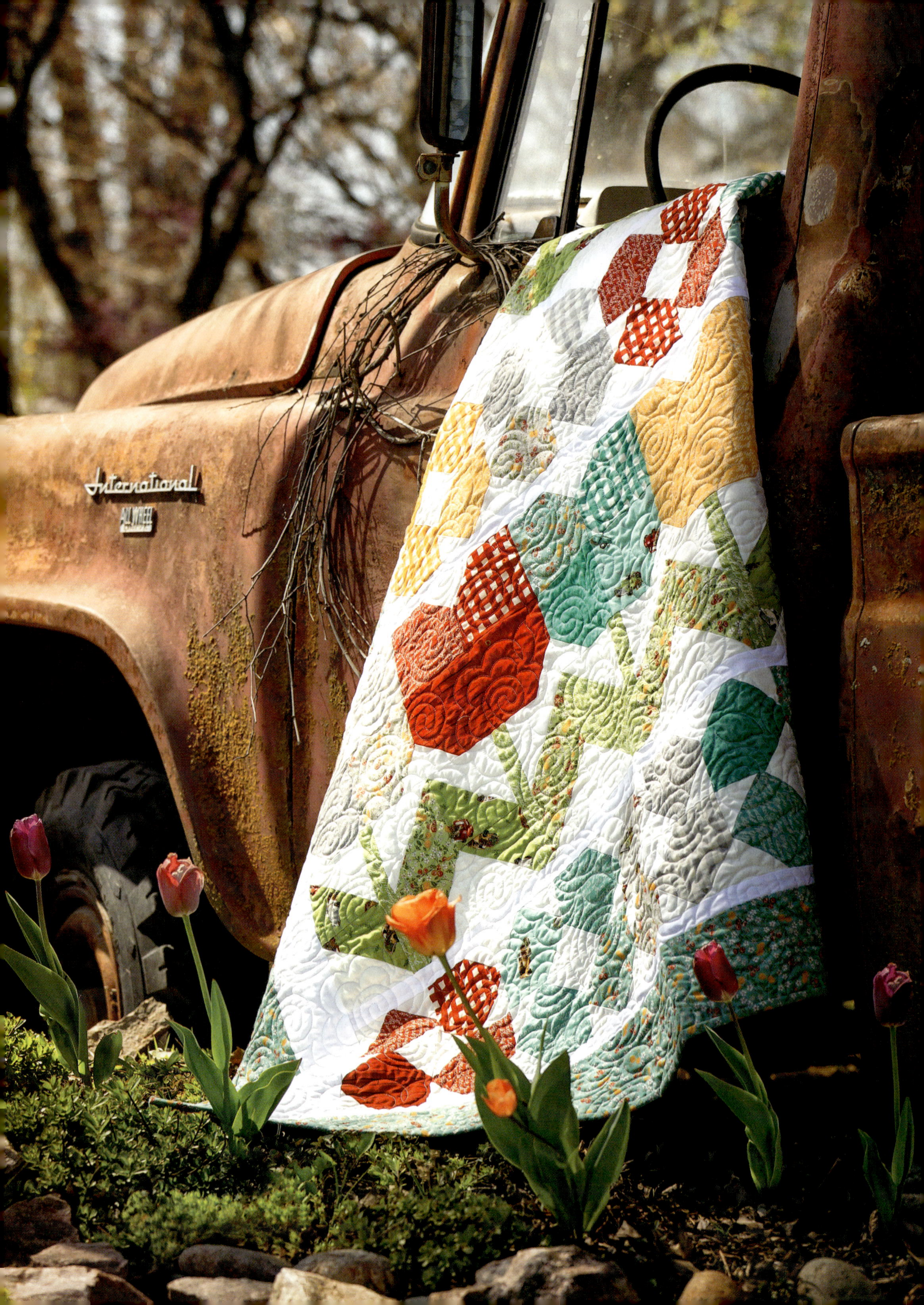
International

Tulip Fields
Natalie's Play

Frolic through patchwork fields of pretty tulips and sunny daisies with a smile on your face. Natalie's cheerful quilt is perfect for a springtime pick-me-up project and it's just the right size for picnics or snuggling up on the couch. Keep on stitching and soon you'll have a blooming flower garden.

materials

QUILT SIZE
61" x 76"

DIZZY DAISIES BLOCK SIZE
9½" unfinished, 9" finished

TOTALLY TULIPS BLOCK SIZE
9½" x 17½" unfinished, 9" x 17" finished

QUILT TOP
1 package 10" print squares
2¼ yards background fabric
  - includes sashing and inner border

OUTER BORDER
1¼ yards

BINDING
¾ yard

BACKING
4¾ yards - vertical seam(s) or
  2½ yards 108" wide

SAMPLE QUILT
Cultivate Kindness by Deb Strain for Moda Fabrics

1 cut

From the package of 10" print squares, select 25 squares for flower blossoms, 5 squares for tulip leaves, and 2 squares for tulip stems. Set the 5 tulip leaf squares aside for the moment. Set the remaining 10 squares aside for another project.

Cut each of the 10" flower blossom squares selected in half vertically and horizontally to create (4) 5" squares from each. Sort the squares into 25 sets of 4 squares with different prints, but matching colors.

From the 2 tulip stem squares, cut (1) 1½" strip from 1 side of each 10" print square. From the remaining 8½" x 10" rectangles, cut 1½" x 8½" stem strips. Each rectangle will yield 6 strips and a **total of (10)** 1½" x 8½" stem strips are needed.

From the background fabric, cut:
- (2) 10" strips across the width of the fabric. Subcut:
  - 1 strip into (4) 10" background squares.
  - 1 strip into (1) 10" square and (4) 2½" strips. From each 2½" strip, cut (12) 2½" background squares.

- (11) 2½" strips. Subcut each strip into (16) 2½" background squares. Add these to the 2½" background squares previously cut. Cut for a **total of (220)** 2½" background squares.

- (7) 1½" strips across the width of the fabric. Set these aside for the horizontal sashing.

Set the remaining background fabric aside for the inner border.

2 make dizzy daisies

Snowball Corners

On the reverse side of each of the 2½" background squares, mark a line from corner to corner once on the diagonal. **2A**

Select a set of 4 coordinating 5" squares. Place a marked 2½" background square on 3 corners of a 5" square with right sides facing, as shown. Sew on the marked sewing lines. Trim the excess fabric away ¼" from the sewn seam and press. **2B**

Repeat with the 3 coordinating squares from your selected set.

Block Construction

Arrange the 4 coordinating snowballed units as shown. Sew the squares together in pairs to form rows. Press the seam of the upper row to the right and the lower row to the left. Nest the seams and sew the rows together. **Make 15** dizzy daisy blocks. **2C 2D**

Block Size: 9½" unfinished, 9" finished

3 make totally tulips

Tulip Blossoms

Select a set of 4 coordinating 5" squares. Place a marked 2½" background square atop a 5" square with right sides facing. Sew on the marked line. Trim the excess fabric away ¼" from the sewn seam. Repeat with the 3 coordinating squares from your selected set. **3A**

Arrange the 4 coordinating snowballed units as shown. Sew the squares together in pairs to form rows. Press the seam of the upper row to the right and the lower row to the left. Nest the seams and sew the rows together. **Make 10** tulip blossoms. **3B 3C**

Leaf Units

On the reverse side of the 10" background squares, draw a line from corner to corner twice on the diagonal. Layer a marked square with a 10" print square right sides together. Sew on either side of both drawn lines using a ¼" seam allowance. **3D**

Cut the sewn squares through the center horizontally and vertically. Then cut on the drawn lines. Open each section to reveal a half-square triangle. Each set of sewn squares will yield 8 half-square triangles and you will need a **total of 40**. Square each half-square triangle unit to 4½" and keep sets of 2 matching half-square triangles together. **3E**

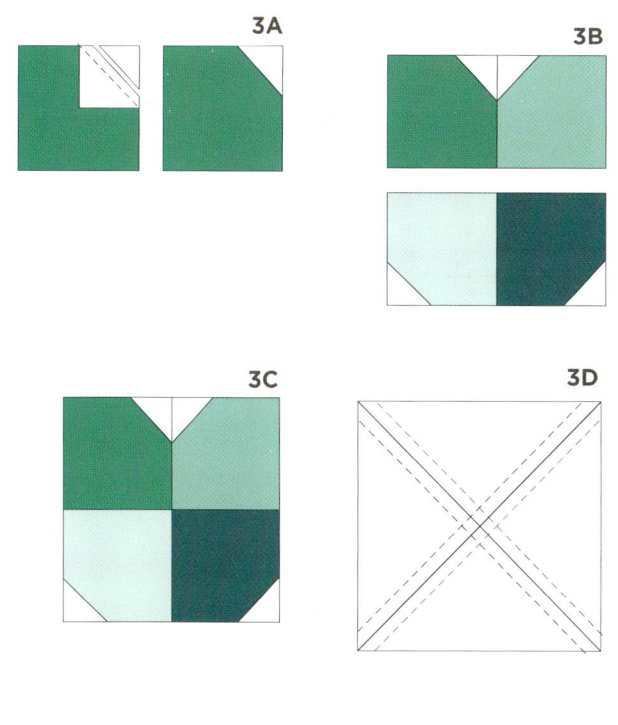

Arrange 2 matching half-square triangles as shown. Sew them together in a vertical row. **3F**

Select 2 other half-square triangles that match each other, but not the pair you just sewed into a vertical row. Sew them together in the same manner. Notice the orientation of the half-square triangles. **3G**

Sew the vertical rows to either side of a 1½" x 8½" stem strip. **Make 10** leaf units. **3H**

Block Construction
Sew a tulip blossom to the top of a leaf unit as shown to complete the block. **Make 10** totally tulip blocks. **3I**

Block Size: 9½" x 17½" unfinished, 9" x 17" finished

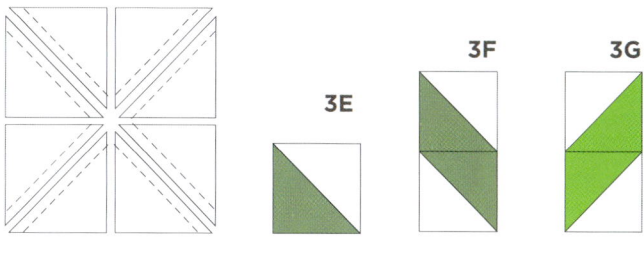

4 sew rows

Arrange 5 dizzy daisy blocks in a row. Sew the row together, matching seams. Press the seams toward the right. **Make 3** dizzy daisy rows. **4A**

Arrange 5 totally tulip blocks in a row. Sew the row together, matching seams. Press the seams toward the left. **Make 2** totally tulip rows. **4B**

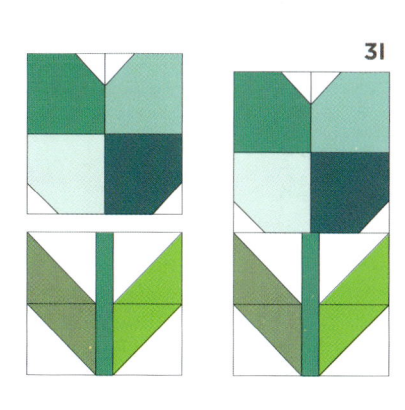

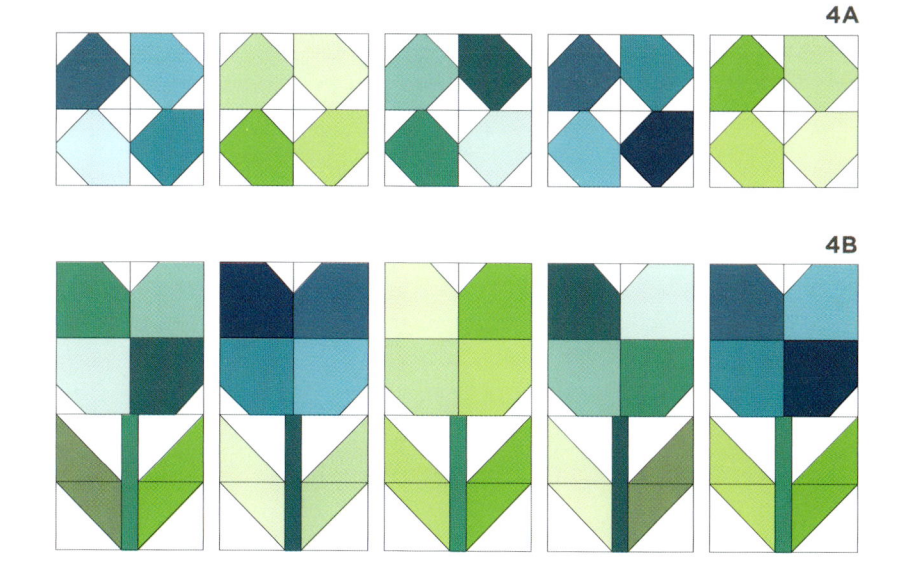

1. Arrange 4 coordinating units with 3 snowballed corners as shown. Sew the squares together in pairs to form rows. Nest the seams and sew the rows together. Make 15 dizzy daisy blocks.

2. Arrange 4 coordinating snowballed units as shown. Sew the squares together in pairs to form rows. Nest the seams and sew the rows together. Make 10 tulip blossoms.

3. Layer a marked square with a 10" print square, right sides together. Sew on either side of both drawn lines using a ¼" seam allowance. Cut the sewn squares through the center horizontally and vertically, then cut on the drawn lines. Open and press each section. Square each half-square triangle to 4½".

4. Arrange 2 matching half-square triangles as shown and sew them together in a vertical row. Select 2 other half-square triangles that match each other, but not the pair just sewn and sew them together in the same manner.

5. Sew the vertical rows to either side of a 1½" x 8½" stem strip. Make 10 leaf units.

6. Sew a tulip blossom to the top of a leaf unit as shown to complete the block. Make 10 totally tulip blocks.

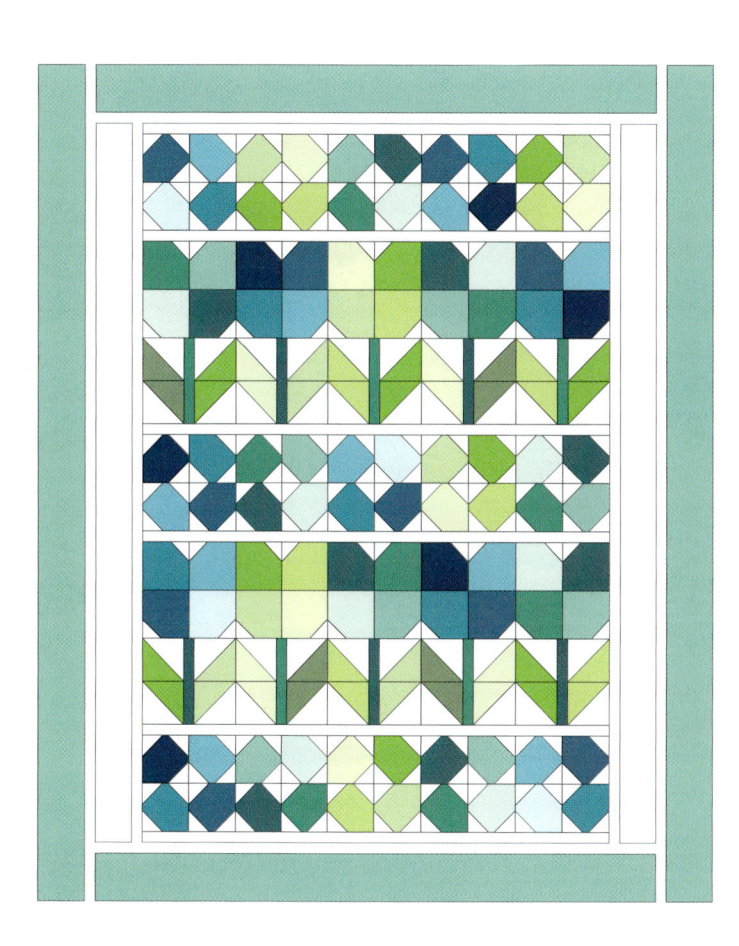

5 arrange & sew

Sew the horizontal sashing strips set aside earlier end-to-end to create 1 long strip. Cut the horizontal sashing from this strip. Measure the width of your rows to determine the length of your horizontal sashing, approximately 45½".

Arrange the rows as shown in the diagram on your left. Sew the rows together with a horizontal sashing strip between each row and to the top and bottom. Press the seams toward the bottom.

6 inner border

From the background fabric, cut (4) 4" strips across the width of the fabric. Sew the strips together to create 1 long strip. Trim the border from this strip. Refer to Borders (pg. 238) in the Construction Basics to measure, cut, and attach the borders. The strip lengths are approximately 67½" for the sides.

7 outer border

From the border fabric, cut (7) 5" strips across the width of the fabric. Sew the strips together to create 1 long strip. Trim the border from this strip.

Note: For this quilt, the top and bottom borders will be sewn first, followed by the side borders.

Refer to Borders (pg. 238) in the Construction Basics to measure and cut the border. The strips lengths are approximately 52½" for the top and bottom and 76½" for the sides.

8 quilt & bind

Layer the quilt with batting and backing, then quilt. After the quilting is complete, see Construction Basics (pg. 238) to finish your quilt.

AMES PATTERSON NOW YOU SEE HER
THE AUDUBON BOOK OF True Nature Stories

Tulip Garden
Misty's Play

Let your creativity bloom with Misty's lovely tulip wall hanging featuring five flowers in a variety of colors and sizes. She makes her tulips in three different heights to give her blocks a unique, staggered effect. Stitch it up and welcome spring into your home!

materials

WALL HANGING SIZE
31" x 21"

BLOCK SIZE
4½" x 12" unfinished, 4" x 11½" finished

PROJECT TOP
1 package 5" print squares or
   at least (8) 5" print squares
¼ yard green print
½ yard background - includes
   sashing and inner border

OUTER BORDER
½ yard

BINDING
½ yard

BACKING
¾ yard

SAMPLE PROJECT
Artisan Batiks - Serenity Lake by
Lunn Studios for Robert Kaufman

1 cut

Select (5) 5" print squares for the tulip blossoms. Cut each in half vertically and horizontally to make 2½" squares. Each 5" square will yield (4) 2½" squares and a **total of 20** are needed.

From the green print fabric:
- Cut a 3" strip across the width of the fabric.

- Cut a 1" strip across the width of the fabric. Subcut the strip into (2) 1" x 8" rectangles, (1) 1" x 6" rectangle, and (2) 1" x 4" rectangles.

From the background fabric:
- Cut a 5" strip across the width of the fabric. Subcut (3) 5" squares. Trim the remainder of the strip to 4½" and then subcut (2) 4½" squares and (1) 4½" x 2½" rectangle.

- Cut (1) 2¼" strip across the width of the fabric. Subcut (4) 2¼" x 4½" rectangles and (2) 2¼" x 2½" rectangles.

- Cut (4) 1½" strips across the width of the fabric. Subcut (3) 1½" x 12" sashing rectangles from 1 strip. Subcut (1) 1½" x 12" sashing rectangle from another strip. Add the rest of the cut strip to the remaining 1½" strips and set them aside for the inner border.

- Cut a 1¼" strip across the width of the fabric. Subcut (20) 1¼" squares.

2 leaf units

On the reverse side of (3) 5" background squares, draw a line from corner to corner twice on the diagonal. Select (3) 5" print squares from your package to create the leaves. Layer a marked square with a 5" print square, right sides facing. Sew on either side of both drawn lines using a *scant* ¼" seam allowance. **2A**

Cut the sewn squares through the center horizontally and vertically. Then cut on the drawn lines. Open each section to reveal a half-square triangle. Each set of sewn squares will yield 8 half-square triangles and a **total of 20** are needed. Square to 2¼" if necessary. **2B**

Note: If your half-square triangles measure differently than ours, don't panic. You can adjust the tulip blossom to account for any slight variances.

Arrange 4 matching half-square triangles in 2 vertical rows as shown. Sew the half-square triangles together in pairs. Press. Repeat to **make 5 pairs** of vertical rows. Set the remaining 4 half-square triangles aside for another project. **2C**

Sew a pair of vertical rows to either side of a 1" x 4" green print rectangle. Press. **Make 2** A units and set them aside for the moment. **2D**

Sew a 2¼" x 4½" background rectangle to the top of each vertical row in a pair of matching rows. Press. Sew each of these vertical rows to either side of a 1" x 8" green print rectangle. Press. **Make 2** B units and set them aside for the moment. **2E**

Sew a 2¼" x 2½" background rectangle to the top of each remaining vertical row. Press the seams toward the top. Sew each of these vertical rows to either side of a 1" x 6" green print rectangle. Press to complete 1 C unit and set it aside for the moment. **2F**

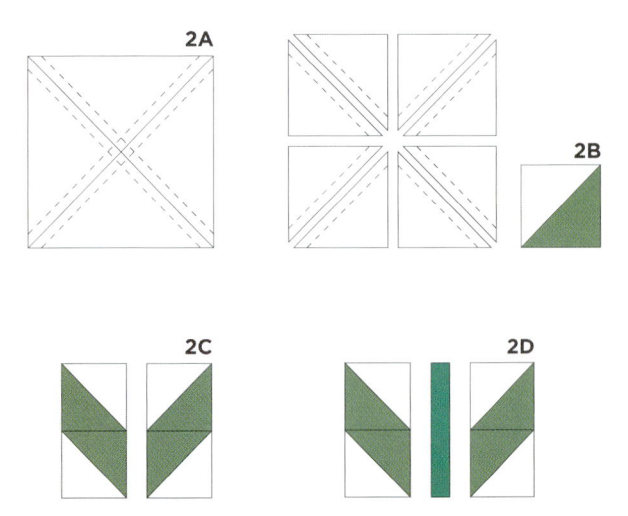

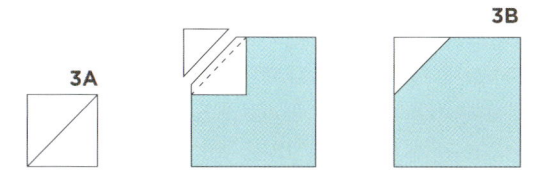

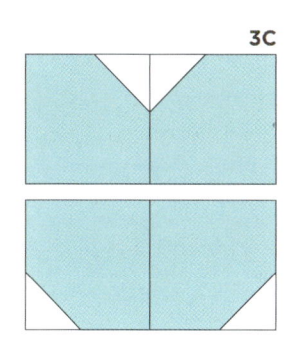

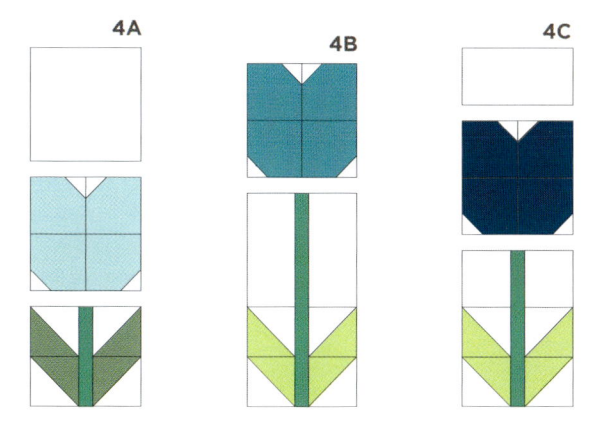

3 tulip blossoms

On the reverse side of the 1¼" background squares, mark a line from corner to corner once on the diagonal either by folding the square and pressing in a crease or by marking it with a pencil. **3A**

Place a marked background square atop a 2½" print square with right sides facing. Sew on the marked line. Trim the excess fabric away ¼" from the sewn seam. **Make 20** snowballed squares. **3B**

Note: You may need to adjust the size of your snowballed squares slightly to match your leaf units. Measure the width of your leaf units and if it is not 4½" wide, you can either trim your snowballed squares before sewing them together or adjust your seam allowance when sewing them together to account for any differences.

Arrange 4 matching snowballed squares in a 4-patch formation as shown. Sew the squares together in pairs to form rows. Press the rows in opposite directions. Nest the seams and sew the rows together. Press the seam towards the bottom to complete the unit. **Make 5** units and set them aside for the moment. These will be used as the tulip blossoms. **3C**

4 block construction

Sew a blossom unit to the top of an A unit. Press the seam. Sew a 4½" background square to the top to complete an A Block. **Make 2** A Blocks. **4A**

Sew a blossom unit to the top of a B unit. Press the seam to complete a B Block. **Make 2** B Blocks. **4B**

Sew the last blossom unit to the top of the C unit. Press the seam. Sew the 4½" x 2½" background rectangle to the top. Press the seam to complete the C Block. **4C**

Block Size: 4½" x 12" unfinished, 4" x 11½" finished

1. Mark a line twice on the diagonal on the reverse side of a 5″ background square. Place the marked square atop a print square, right sides facing. Sew along both sides of the marked lines with a ¼″ seam allowance. Cut in half in both directions and then on each marked line. Open and press.

2. Arrange 4 half-square triangles in 2 vertical rows of 2 as shown. Sew them together in pairs. Press.

3. Sew a 2¼″ x 4½″ background rectangle to the top of each pair of half-square triangles. Press. Sew the 2 vertical rows to either side of a 1″ x 8″ green print rectangle and set this aside for now.

4. Mark a line once on the diagonal on the reverse side of a 1¼″ background square. Palace the marked square atop a 2½″ print square, right sides facing. Sew on the marked line and then trim the excess fabric away. Open and press. Make 4 identical units.

5. Arrange the 4 units in 2 rows of 2 as shown. Sew the units together in rows. Press the seams in opposite directions. Nest the seams and sew the rows together.

6. Sew the blossom unit you just created on top of the unit you set aside earlier. Press.

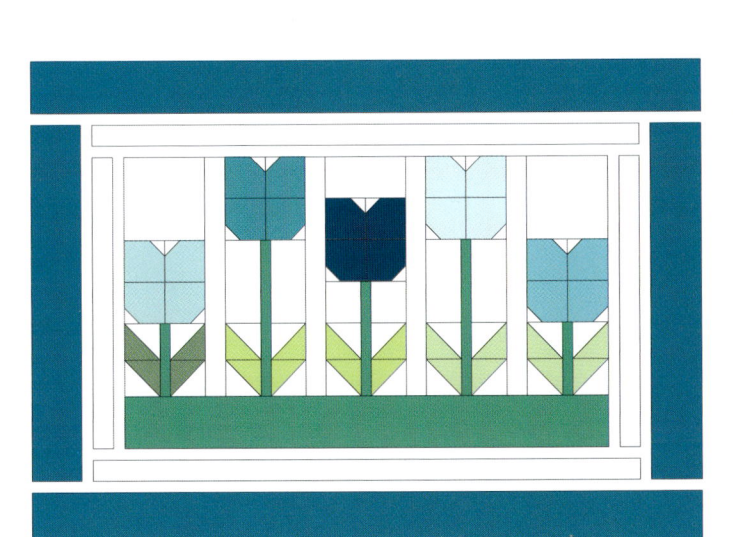

5 arrange & sew

Lay out your blocks in a single row as shown in the diagram below. Sew the blocks together with a 1½"x 12" sashing rectangle between each block. Press the seams.

Measure the width of your project in 3 places. See the instructions for measuring a project for borders in the Construction Basics (pg. 238) if you need additional guidance. Your project should be approximately 24½" wide. Trim the 3" green print strip to the same width as your project.

Sew the green print rectangle to the bottom of your project. Press the seam.

6 inner border

Pick up the 1½" background strips you set aside earlier. Sew the strips to make 1 long strip. Trim the borders from this strip. Refer to Borders (pg. 238) in the Construction Basics to measure, cut, and attach the borders. The lengths are approximately 14" for the sides and 26" for the top and bottom.

7 outer border

Cut (3) 3" strips across the width of the outer border fabric. Sew the strips to make 1 long strip. Trim the borders from this strip. Refer to Borders (pg. 238) in the Construction Basics to measure, cut, and attach the borders. The lengths are approximately 16" for the sides and 31" for the top and bottom.

8 quilt & bind

Layer the wall hanging with batting and backing, then quilt. After the quilting is complete, see Construction Basics (pg. 238) to finish your project.

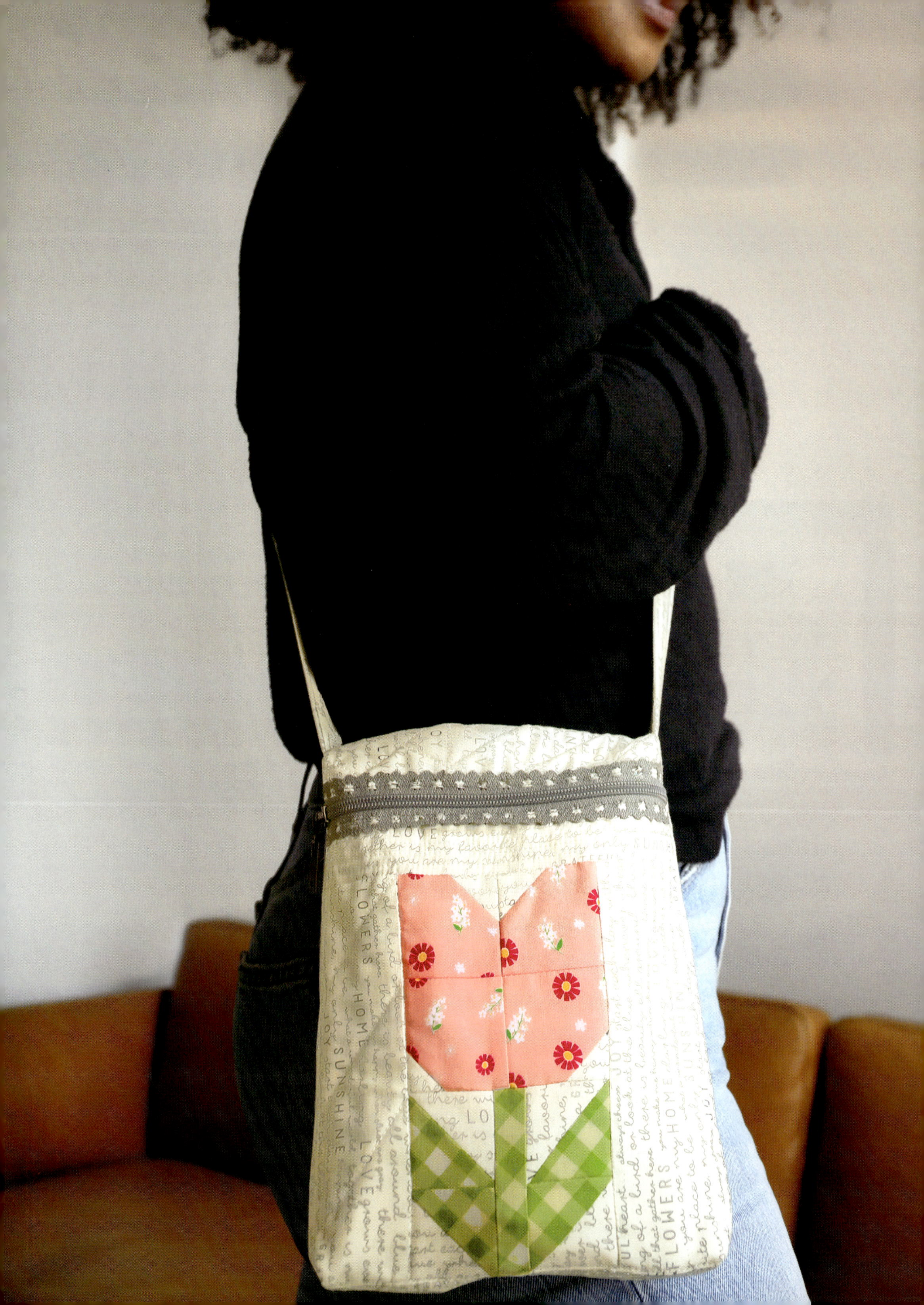

Mini Tulip Crossbody Bag

HOME RUN

materials

BAG SIZE
7" x 9" x 1½"

BLOCK SIZE
4½" x 8" unfinished, 4" x 7½" finished

PROJECT SUPPLIES
(1) 5" print square for the tulip blossom
(1) 5" print square for the leaves
½ yard of print background fabric
½ yard of fabric for the lining
1¼ yards of batting - at least 14½" wide
Missouri Star Fancy Zip - 14"

SAMPLE PROJECT
Gingham Gardens by My Mind's Eye for Riley Blake
Pure Delight Pink by Melanie Collette of Hello Melly Designs for Riley Blake Designs

1 cut

From the background fabric, cut:

- (1) 10½" strip across the **width** of the fabric. Subcut (1) 10½" x 9½" rectangle. From the remainder of the strip, cut:
  - (1) 5" strip across the **width** of the fabric. Subcut (1) 5" x 9½" rectangle and (1) 5" x 4" rectangle. Trim the 5" x 4" rectangle to 4" square.
  - (1) 3" strip across the **width** of the fabric. Subcut (2) 3" x 8" rectangles.
  - (1) 1½" strip across the **width** of the fabric. Subcut (1) 1½" x 9½" rectangle and (4) 1½" x 1¼" rectangles. Trim the small rectangles to 1¼" square.
- (1) 4" strip across the **width** of the fabric. Set this aside for the strap.
- From the lining fabric, cut (1) 9½" strip across the **width** of the fabric. Subcut (1) 9½" x 23½" rectangle.

From the batting, cut (1) 1" strip along the **length** of the batting. Trim to the same length as your 4" background strip that was set aside for the strap. From the remaining batting, cut (1) 23½" strip across the **width** of the batting. Subcut (1) 23½" x 9½" rectangle.

2 make the strap

Fold the 4" background strip in half lengthwise, wrong sides together. Press along the fold to crease the centerline. Open, then fold each long raw edge in to meet the centerline. Press along the folds. **2A**

Open and place the 1" batting strip inside with 1 long edge lined up with the centerline. Refold the fabric strip where you creased before to enclose the batting strip and create a 1" folded strap. Press. Topstitch the strap ⅛" from each long edge. Set the finished strap aside for now. **2B**

Note: You can trim this strap to the desired length that best fits your body.

2A

2B

3 block construction

Leaf Unit

From the 5" print square for the leaves, cut (1) 1" strip and (1) 4" strip across the width of the square.

- From the 1" strip, subcut (1) 1" x 4" rectangle.
- From the 4" strip, subcut (1) 4" square.

Lay the 4" background square atop the 4" leaf square. Sew around the perimeter using a ¼" seam. Cut the sewn squares twice on the diagonal. Square to 2¼". **3A**

Arrange the half-square triangles in 2 vertical rows as shown and sew them together in pairs. Press toward the bottom. **3B**

Sew the vertical rows to either side of the 1" x 4" leaf rectangle. Press toward the rectangle. Set aside for the moment. **3C**

Tulip Blossoms

Cut the 5" print square for the tulip blossom in half vertically and horizontally to yield (4) 2½" squares.

Note: You may need to adjust the size of your snowballed squares slightly to match your leaf unit. Measure the width of your leaf unit and if it is not 4½" wide, you can either trim your snowballed squares before sewing them together or adjust your seam allowance when sewing them together to account for any differences.

Fold each 1¼" background square in half on the diagonal and press a crease. Place a marked background square atop a 2½" blossom square as shown, right sides facing. Sew on the marked line. Trim the excess fabric away ¼" from the sewn seam. **Make 4** snowballed squares. **3D**

Arrange the snowballed squares as shown. Sew the squares together in pairs to form rows. Press the rows in opposite directions. Nest the seams and sew the rows together. Press to complete the blossom unit. **3E**

Tulip Block

Sew the blossom unit to the top of the leaf unit. Press. **3F**

Block Size: 4½" x 8" unfinished, 4" x 7½" finished

4 bag construction

Sew a 3" x 8" background rectangle to each side of the tulip block. Press towards the rectangles. **4A**

Sew the 1½" x 9½" background rectangle to top and the 5" x 9½" background rectangle to bottom. Press towards the rectangles to complete the bag front. **4B**

Sew the 9½" x 10½" rectangle to the bottom of the bag front. Press towards the bottom. **4C**

Layer the lining fabric right side down, the batting, and the bag front right side up. Baste, then quilt as desired. Trim the edges even as needed.

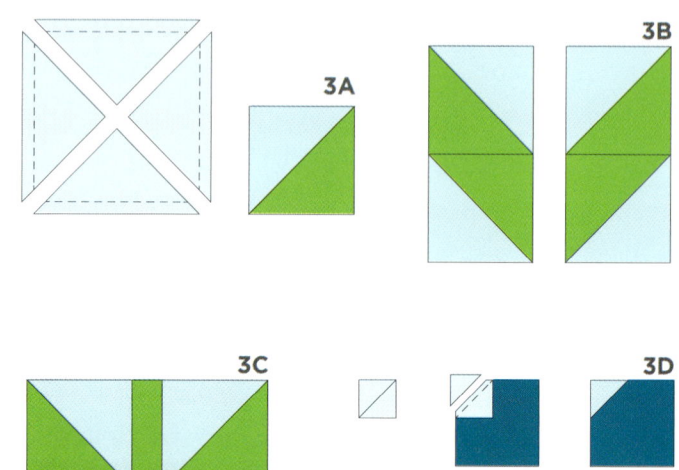

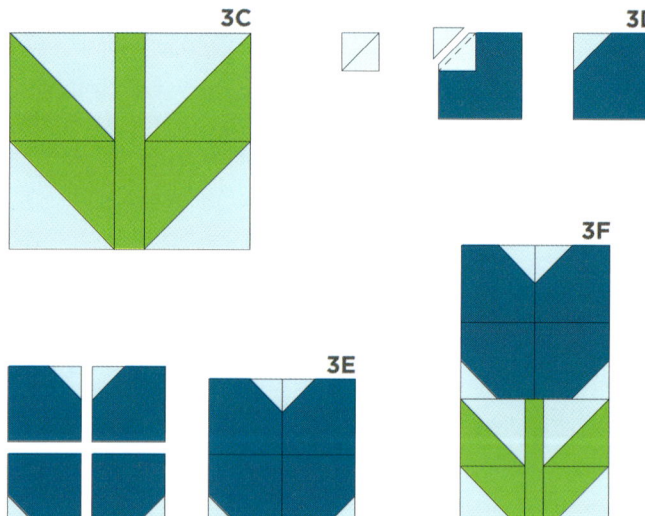

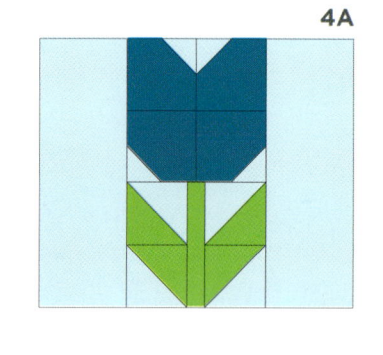

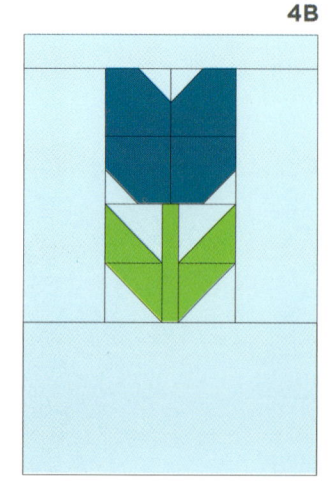

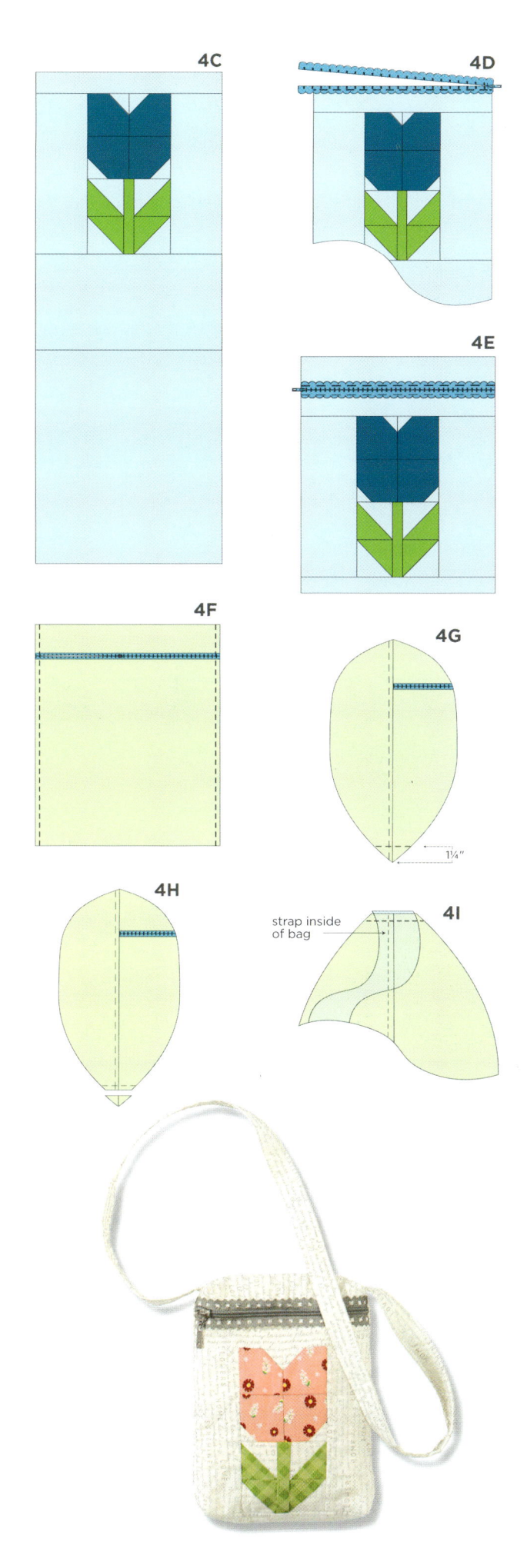

Missouri Star Fancy Zips may be sewn directly over the top of the bag's raw edges. Lay the bottom of the unzipped decorative zipper along the top raw edge of the bag face, making sure the zipper teeth extend just off the fabric. Pin and stitch using a zigzag or straight stitch. **Note**: Make sure to line up the zipper pull with 1 side of the bag. The other end may extend off the side to be trimmed later. **4D**

Fold the bottom of the bag back, bringing it from behind toward the top to make a tube. Pin, then stitch the other side of the zipper along the raw edge of the bag back. Close the zipper to be sure everything is lined up and works well, then move the zipper to the middle of the bag before trimming the zipper ends flush with the fabric. **4E**

Turn the quilted bag so the lining is on the outside. Before sewing the sides of the tube together, roll the zipper down so it is positioned on the bag front, 1½" down from its previous position. Flatten the bag and pin or clip the sides together, then sew them together using a ¼" seam allowance. **4F**

While the bag is wrong sides out, open 1 bottom corner of the bag by pulling the top and bottom in opposite directions and make a point with the end seam running vertically down the center. Measure and mark 1¼" from the corner point. Line the 45° mark of your ruler with the angled edge of the corner and draw a horizontal line at the mark previously made. Sew along this line to box the corner, backstitching twice at the beginning and end. **4G**

Repeat for the remaining bottom corner. Trim each corner ¼" away from the sewn seam and zigzag the raw edges if desired. **4H**

Flatten 1 top corner as you did earlier, marking a line that extends 1¼" across the triangle point. Before stitching, cut the corner off ¼" from the drawn line to create an opening for the bag strap. Insert the 1 end of the strap from inside the bag, line up the raw edges, and pin. Stitch across the opening, backstitching at both ends. Repeat with the other top corner, being careful not to twist the strap inside the bag. **4I**

Turn the bag right side out through the zipper. Gently poke the corners out and press the bag. Fill your Mini Tulip Crossbody Bag with essentials and you're ready to tiptoe through the tulips!

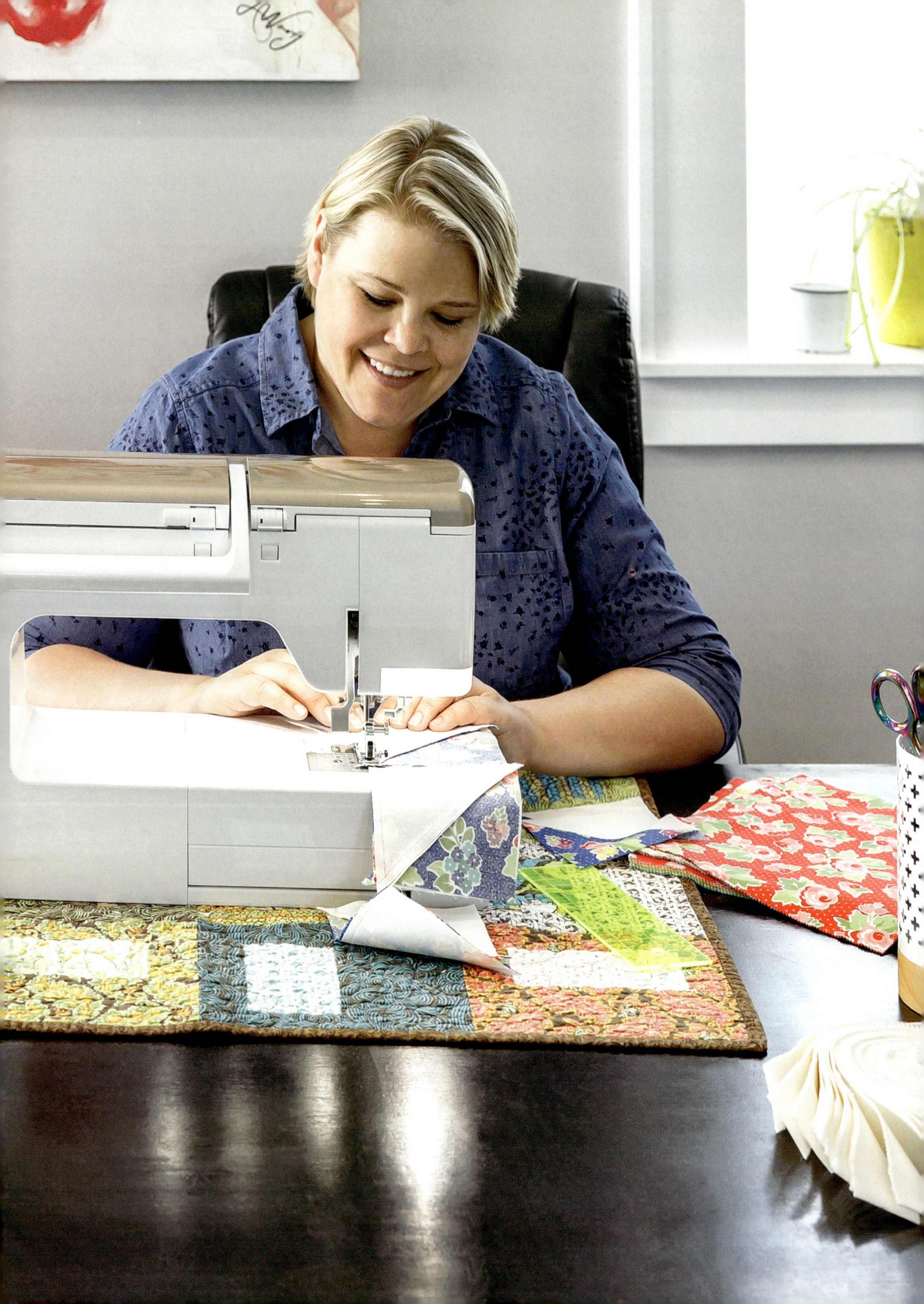

Natalie Earnheart

Finding Inspiration in Unlikely Places

Natalie Earnheart is the oldest daughter in the Doan family. Growing up with Jenny as her mother definitely influenced her to take up the art of sewing and she's become a talented sewist and quilter in her own right. As a child, she learned how to sew with her mother's guidance and as she grew up, she quickly picked up quilting too. Over a decade ago, when Missouri Star had just started creating online quilting tutorials, Jenny tripped while filming and broke her leg and Natalie was right there to step in and help out. Natalie continues to teach quilting tutorials to this day and even has her own tutorial series called The Final Stitch that focuses on in-depth quilt finishing techniques.

Collaborating to create the Triple Play tutorials once a month was a natural extension of what Natalie had already been doing. Working in close proximity with her mother and with her sister-in-law in the same studio space while they were each doing their own tutorials was always helpful for them all and it just made sense. Why not do a tutorial together? That's how the Triple Play came about.

We took a moment to sit down and chat with Natalie to get a glimpse into her perspective on creativity and how she has the fortitude to constantly be involved in coming up with ideas for new quilt designs. As she explains, it has become a part of her life, something that she's become attuned to. Natalie can dream up new quilt designs just about anywhere and they even come to her while she's simply walking down the street. She says, "Architecture is super inspiring. I love looking at the way architects combine geometric shapes with curves and art to create something beautiful and functional. All of our quilt designs come from somewhere, but I am also very purpose-driven. I don't just do things to do them. We usually have a challenge to tackle. It could be a challenging pattern we want to simplify, or a new way to use a template. I'm inspired by a need to disrupt the difficulty in this industry. Meaning, I want to remove the barriers that create the idea that quilting is hard, and has to be done a certain way. I want everyone to feel welcome in our industry. We are creatives, artists, and dreamers. Everything and everyone is celebrated, because quilting is personal. We don't have to be the same, I prefer the variety. I am inspired by the entire quilting community."

Simplifying complex quilting techniques runs in the family and Natalie is quick to share her wisdom with newcomers to the craft. She explains, "Don't be afraid to try something new. Don't be afraid to make mistakes. There's a world of creative possibilities; try a different technique or style and learn to create what makes you happy." And Natalie loves trying new types of art as well. She has a talent for working with stained glass and has created many beautiful pieces. She also enjoys baking, to her childrens' delight. Nobody can resist when she pulls a hot sourdough loaf out of the oven!

> "Don't be afraid to try something new. Don't be afraid to make mistakes. There's a world of creative possibilities."

> "I want to remove the barriers that create the idea that quilting is hard, and has to be done a certain way. I want everyone to feel welcome in our industry. We are creatives, artists, and dreamers."

Natalie began quilting herself soon after she became a mother. "I started quilting when my mom started taking her quilting classes. I came over one time and we made some quilts for my little boys—they were toddlers at the time. I don't think I did much of the sewing, I did the cutting and the pressing. So, I didn't make my own quilts until after we started the shop. Mom took a log cabin class at the Vo-tech school, so she was into it and wanted to make quilts for everybody." That Log Cabin class at the Vo-tech school in Chillicothe, Missouri, back in the late 1990s was the first step into the wonderful world of quilting that Natalie has since fully embraced. Her favorite thing about quilting is this: "I enjoy the act of creating something that didn't exist before. I like being able to play with color and create patterns. I like the art side of it, but I like that you can snuggle up with it and use it. There are SO many possibilities!" A quilt is much more than a blanket, as we all know. It's an artform. It's tangible. It's a way of showing you care, expressing yourself, experimenting with color and pattern, and so much more.

Natalie pictured with a quilt she made for one of her sons

> "It's okay to have failures in quilting ... It's about being a problem-solver and having fun with it." So much of creativity really is about finding creative solutions to life's challenges.

At times it may seem like creativity comes easily to someone like Natalie, but she'll have you know that there is a lot more trial and error than you might think. Good ideas take a lot of experimentation. She adds, "It's okay to have failures in quilting. You'll get to be a much better quilter. Being inspired by something you see and creating something new and different, something that excites you, something that could be a gift, something for a friend. There's a lot of nuance there. It's doing the best you can with what you have and being willing to try new things. It's about being a problem-solver and having fun with it." So much of creativity really is about finding creative solutions to life's challenges.

Finding the time to be creative also takes careful planning for Natalie. She doesn't have the time to wait for inspiration to strike, so she plans it into her schedule. As many creative professionals know, sometimes you need to show up before creativity does, and that's okay. For her, designing a quilt "starts with creative limitations like a ruler or a fabric line." She continues, "Before we start creating we have a planning session where we develop ideas about what blocks, quilts, or templates we want to challenge ourselves to make into new quilts. Then as we think about what we are going to make, we will often have spontaneous brainstorm sessions and discuss our ideas. We'll give each other feedback, help solve construction problems, contribute to layout and color design, etc. It's a really fun collaborative process." And it helps to have Jenny and Misty nearby. Natalie says, "Everything we do is built on a framework of release dates and deadlines. A lot of times we work together, but we often work independently. We ask each other for help with challenges we have. We brainstorm together. We talk to each other a lot. We cut and sew for each other at times. We get more work done together."

And what if inspiration remains elusive? Here's Natalie's ingenious solution: "I light a candle, turn on music, and get a favorite snack. I tell myself I'll work on my project for 10 minutes. As soon as I get started, suddenly I'm into it. I can find the motivation by doing it. I'm a big proponent of doing the thing you don't want to do first." Isn't that the way it goes? So much time can be spent avoiding the task at hand, but when we simply start, suddenly we're halfway through. Or as the famous saying by Aristotle goes (quoted famously by Mary Poppins), "Well begun is half done."

And speaking of Mary Poppins, of all the Triple Play projects so far, Natalie's favorite is the West Wind. She says, "To me, the block looks like arrows on a compass, like a weathervane. It reminds me of Mary Poppins and the wind blowing in and bringing her with it." After hearing about Natalie's sources of inspiration, it feels very appropriate. No matter which way the wind blows in her life, she is able to orient herself well and explore her creativity in any direction she chooses.

"I can find the motivation by doing it. I'm a big proponent of doing the thing you don't want to do first."

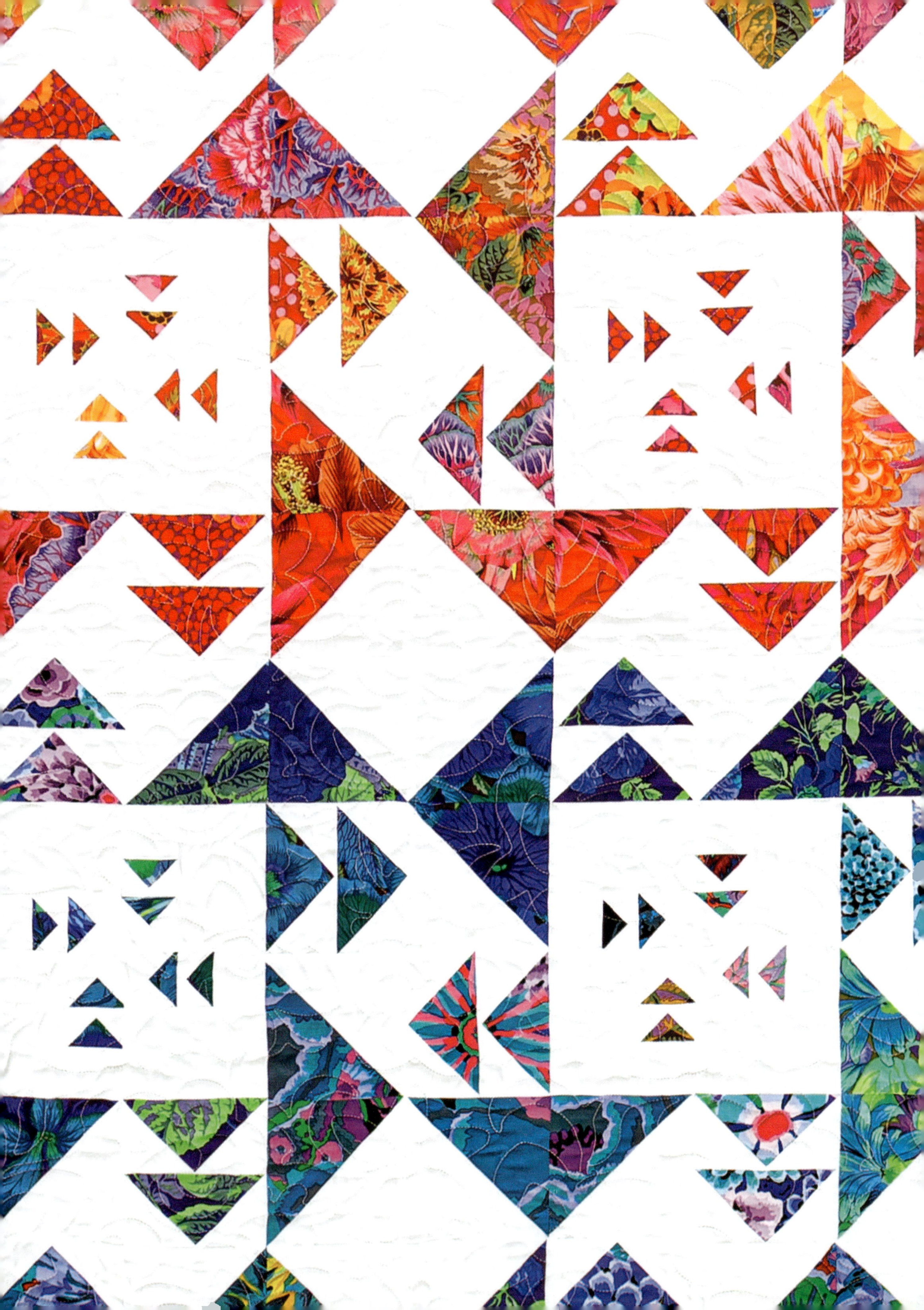

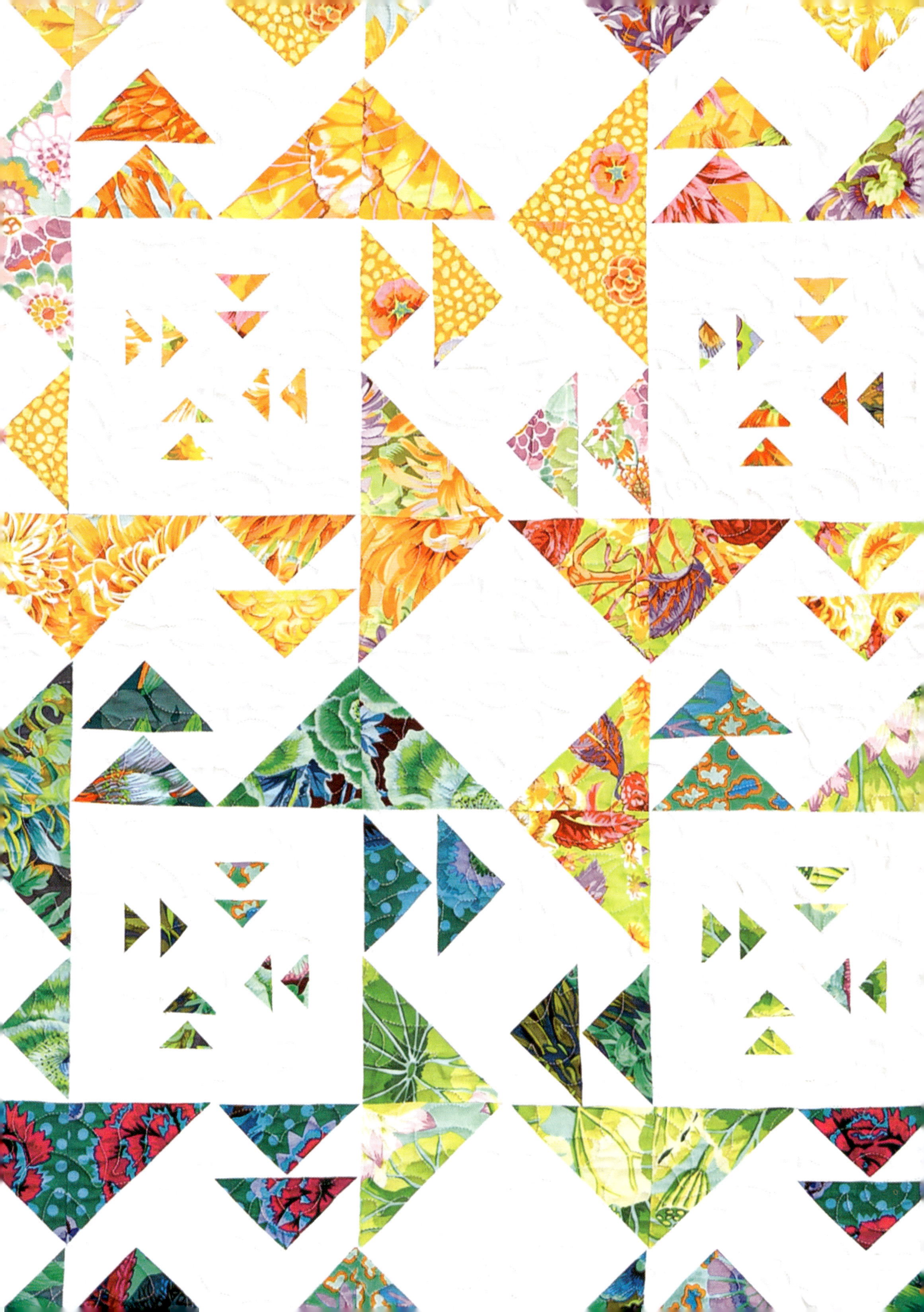

102

Flying Geese

TRIPLE PLAY

Duck. Duck. Goose! Don't be afraid to chase your dreams and stitch up a gorgeous flying geese quilt. This classic pattern may elude many, but we're here to help make it easy and approachable. As three different quilters, we've all made this quilt block a little differently, so whichever method works best for you is fine by us! After all, what's good for the goose is good for the gander.

Whether you like to create your flying geese out of two half-square triangles, you like to snowball two corners of a rectangle for each goose, or you like to use our fancy method of making four flying geese all at once with some clever piecing and cutting, it's all up to you. The results are always beautiful! That's the fabulous thing about learning from three different quilters. When we combine our unique perspectives, you'll learn something new from each of us.

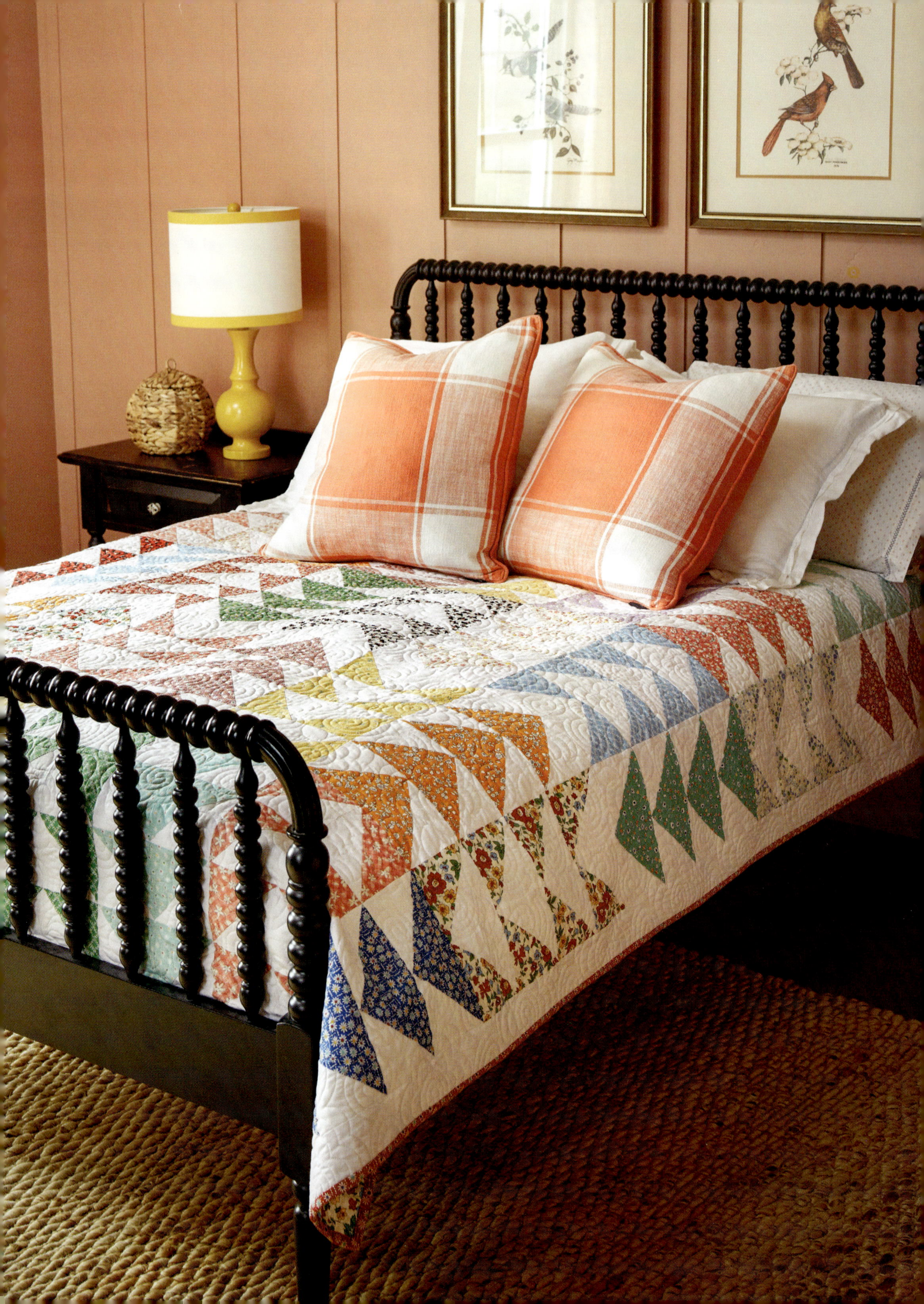

Every Which Way But Goose

Jenny's Play

Take a gander at Jenny's gorgeous flying geese quilt! Created with sections of four flying geese units stacked and flipped, it creates a fun pattern you won't squawk at. You're in for a truly quack-tacular quilt!

materials

QUILT SIZE
76" x 84"

BLOCK SIZE
8½" x 16½" unfinished, 8" x 16" finished

QUILT TOP
4 packages 5" print squares
4 packages 5" background squares
½ yard coordinating print fabric
1 yard background fabric
  - includes border

BINDING
¾ yard

BACKING
5¼ yards - vertical seam(s) or
  2½ yards 108" wide

SAMPLE QUILT
Aunt Grace's Apron by Judie Rothermel for Marcus Fabric

1 sort & cut

From the coordinating print fabric, cut (2) 5" strips across the width of the fabric. Subcut 5" squares from the strips. Each strip will yield 8 squares and a **total of 12** are needed. Add these squares to your packages of 5" print squares. Set the remainder of the fabric aside for another project.

Sort the 5" print squares into a **total of 45** sets of 4 matching squares.

From the background fabric, cut (2) 5" strips across the width of the fabric. Subcut into 5" squares. Each strip will yield 8 squares and you will need to add 12 squares to your packages for a **total of 180** background squares. Set the remaining background fabric aside for the border.

2 make half-square triangles

Mark a line from corner to corner once on the diagonal on the reverse side of each background square. **2A**

Choose 1 set of print squares. Place a marked background square atop a print square with right sides facing. Sew on both sides of the marked line using a ¼" seam allowance. Cut on the marked line. Open each unit and press. Trim the units to 4½" square. Each pair of sewn squares will yield 2 half-square triangles. Repeat with the remaining print squares in your selected set to **make 8** matching half-square triangles. Keep the set of matching units together. **2B**

Repeat to make a **total of 45** sets of 8 matching half-square triangles with all of the remaining squares.

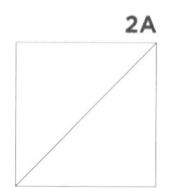

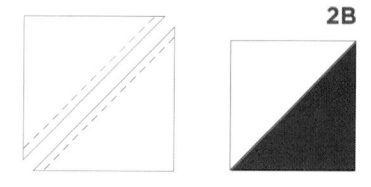

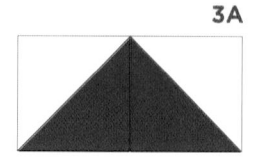

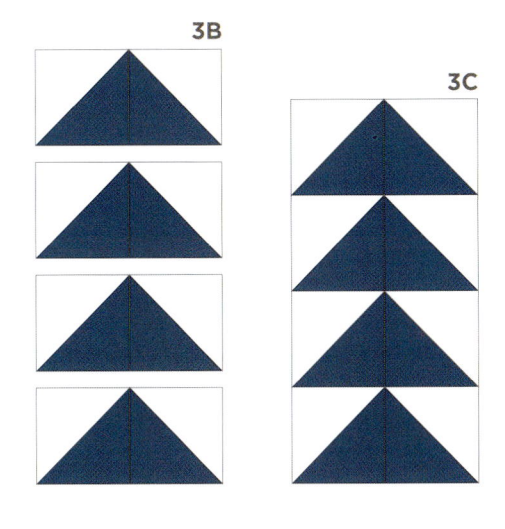

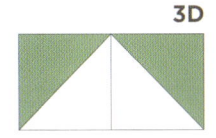

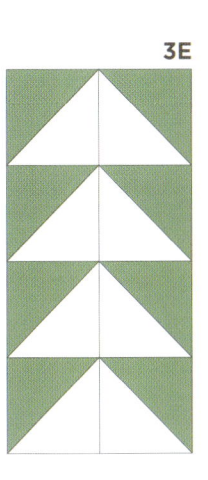

3 block construction

Select 1 set of matching half-square triangles. Sew 2 half-square triangles together as shown with the print sides together. **Make 4** flying geese units. Press. **3A**

Arrange the 4 units as shown with the seams alternating left and right. Nest the seams and sew the 4 units together. Press. **Make 23** A blocks. **3B 3C**

Select another set of matching half-square triangles. Sew 2 half-square triangles together as shown, this time with the background sides together. **Make 4** flying geese units. **3D**

In the same manner as before, sew the 4 units together. Press. **Make 22** B blocks. **3E**

Block Size: 8½" x 16½" unfinished, 8" x 16" finished

4 arrange & sew

Referring to the diagram on page 109, lay out your blocks in **5 rows of 9 blocks** each.

Each odd-numbered row will begin with an A block and alternate with B blocks which are turned 180° so the arrows point down.

Each even-numbered row will begin with a B block and alternate with A blocks which are turned 180° so the arrows point down.

Sew the blocks together in rows. Press. Nest the seams and sew the rows together to complete the quilt center. Press.

1. Mark a line from corner to corner once on the diagonal on the reverse side of each background square.

2. Place a marked background square atop a print square, right sides facing. Sew on both sides of the marked line using a ¼" seam allowance. Cut on the marked line and press. Trim to 4½". Repeat to make a total of 45 sets of 8 matching half-square triangles with all of the remaining squares.

3. Select 1 set of matching half-square triangles. Sew 2 half-square triangles together as shown, print sides together. Make 4 flying geese units.

4. Arrange the 4 units as shown with the seams alternating left and right. Nest the seams and sew the 4 units together. Press the seams toward the bottom. Make 23 A blocks.

5. Sew 2 half-square triangles together as shown, this time with the background sides together. Make 4 flying geese units. In the same manner as before, sew the 4 units together. Make 22 B blocks.

5 border

Cut (8) 2½" strips across the width of the background fabric. Sew the strips together to make 1 long strip. Trim the borders from this strip. Refer to Borders (pg. 238) in the Construction Basics to measure, cut, and attach the borders. The approximate lengths of the strips are 80" for the sides and 76" for the top and bottom.

6 quilt & bind

Layer the quilt with batting and backing, then quilt. See Construction Basics (pg. 238) to finish your quilt.

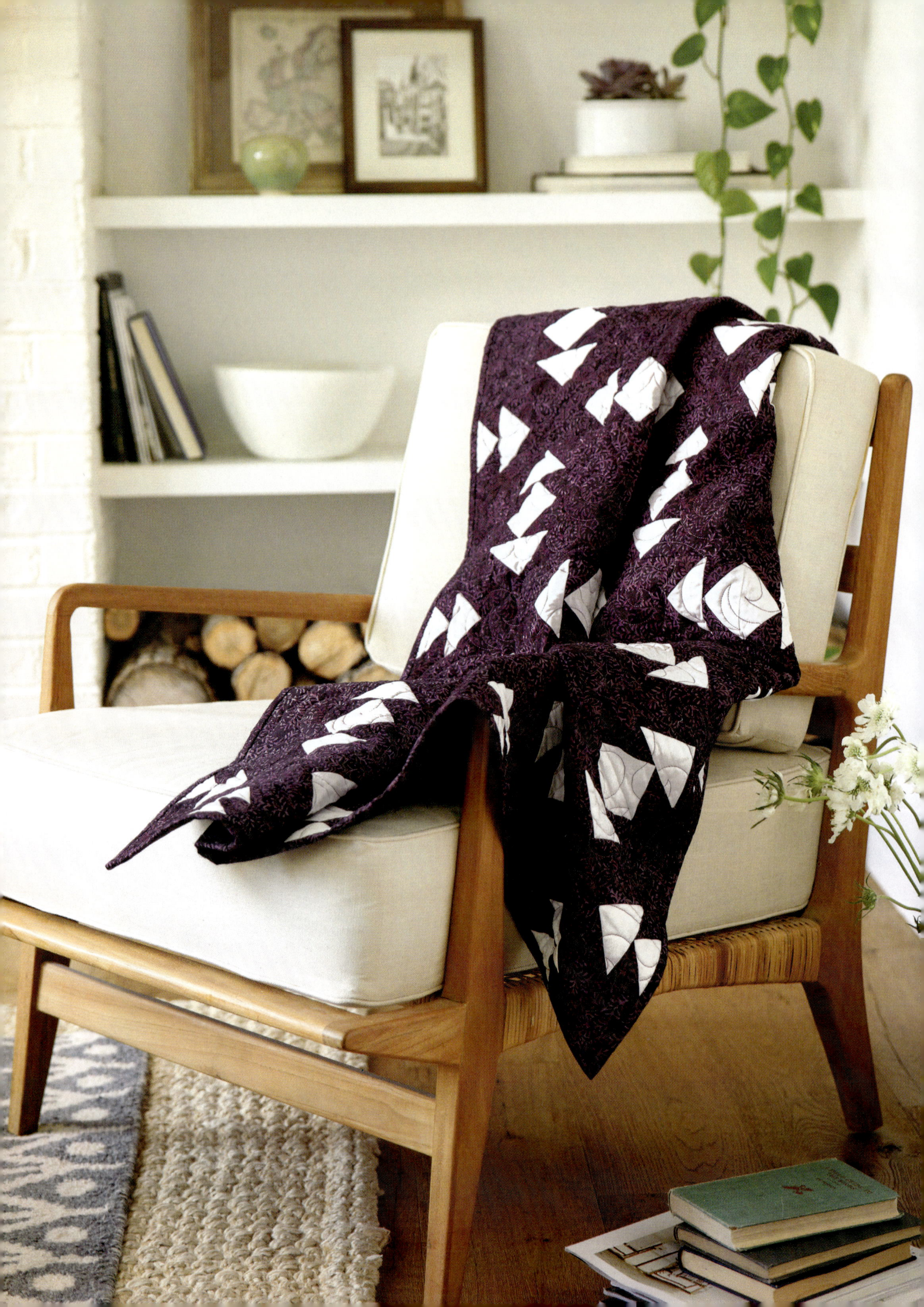

West Wind
Natalie's Play

Stitch up a flock of colorful flying geese with Natalie and watch them come together quickly and easily in her gorgeous West Wind quilt. It's amazing what you can do with these pretty triangles when you follow our easy method of making four flying geese units at once for im-peck-able results.

materials

QUILT SIZE
42" x 52½"

BLOCK SIZE
11" unfinished, 10½" finished

QUILT TOP
1 package 5" white solid squares
2¼ yards print fabric

OUTER BORDER
1¼ yards

BINDING
½ yard

BACKING
2¾ yards - horizontal seam(s)

SAMPLE QUILT
Fiery Sunset Batiks by Kathy Engle for Island Batik

1 cut

Set (2) 5" white solid squares aside for another project.

From the print fabric:
- Cut (10) 4" strips across the width of the fabric. Subcut 4" squares from the strips. Each strip will yield 10 squares and a **total of 100** are needed.

- Cut (12) 2¾" strips across the width of the fabric. Subcut 2¾" squares from the strips. Each strip will yield 14 squares and a **total of 160** are needed.

2 make flying geese units

Mark a diagonal line on the reverse side of each 2¾" print square. **2A**

Pick up a 5" white solid square and 4 marked print squares. Place 2 of the marked squares on opposite corners of the white solid square as shown, right sides facing. Notice the 2 smaller squares will overlap in the middle. Pin in place if necessary. **2B**

Sew on both sides of the marked lines using a ¼" seam allowance. Cut on the marked line to yield 2 partial units. Press towards the print triangles. **2C 2D**

Place a marked square on top of the white solid corner of 1 of the partial units as shown, right sides facing. Sew on both sides of the marked line using a ¼" seam allowance. Cut on the marked line. **2E 2F**

Press towards the print triangles to yield 2 flying geese units. **2G**

Repeat with the remaining partial unit.

Repeat to **make 160** flying geese units from the remaining 5" white solid squares and marked print squares.

Square each flying geese unit to 4" x 2¼". Be sure to leave ¼" past the point for the seam allowance.

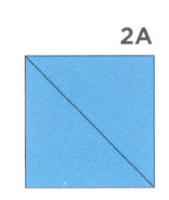

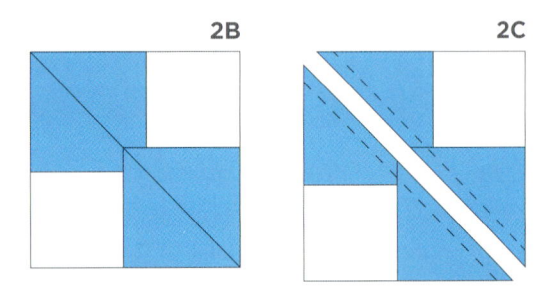

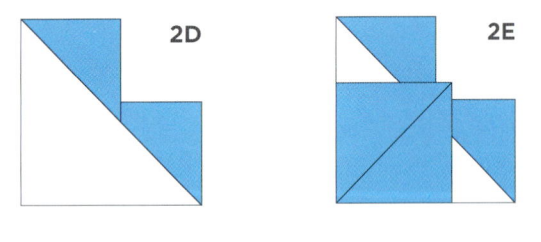

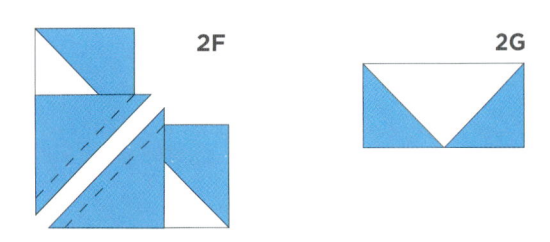

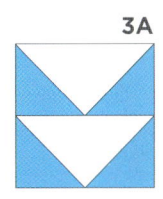

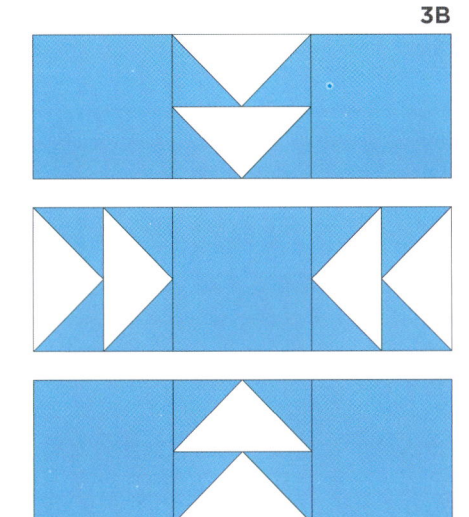

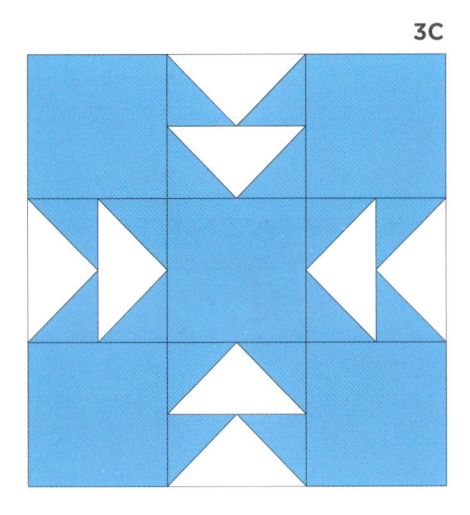

3 block construction

Pick up 8 flying geese units and sew them together as shown. Press. **Make 4** units. **3A**

Pick up (5) 4" print squares and add them to the 4 units you just made. Arrange the units in a 9-patch formation as shown. Notice how all of the flying geese point towards the center square. Sew the units together in rows. Press the seams of the upper and lower rows toward the outside. Press the seams of the center row towards the center square. **3B**

Nest the seams and sew the rows together. Press. **Make 20** blocks. **3C**

Block Size: 11" unfinished, 10½" finished

4 arrange & sew

Use the diagram on page 115 to lay out the blocks in **5 rows** of **4 blocks**. Sew the blocks together to form rows. Press the rows in alternating directions. Sew the rows together and press.

5 quilt & bind

Layer the quilt with batting and backing, then quilt. After quilting is complete, see Construction Basics (pg. 238) to finish your quilt.

1. Lay 2 marked 2¾" print squares on opposite corners of a 5" background square, as shown. Sew on either side of the marked line with a ¼" seam allowance. Cut on the marked line.

2. Press the seam of each unit towards the print triangles. Lay another marked 2¾" print square on the background corner of the unit, as shown. Sew on either side of the marked line with a ¼" seam allowance and then cut on the marked line.

3. Press the seam of each unit towards the print triangles. Leave ¼" past the point for the seam allowance and trim each unit to 4" x 2¼". Repeat to make a total of 160 flying geese units.

4. Select 2 flying geese units. Sew the 2 units together along 1 long side, as shown. Press the seam towards the bottom. Make 4 units.

5. Arrange the 4 units and (5) 4" background squares in a 9-patch formation, as shown. Sew the pieces together to form rows and press.

6. Nest the seams and sew the rows together. Press to complete the block.

115

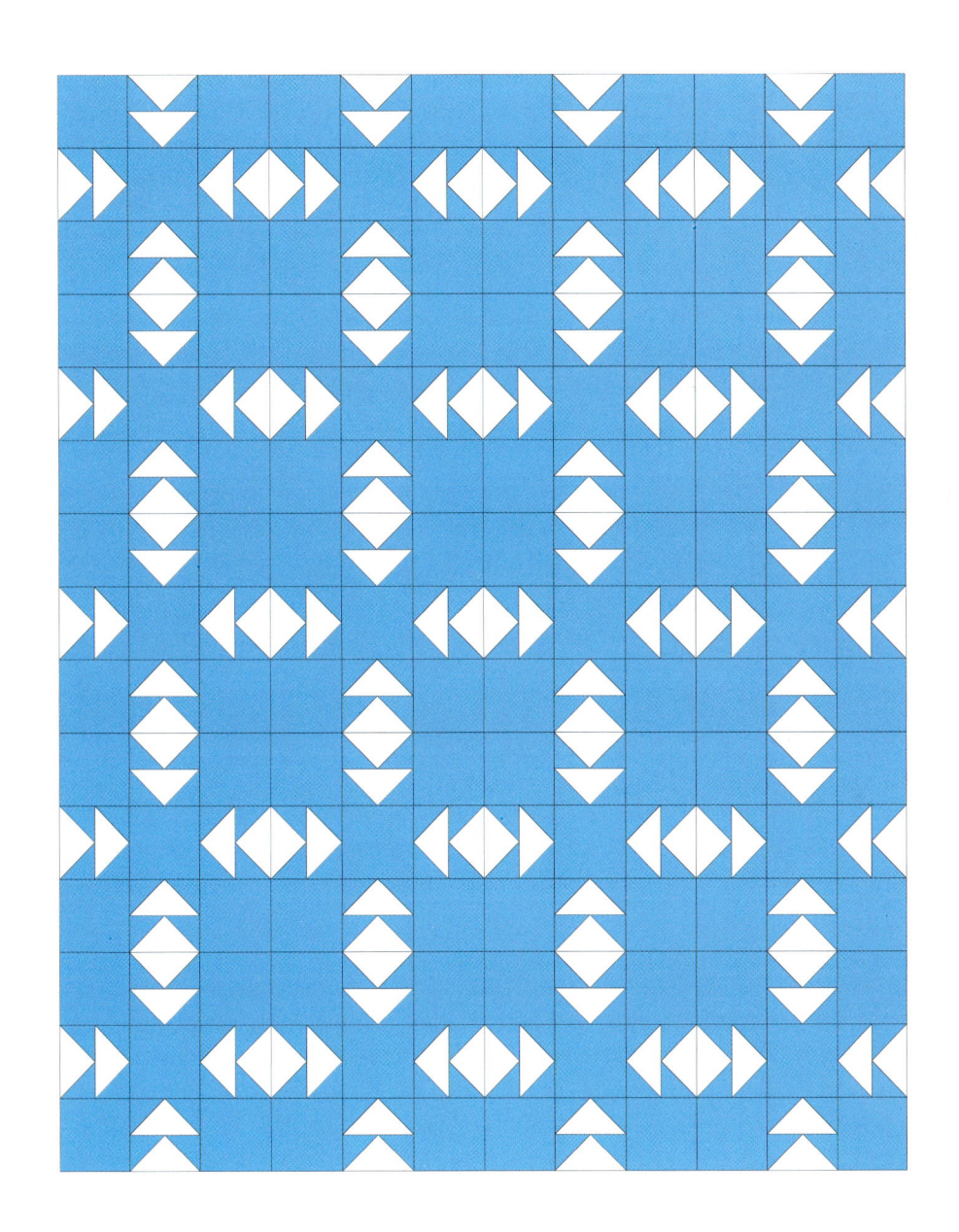

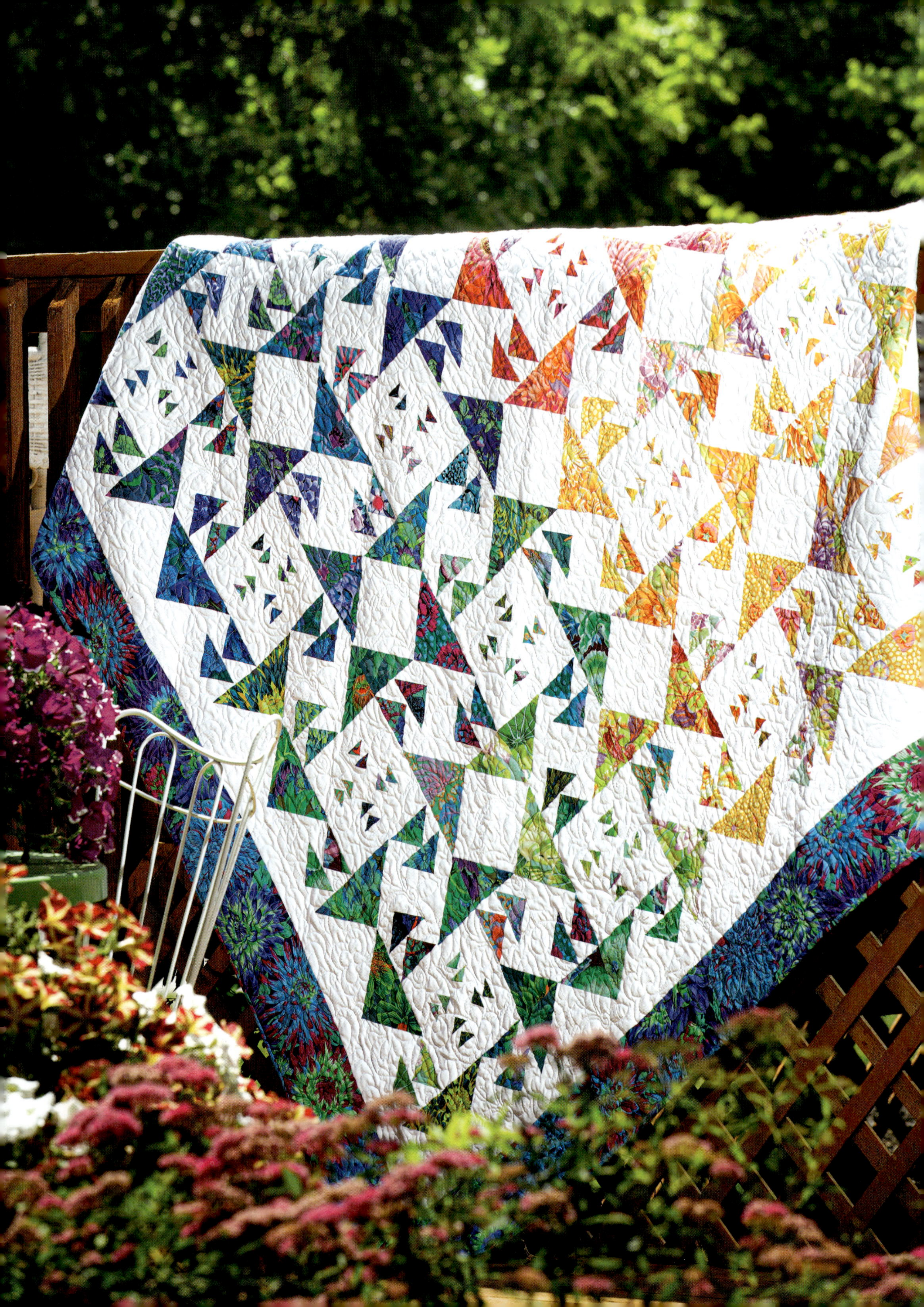

Gaggle of Geese
Misty's Play

Birds of a feather flock together, and this Gaggle of Geese quilt comes together with differently sized flying geese units for an intricate pattern that's easier to create than you might imagine. Begin with 4 packages of 5" print squares, 4 packages of 5" background squares, and 1½ yards of background fabric and watch your creativity take flight.

materials

QUILT SIZE
79" x 79"

BLOCK SIZE
16½" unfinished, 16" finished

QUILT TOP
4 packages 5" print squares
4 packages 5" background squares
1½ yards background fabric
  - includes inner border

OUTER BORDER
1½ yards

BINDING
¾ yard

BACKING
5 yards - vertical seam(s) or
  2½ yards 108" wide

SAMPLE QUILT
Kaffe Florals Rainbow by Kaffe Fassett for FreeSpirit Fabrics

1 cut

From the background fabric:

- Cut (8) 3" strips across the width of the fabric. Subcut each strip into 3" x 4½" rectangles. Each strip will yield 8 rectangles and a **total of 64** are needed.

- Cut (3) 2" strips across the width of the fabric. Subcut each strip into 2" x 1½" rectangles. Each strip will yield 26 rectangles and a **total of 64** are needed. Set the remainder of the fabric aside for the inner border.

2 sort

Note: This quilt is made using like-colored print fabrics within each block. This pattern is written to create a single block at a time in order to simplify the fabric organization.

Make 16 stacks of (9) 5" print squares that are like-colored, (10) 5" background squares, (4) 2" x 1½" background rectangles, and (4) 3" x 4½" background rectangles. Each stack contains all of the pieces you'll need to complete 1 block.

3 make small flying geese

Select (1) 5" print square and (2) 5" background squares from a single stack you sorted in the last section.

Cut each of your selected 5" squares in half horizontally and vertically. Each square will yield (4) 2½" squares.

Mark a line once on the diagonal on the reverse side of each selected 2½" background square. **3A**

Lay a marked background square atop a 2½" print square with right sides facing. Sew on the marked line. Trim away the excess fabric ¼" from the sewn seam. Press. Notice your half-square triangle unit is still 2½". **3B**

Lay another marked background square atop the half-square triangle unit with right sides facing. Be sure the marked line is perpendicular to the sewn seam. Sew on each side of the marked line using a ¼" seam allowance. **3C**

Cut on the marked line. Press. Trim each unit to 2" square. **3D**

Sew the units together as shown. Press. **3E**

Sew a 2" x 1½" background rectangle to the left side of the unit as shown. Press. **3F**

Sew a 3" x 4½" background rectangle to the top of the unit. Press to complete the small flying geese unit. **Make 4** and set them aside for the moment. **3G**

4 make medium flying geese

Select (4) 5" print squares and (4) 5" background squares from the same stack you chose the pieces for the small flying geese units you just made.

Cut each of your selected 5" print squares in half once horizontally to yield 5" x 2½" rectangles. Each square will yield 2 rectangles and a **total of 8** are needed. Trim each rectangle to measure 4½" x 2½".

3A

3B

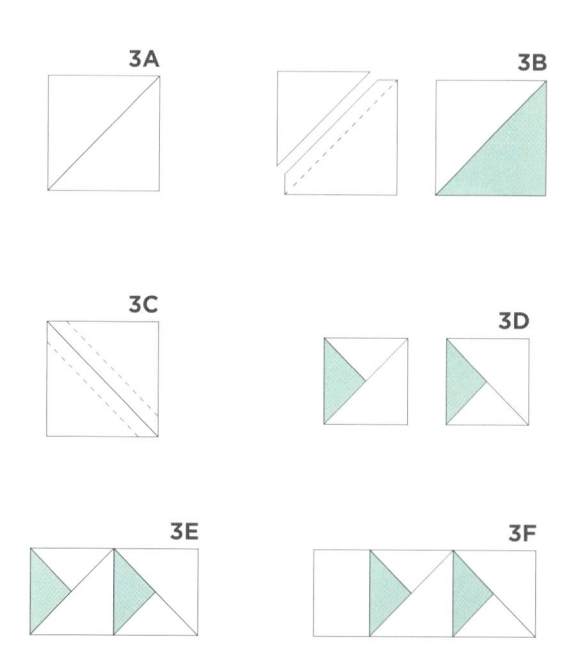

3C

3D

3E

3F

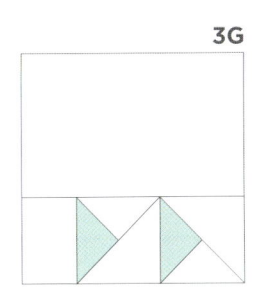

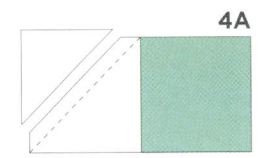

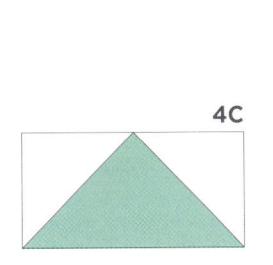

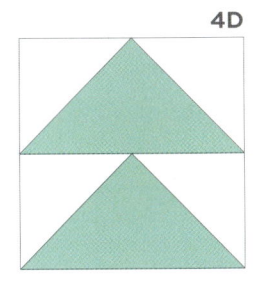

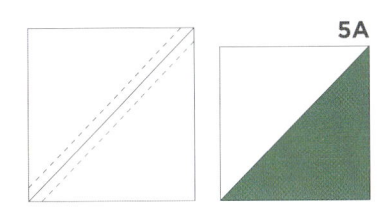

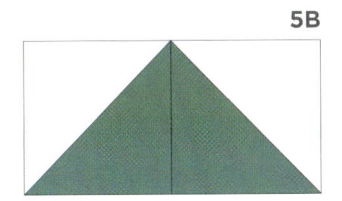

Cut each of your selected background squares in half horizontally and vertically. Each square will yield (4) 2½" squares and a **total of 16** are needed. Mark a line once on the diagonal on the reverse side of each 2½" background square. Refer to **3A** if necessary.

Place a marked background square atop a print rectangle with right sides facing and left edges aligned. The marked line should extend from the lower-left corner to the top-right of the square. Sew on the marked line. Trim away the excess fabric ¼" from the seam line. Press to snowball the corner of the rectangle. **4A 4B**

Place another marked background square atop the unit with right sides facing and right edges aligned. The marked line should extend from the upper-left corner to the lower-right of the square. Sew on the marked line and trim away the excess fabric ¼" from the sewn seam. Press. **Make 8** units. **4C**

Sew 2 units together as shown. Press to complete the medium flying geese unit. **Make 4** and set them with the 4 small flying geese units you just made. **4D**

5 make large flying geese

Pick up the rest of the stack you used to create the small and medium flying geese units. There should be (4) 5" print squares and (4) 5" background squares remaining.

Mark a line once on the diagonal on the reverse side of each selected background square. Refer to **3A** if necessary.

Lay a marked background square atop a print square with right sides facing. Sew on each side of the marked line using a ¼" seam allowance. Cut on the marked line. Press. Trim each unit to 4½" square. **5A**

Sew the 2 half-square triangle units together as shown. Press. **Make 4** large flying geese units. **5B**

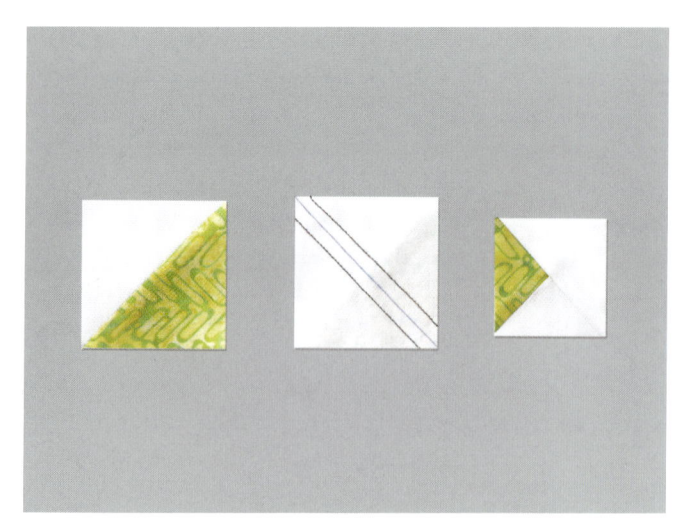

1. Follow the instructions to make a half-square triangle. Lay a marked background square atop the half-square triangle with the marked line perpendicular to the seam. Sew ¼" away from the marked line on both sides. Cut on the marked line and trim each unit to 2".

2. Sew the 2 units together and then sew a 2" x 1½" background rectangle to the left side of the row. Press. Sew a 3" x 4½" background rectangle to the top of the row to complete the small flying geese unit. Make 4 small flying geese.

3. Place a marked background square atop a print rectangle and sew on the marked line. Trim the excess fabric and press. Repeat on the other side of the rectangle. Make 8. Sew 2 matching units together. Make 4 medium flying geese.

4. Lay a marked background square atop a print square, right sides facing. Sew ¼" away from the marked line on both sides. Cut on the marked line and press each unit. Sew the 2 units together. Make 4 large flying geese.

5. Sew a small flying geese unit to the bottom of a medium flying geese unit. Press. Sew the large flying geese unit to the left and press to complete the quadrant. Make 4 quadrants.

6. Sew the 4 quadrants together to complete the block. Make 16 blocks.

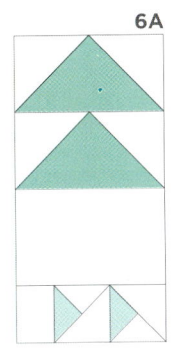

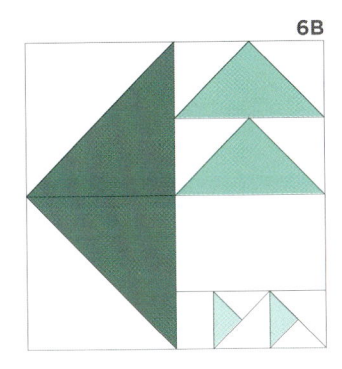

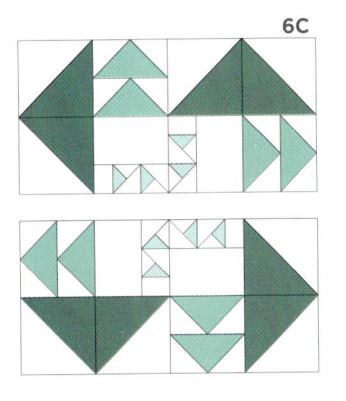

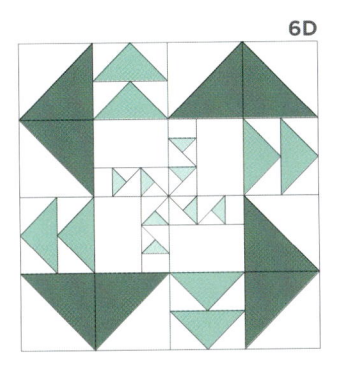

6 block construction

Pick up the small, medium, and large flying geese units you made for this block in sections 3-5. Sew a small flying geese unit to the bottom of a medium flying geese unit as shown. Press. **6A**

Sew a large flying geese unit to the left side of the small/medium unit as shown. Press to complete a quadrant. **Make 4** quadrants. **6B**

Arrange the 4 quadrants into a 4-patch formation as shown, paying close attention to the orientation of each quadrant. Sew the quadrants together to form rows. Press. **6C**

Sew the 2 rows together and press. Repeat sections 3-6 to **make 16** blocks. **6D**

Block Size: 16½" unfinished, 16" finished

7 arrange & sew

Use the diagram below to lay out the blocks in **4 rows** of **4 blocks**. Sew the blocks together to form rows. Press. Sew the rows together and press.

8 inner border

From the background fabric, cut (7) 2½" strips across the width of the fabric. Sew the strips together to form 1 long strip. Trim the borders from this strip. Refer to Borders (pg. 238) in the Construction Basics to measure, cut, and attach the borders. The approximate lengths of the strips are 64" for the sides and 68" for the top and bottom.

9 outer border

From the outer border fabric, cut (8) 6" strips across the width of the fabric. Sew the strips together end-to-end to form 1 long strip. Trim the borders from this strip. Refer to Borders (pg. 238) in the Construction Basics to measure, cut, and attach the borders. The approximate lengths of the strips are 68" for the sides and 79" for the top and bottom.

10 quilt & bind

Layer the quilt with batting and backing, then quilt. See Construction Basics (pg. 238) to finish your quilt.

FINISHED IS BETTER THAN PERFECT!

Finished is Better than Perfect Wall Hanging

HOME RUN

materials

WALL HANGING SIZE
26" x 26"

BLOCK SIZE
4½" x 2½" unfinished, 4" x 2" finished

PROJECT TOP
1 package 5" solid squares*
¾ yard of background fabric
1 package of 2½" background squares - optional**
½ yard black solid fabric - includes inner border and binding
"Finished is Better than Perfect!" Precut Fusible Appliqué Pack or alternative supplies:
- ½ yard Heat n Bond Lite
- ¼ yard aqua solid fabric
- ¼ yard purple solid fabric

BACKING
¾ yard

SAMPLE PROJECT
Kona Cotton Solids - Over the Rainbow
by Robert Kaufman Fabrics

*Note: At least 11 matching pairs of 5" squares are needed to obtain the same fabric placement used in our project.

**Note: You can cut your own 2½" background squares from the background yardage listed if you prefer.

1 cut

Select (22) 5" squares—11 pairs of matching 5" squares are needed to get the same fabric placement as our project. Cut ½" off 1 side of each square and then subcut (2) 2½" x 4½" rectangles from each for a **total of 44** rectangles.

From the background fabric, cut (1) 17½" strip across the width of the fabric. Subcut (1) 17½" square from the strip.

- If you are using precut background squares, you'll need 4 additional 2½" squares. Trim the remainder of the 17½" strip to 2½" and subcut (4) 2½" background squares. Add these to your precut squares for a **total of 88**.

- If you are not using precut background squares:
  ◦ Cut (7) 2½" strips across the remainder of the 17½" strip. Subcut (8) 2½" squares from each of these strips.
  ◦ Cut (2) 2½" strips across the width of the fabric. Subcut (16) 2½" squares from the strips. You will have a **total of (88)** 2½" squares.

If creating your own appliqué letters:
- From the aqua solid fabric, cut (1) 4" strip across the width of the fabric. Set the remainder aside for another project.

- From the black solid fabric, cut (1) 3" strip across the width of the fabric. Set the remainder aside for the inner border.

- From the purple solid fabric, cut (1) 4" strip across the width of the fabric. Set the remainder aside for another project.

- From the Heat n Bond Lite, cut (2) 3½" strips and (1) 2½" strip across the width of the fusible web.

2 appliqué

Note: The templates for the letters can be found on pages 235-237.

If you are using Heat n Bond Lite to create your own fusible letters, trace the letters F I N I S H E D onto the paper side of (1) 3½" strips of fusible web. Trace the letters P E R F E C T and the ! onto the paper side of the other 3½" strip of fusible web. Trace the letters I S   B E T T E R   T H A N onto the paper side of the 2½" strip of fusible web. Follow the manufacturer's instructions and adhere the fusible web onto the reverse side of the appropriate solid fabric. **2A**

After you have fused all of the letters, cut them out on the line.

Remove the paper backing from the letters. Arrange all the letters in 3 rows on the 17½" background square as shown. **2B**

Tip: You may find it helpful to fold the 17½" background square in half to mark the center in both directions.

When you are happy with the arrangement, follow the manufacturer's directions to fuse the letters to the background square. After all of the letters are fused in place, stitch around all of the edges with a small zigzag or blanket stitch. **2C**

3 inner border

From the black solid fabric, cut (2) 1" strips across the width of the fabric and set the remainder aside for the binding. Cut the inner borders from these strips. Refer to Borders (pg. 238) in the Construction Basics to measure, cut, and attach the inner borders. The strip lengths should be approximately 17½" for the sides and 18½" for the top and bottom.

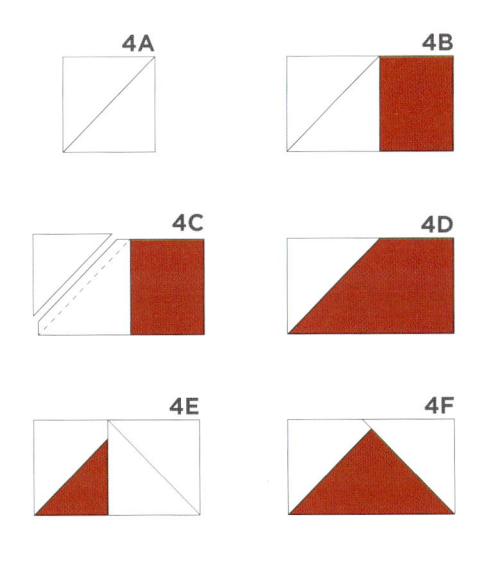

4 block construction

Mark a diagonal line on the reverse side of each 2½″ background square. **4A**

Place a marked square on the left end of a 2½″ x 4½″ rectangle, right sides facing, as shown. **4B**

Sew on the marked line and then trim the excess fabric ¼″ away from the sewn seam. Press. **4C 4D**

Place another marked square on the opposite end of the rectangle, right sides facing, as shown. **4E**

Sew, trim, and press as before. **Make 44**. **4F**

Block Size: 2½″ x 4½″ unfinished, 2″ x 4″ finished

5 pieced border

Note: You may find it helpful to arrange the flying geese around the appliqué center on a design wall before sewing them together to form the borders. See the diagram on your left for placement and orientation.

Select the 9 flying geese needed to make 1 side border. Sew them together in order and press. Repeat to make a second side border. Sew them to the sides of the appliquéd center and press.

Select the 11 flying geese needed to make the top border. Notice the last 2 flying geese in this border are turned perpendicular to the rest. Sew the flying geese together in order and press. Repeat to make the bottom border. Sew these borders to the top and bottom of the project.

6 quilt & bind

Layer the project with batting and backing, then quilt. See Construction Basics (pg. 238) to finish your project.

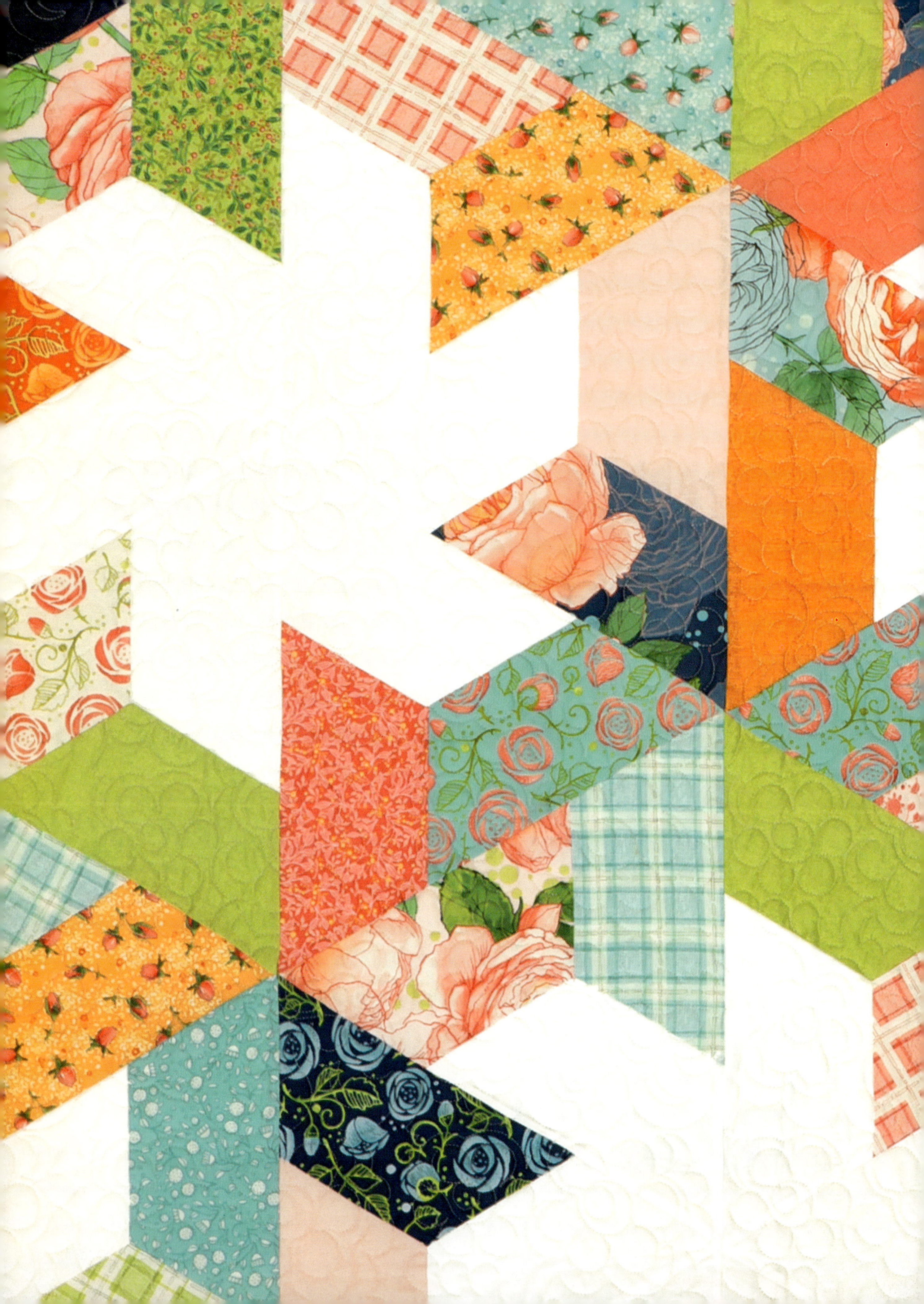

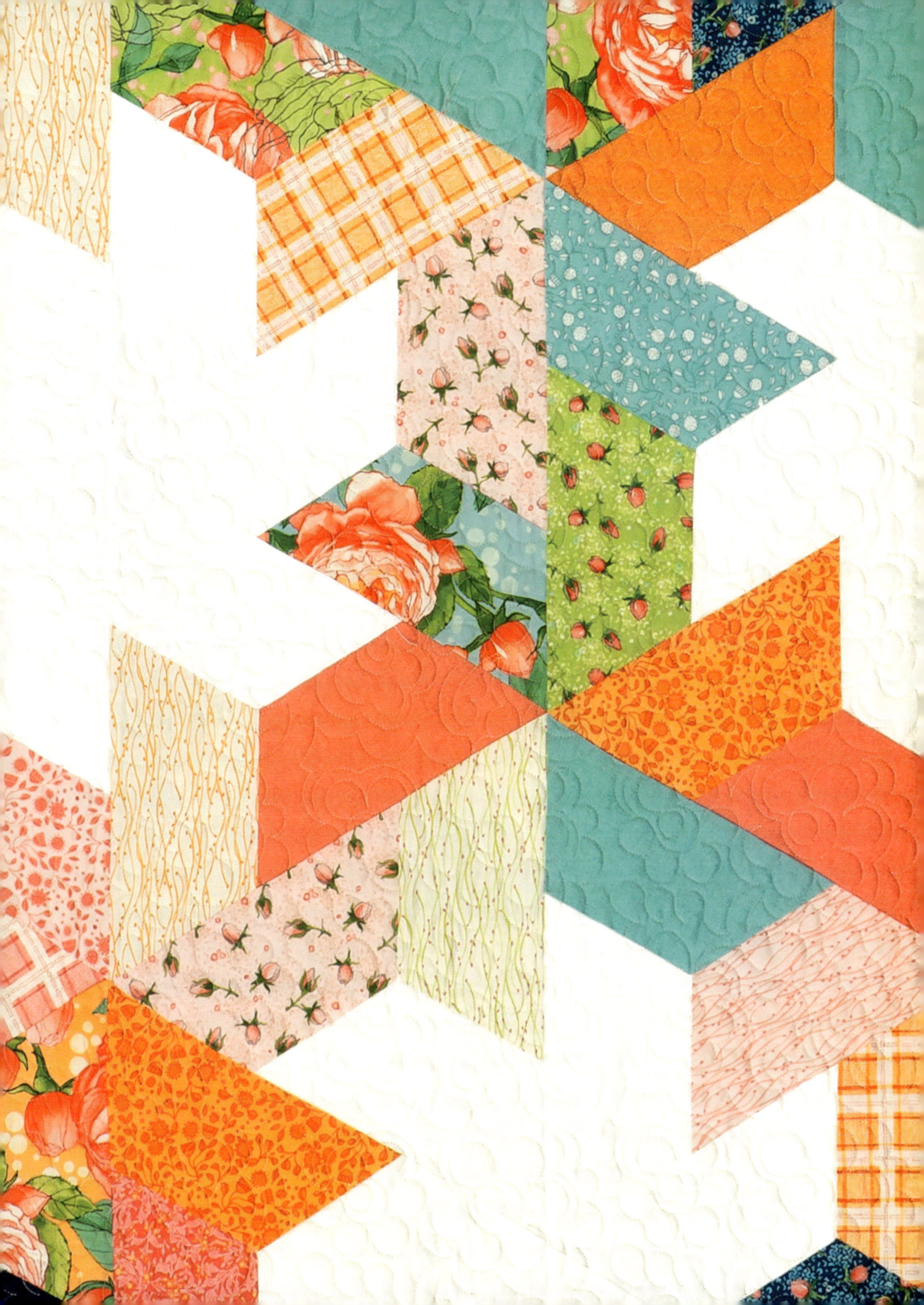

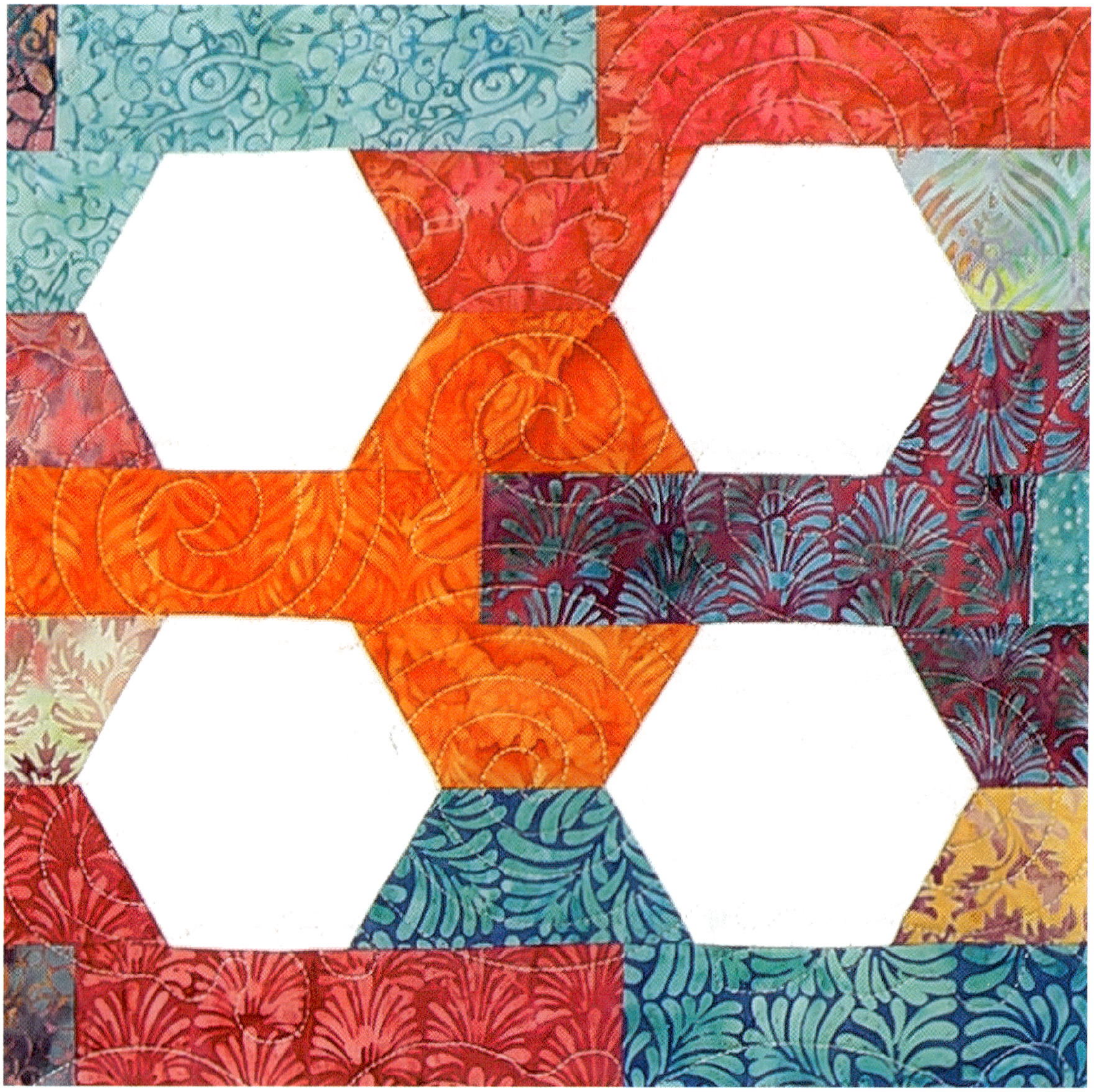

Half-Hexagon

TRIPLE PLAY

Hexagons used to be one of those quilt blocks that made us groan. The Y-seams! The paper piecing! But it's time to put all those moans and groans to rest with our modern update to the hexagon block. By splitting it in two, suddenly, it becomes so much more adaptable. This is not one of those templates you'll use once and forget about in a drawer. Hexagons are back, and they're more versatile than ever!

We have a long history of loving hexagons and despite the fact that we've created many quilts featuring this block already, we just keep coming up with new ideas. That's why doing a Triple Play tutorial featuring hexagons just made sense. We'll never get tired of it! This amazing six-sided shape is so much fun. We hope you love it too.

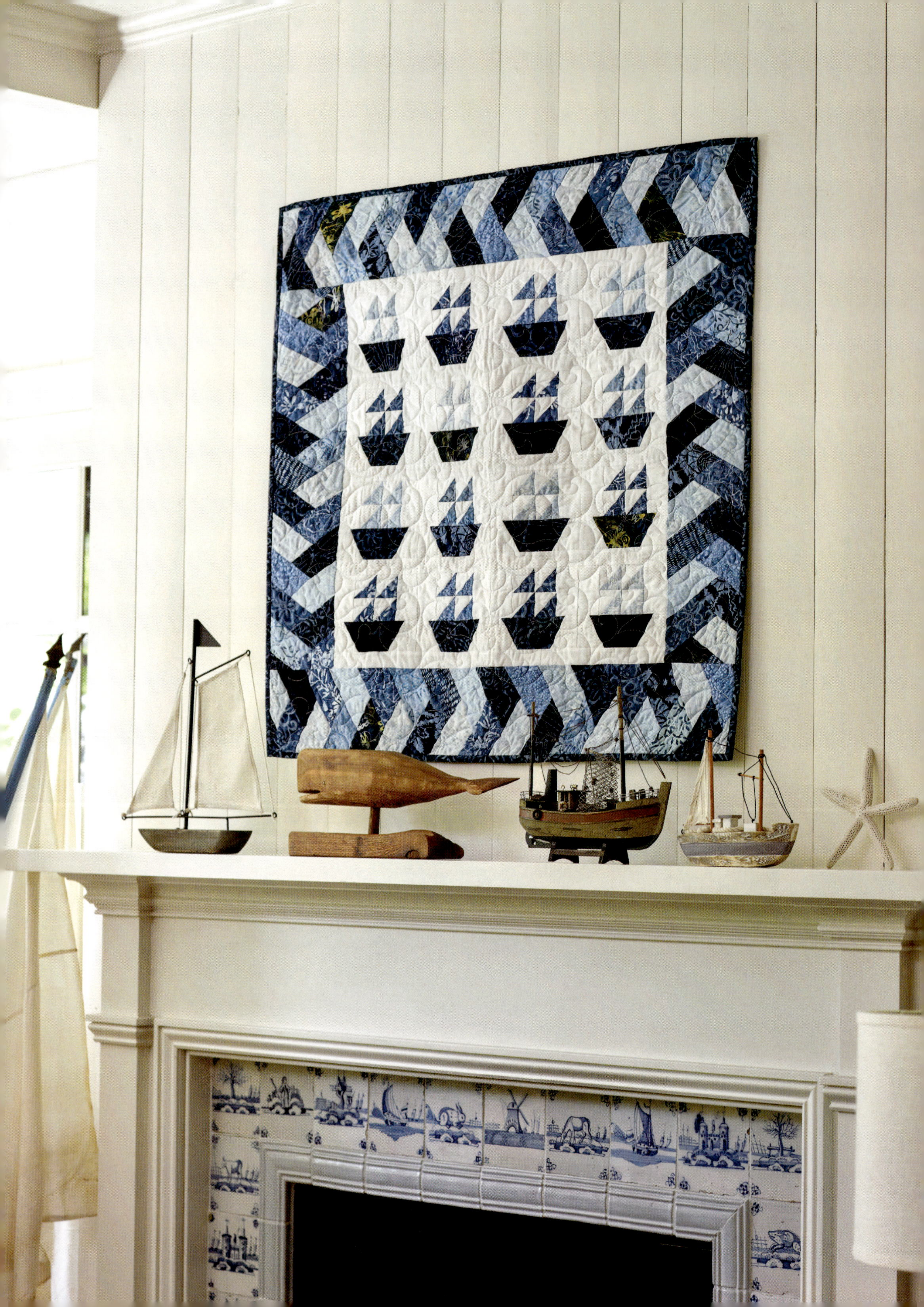

Half-Hexagon Boats and Braids
Jenny's Play

Ahoy there quilter! Adjust your sails and get ready to seas the day. Jenny's adorable quilt design features four half-square triangle sails atop half-hexagon boats surrounded by a herringbone border. It's perfect for your favorite sailor! Begin your journey and let your dreams set sail.

materials

QUILT SIZE
35½" x 36½"

BLOCK SIZE
6½" x 5½" unfinished, 6" x 5" finished

QUILT TOP
1 package 10" print squares
  - includes pieced border
¾ yard background fabric
  - includes sashing

BINDING
½ yard

BACKING
1¼ yards

OTHER
Missouri Star Small Half Hexagon Template for 5" Charm Packs & 2½" Jelly Rolls

SAMPLE QUILT
Tonga Batiks - Blue Moon by Timeless Treasures for Timeless Treasures

1 cut

Select (19) 10" print squares and set the remaining print squares aside for another project. Cut each 10" print square in half vertically and horizontally to yield a **total of (76)** 5" squares.

- Subcut 68 of the 5" print squares in half to yield 5" x 2½" rectangles. Use the half-hexagon template to subcut a half-hexagon shape from each of the rectangles. A **total of 136** half-hexagons are needed.

Set 16 of these half-hexagons aside for the boat shapes and set the other 120 aside for the pieced border.

- Set the remaining (8) 5" squares aside to make the sails.

From the background fabric, cut:
- (1) 5" strip across the width of the fabric. Subcut a **total of (8)** 5" squares from the strip.

- (2) 2½" strips across the width of the fabric. Use the template to subcut a **total of 16** half-hexagons from the strips. Be sure to rotate the template 180° after cutting each shape.

Subcut each half-hexagon in half to yield a **total of 32** quarter-hexagons.

- (3) 2" strips across the width of the fabric. Subcut a **total of (32)** 2" x 3½" rectangles from each strip.

- Set the remainder of the fabric aside for the sashing.

2 make boat units

Sew a quarter-hexagon unit to both sides of a print half-hexagon. Press. **Make 16**. **2A**

3 make sail units

Mark each of the (8) 5" background squares twice on the diagonal. **3A**

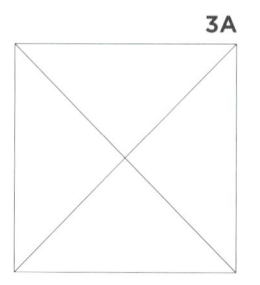

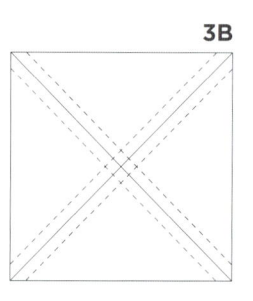

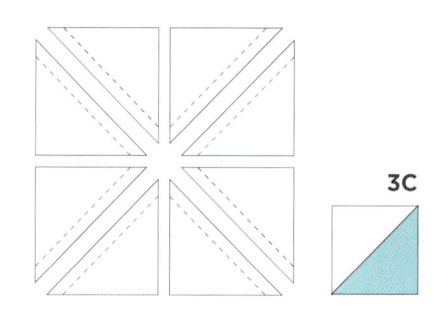

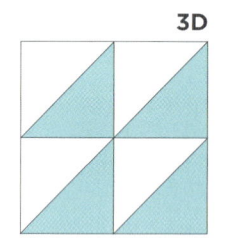

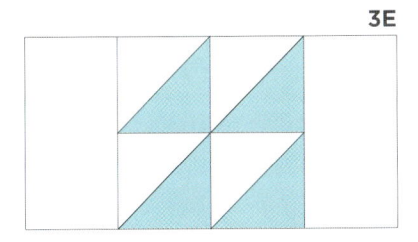

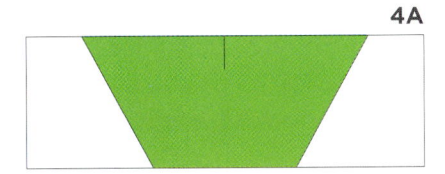

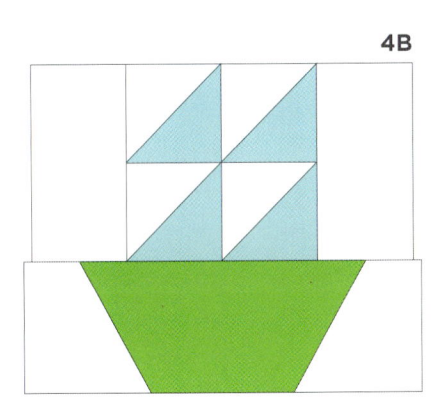

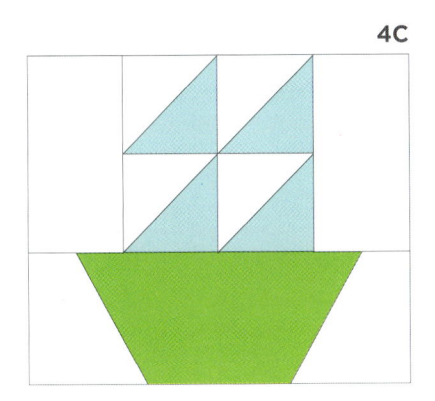

Lay a marked background square atop a 5" print square, right sides facing. Sew on each side of both marked lines using a ¼" seam allowance. **3B**

Without disturbing the fabric, cut each sewn square in half vertically, in half horizontally, and along both diagonal lines. Open, press, and trim each unit to 2". **3C**

Arrange 4 of the half-square triangle units in 2 rows of 2, as shown. Sew the units together in rows. Press the seams in opposite directions. Nest the seams, sew the rows together, and press. **Make 16** sails. **3D**

Sew a 2" x 3½" background rectangle to each side of a sail. Press. Repeat the process to **make 16** sail units. **3E**

4 block construction

Fold each boat unit in half. Finger press to mark the center. **4A**

Align the center of the boat unit with the center of a sail unit, right sides together and sew them together. Press the seam towards the bottom of the block. **4B**

Trim the edges of the boat unit portion of the block even with the sail portion. **Make 16** blocks. **4C**

Block Size: 6½" x 5½" unfinished, 6" x 5" finished

5 arrange & sew

Arrange the blocks in **4 rows of 4** as shown in the diagram on page 135. Sew the blocks together to form rows and press.

From the background fabric, cut (3) 1½" strips across the width of the fabric. Sew the strips together to form 1 long strip. Measure the length of your rows and trim 5 sashing strips to match this length. They should measure approximately 24½".

Sew a sashing strip to the bottom of each row and press towards the bottom. Sew the remaining sashing strip to the top edge of the top row and press towards the top. Sew the rows together and press.

1. Sew a quarter-hexagon unit to both sides of a print half-hexagon and press the seams towards the outer edges of the boat unit.

2. Mark both diagonal lines on the reverse side of a 5″ background square. Lay the marked square atop a 5″ print square and sew ¼″ away from each marked line. Cut the sewn square in half horizontally, vertically, and on both marked lines. Open and press each half-square triangle.

3. Arrange 4 half-square triangles in a 4-patch formation, as shown. Sew the units together in pairs to form rows and press in opposite directions. Nest the seams and sew the rows together to form a sail.

4. Sew a 2″ x 3½″ background rectangle to each side of the sail. Press to complete the sail unit.

5. Fold the boat unit in half and finger press to mark the center. Line up the center of the boat unit with the center seam of the sail unit.

6. Sew the 2 units together. Press the seam towards the bottom and then trim the edges of the boat portion of the block even with the sail portion to complete the block.

6 pieced border

Pick up the remaining half-hexagons. Sew 2 of them together as shown. Press to 1 side. **6A**

Add another half-hexagon as shown. Press towards the right half-hexagon. **6B**

Continue adding the remaining half-hexagons in the same fashion until you have 1 long strip. **6C**

Trim the end of the strip so that you have a square edge to start measuring from. You will trim the borders from this strip. **6D**

Refer to Borders (pg. 238) in the Construction Basics to measure, cut, and attach the borders. The approximate strip lengths are 25½" for the sides and 36" for the top and bottom. Pay close attention to the orientation of the strips when sewing them onto your quilt top.

7 quilt & bind

Layer the quilt with batting and backing, then quilt. See Construction Basics (pg. 238) to finish your quilt.

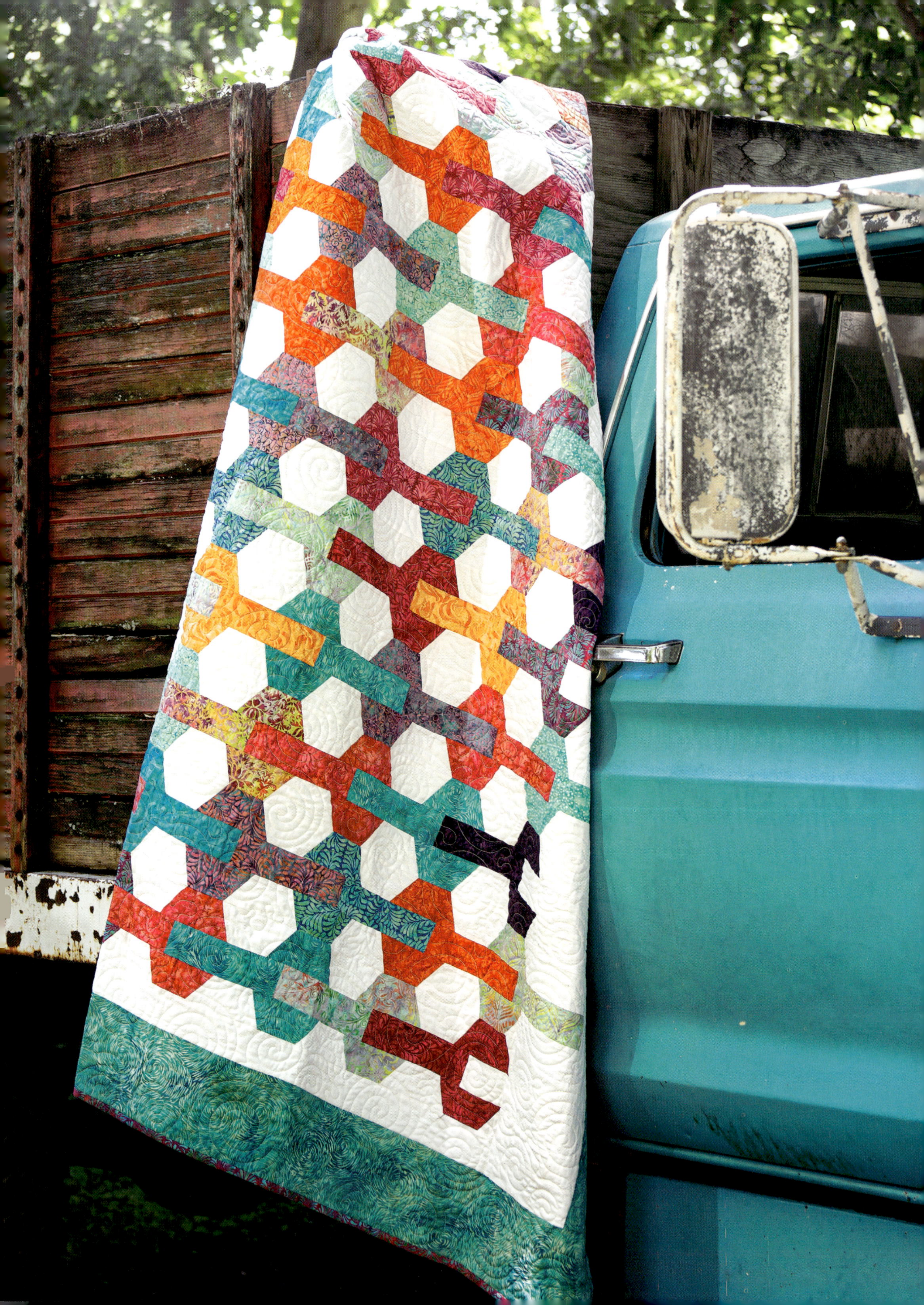

Half-Hexi Links
Natalie's Play

Find the missing link! Natalie's amazing quilt project connects half-hexis in a unique way to create a totally fresh, modern pattern made with easy 2½" strips. Let the good times roll with this fun quilt!

materials

QUILT SIZE
71¾" x 81"

QUILT TOP
1 roll 2½" print strips
1 roll 2½" background strips
  - includes inner border

OUTER BORDER
1½ yards

BINDING
¾ yard

BACKING
5 yards - vertical seam(s)
  or 2½ yards 108" wide

OTHER
Missouri Star Small Half Hexagon Template for 5" Charm Packs & 2.5" Jelly Rolls

SAMPLE QUILT
Floralicious Batiks by Kathy Engle for Island Batik

1 cut

Set 1 print strip from your roll aside for another project.

Keep the print strips folded in half for cutting. From the 39 folded 2½" print strips, cut (1) 2½" x 7½" rectangle and 2 half-hexagons using the template. Each strip will yield (2) 2½" x 7½" rectangles and 4 half-hexagons. A **total of 77** print rectangles and a **total of 154** print half-hexagons are needed.

From the 2½" background strips:
- Cut 12 strips using the half-hexagon template. Be sure to rotate the template 180° after cutting each shape so that each strip will yield 11 half-hexagons. A **total of 132** background half-hexagons are needed.

- Cut 9 strips into 2½" x 7½" rectangles. Each strip will yield up to 5 rectangles and a **total of 44** are needed. Stack 2 rectangles on top of each other, right sides facing. Place the template on top of the stacked rectangles, all the way to 1 edge. Trim off the slanted angle as shown. This will yield a mirrored pair of rectangles with 1 slanted end. **1A**

- Cut 3 strips into 2½" x 8¼" rectangles. Each strip will yield up to 5 rectangles and a **total of 11** are needed.

- Set 7 strips aside for the inner border. Set the remaining strips aside for another project.

2 make rows

Arrange 7 print half-hexagons of varying fabrics in a row separated by 6 background half-hexagons. Add a background rectangle with a slanted end to each end of your arrangement. **2A**

Pick up the first 2 pieces in the row you have laid out. Notice that the 2 corners on the long edge are squared off rather than pointed. Place the second piece atop the first with right sides facing. Align the edges of the 2 pieces, then sew the 2 together. The pointed corner of the bottom shape should peek out from behind the squared-off edge of the top half-hexagon. Press. **2B 2C**

Continue sewing the half-hexagons together until you have completed the upper portion of the row. **2D**

Pick up 7 print half-hexagons that match the fabrics of the row you just sewed. Arrange them in a row that mirrors the row you just sewed. Add 6 background half-hexagons and 2 rectangles with slanted edges to your row. Sew the lower portion of the row together and press. **2E**

Select (7) 2½" x 7½" print rectangles that match the prints used in the 2 previous rows. Arrange the rectangles in the same order as the first row you sewed. Add a 2½" x 8¼" background rectangle to the left side of the row. Sew the pieces together and press. **2F**

Place the center portion of the row between the upper and lower portions so that the like fabrics are touching each other. Sew the 3 portions together and press the seams to 1 side. **Make 11** complete rows. **2G**

3 arrange & sew

Arrange the **11 complete rows** 1 on top of the next as shown in the diagram on page 141. Notice that every other row has been rotated 180°. Sew the rows together and press.

4 inner border

Pick up the (7) 2½" background strips set aside earlier and sew them together end-to-end to make 1 long strip. Trim the borders from this strip. Refer to Borders (pg. 238) in the Construction Basics to measure, cut, and attach the borders. The approximate lengths of the strips are 66½" for the sides and 61¼" for the top and bottom.

5 outer border

From the border fabric, cut (8) 6" strips across the width of the fabric. Sew the strips together to form 1 long strip. Trim the borders from this strip. Refer to Borders (pg. 238) in the Construction Basics to measure, cut, and attach the borders. The approximate lengths of the strips are 70½" for the sides and 72¼" for the top and bottom.

6 quilt & bind

Layer the quilt with batting and backing, then quilt. After the quilting is complete, see Construction Basics (pg. 238) to finish your quilt.

1A

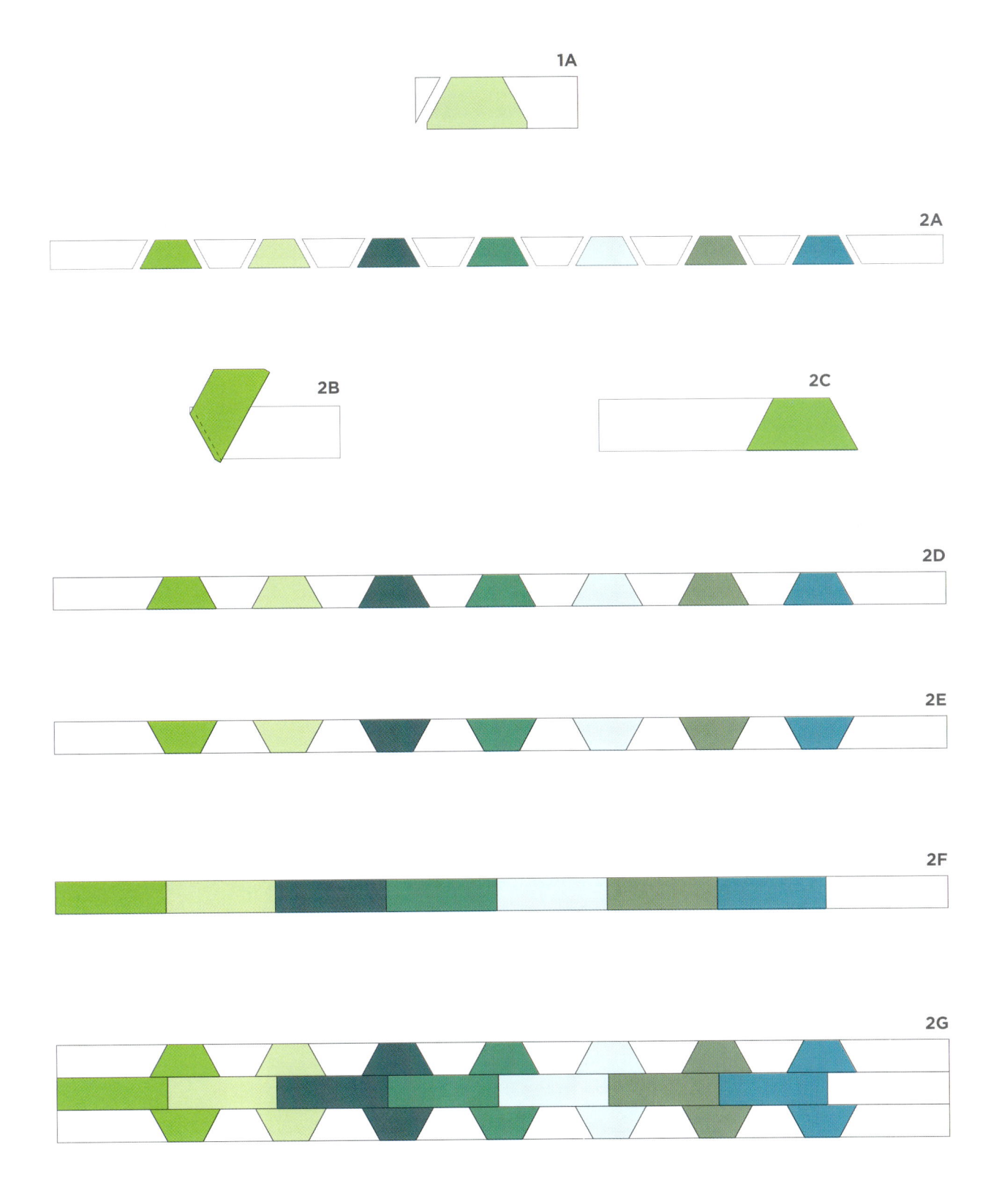

2A

2B **2C**

2D

2E

2F

2G

1 Follow the instructions to lay out the pieces for a row. Lay the second piece in the row on top of the first, as shown. Sew along the edge of the pieces. Open and press towards the darker fabric.

2 Continue in a similar manner to add the rest of the pieces in the row. Always press towards the darker fabric.

3 Follow the instructions to arrange another row. The placement of the half-hexagons of the second row should mirror those in the first row. Sew the pieces together, similar to before, to form the row.

4 Select the 2½"x 7½" rectangles that match the fabrics of the half-hexagons used in the previous 2 rows. Arrange the rectangles matching the order of fabrics used in the other 2 rows. Place a 2½" x 8¼" background rectangle at the start of the row and sew the pieces together. Press.

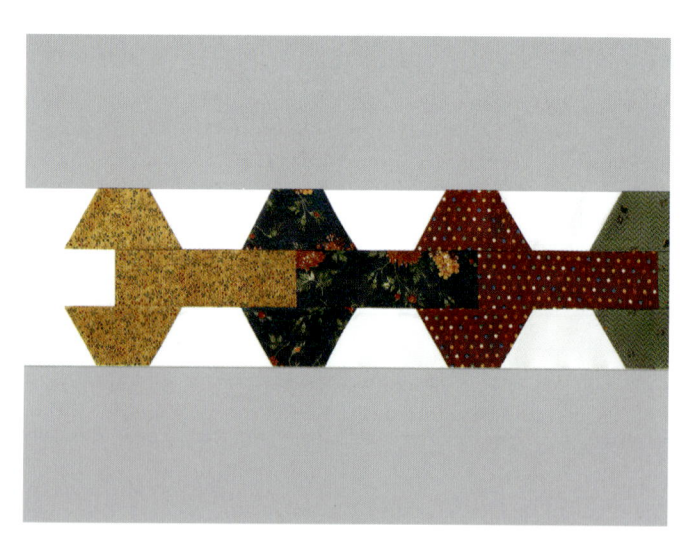

5 Lay the 3 rows out 1 on top of the other so that the like fabrics are touching each other. Sew the 3 rows together and press the seams to 1 side.

141

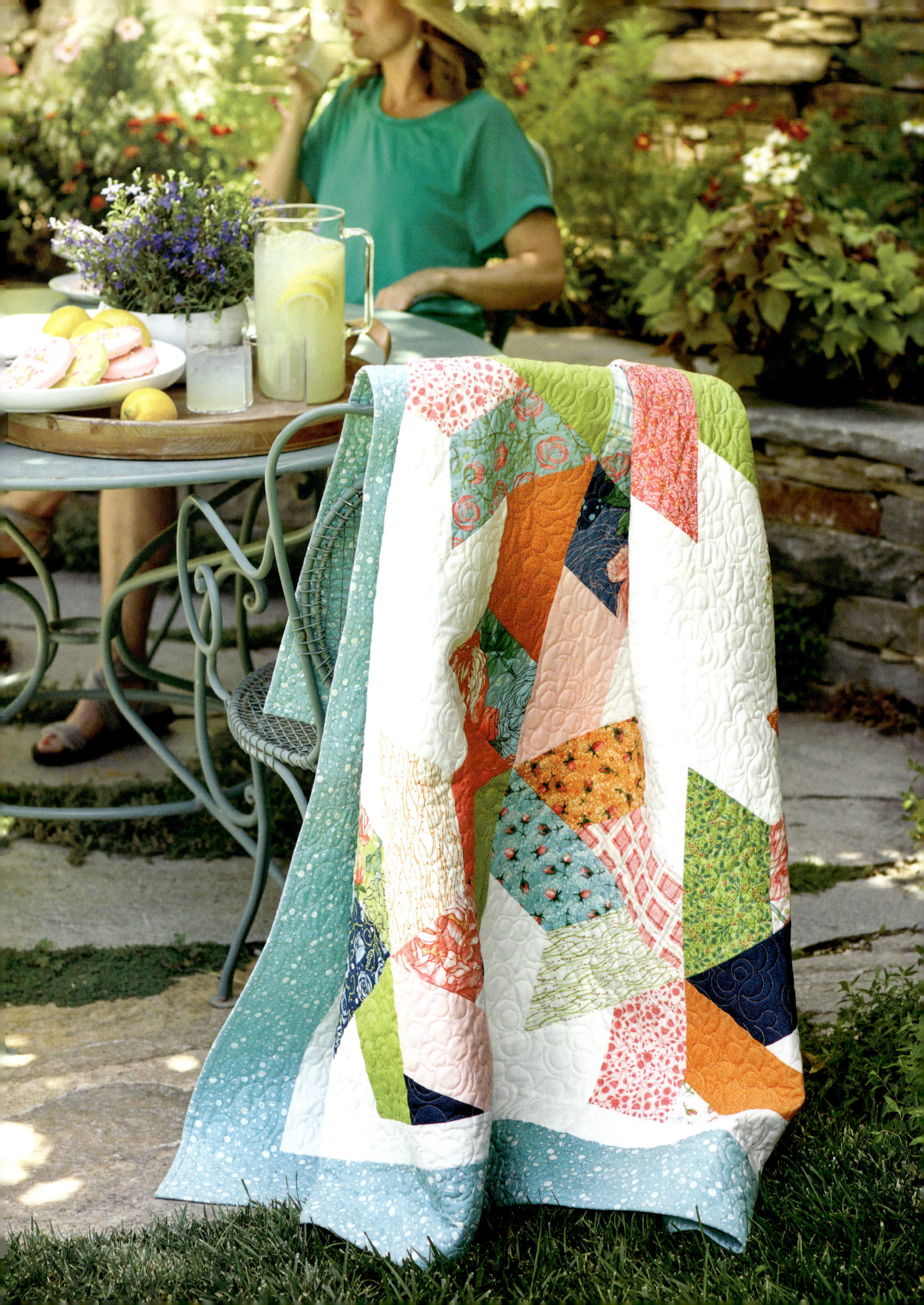

Half-Hexi Whirligigs
Misty's Play

Put your half-hexis to work with this whimsical whirligig quilt by Misty! It takes a template that's become a Missouri Star favorite and puts a whole new twist on it for a fun design you'll love. Three half-hexis are constructed into triangles and pieced into a unique pattern that will amaze you. Go ahead, give it a whirl!

materials

QUILT SIZE
63" x 74½"

BLOCK SIZE
14¾" unfinished triangle,
14¼" finished triangle

QUILT TOP
1 package 10" print squares
1½ yards background fabric
  - includes inner border

OUTER BORDER
1¼ yards

BINDING
¾ yard

BACKING
4¾ yards - vertical seam(s) or
  2½ yards 108" wide

OTHER
Missouri Star Large Half Hexagon
  Template for 10" Squares
Disappearing fabric pen or pencil

SAMPLE QUILT
Abby Rose by Robin Pickens
for Moda Fabrics

1 cut

From the background fabric, cut (8) 4⅝" strips across the width of the fabric. Set the remaining fabric aside for the inner border.

Stack 2 strips on your cutting surface and line up all the edges. Lay the large half-hexagon template atop the strips and line up the top and bottom edges of the template with the strips. Carefully cut along both short sides of the template. **1A**

Move the cut shapes and template away from the stacked strips to trim the 2 corners of the shapes along the long edge of the template, then stack the shapes out of the way of your cutting. Without disturbing the stacked strips, rotate the template 180° and align the left edges of the template and strips. Cut along the right side of the template. **1B**

Continue in this manner to cut 5 half-hexagons from each strip for a **total of 40** background half-hexagons.

Set (2) 10" print squares aside for another project. Cut 2 half-hexagons from each remaining 10" square as shown for a **total of 80** print half-hexagons. **1C**

2 block construction

On the reverse side of each half-hexagon, mark a point ¼" from the top and right sides using a disappearing fabric pen or pencil. **Hint:** You may find it helpful to mark a faint line along the top and right sides at ¼" then make a slightly darker point where they intersect. **2A**

Lay a print half-hexagon face up as shown. We'll call this unit A for clarity. **2B**

Lay a contrasting print half-hexagon face down atop unit A as shown. We'll call this unit B for clarity. Line up the right edges. The bottom point of unit B may extend just slightly past the unit A half-hexagon. Start your needle at the marked point and sew the units together along the right edges using a ¼" seam allowance, backstitching at the beginning. Be sure that you do not backstitch past your marked point. **2C**

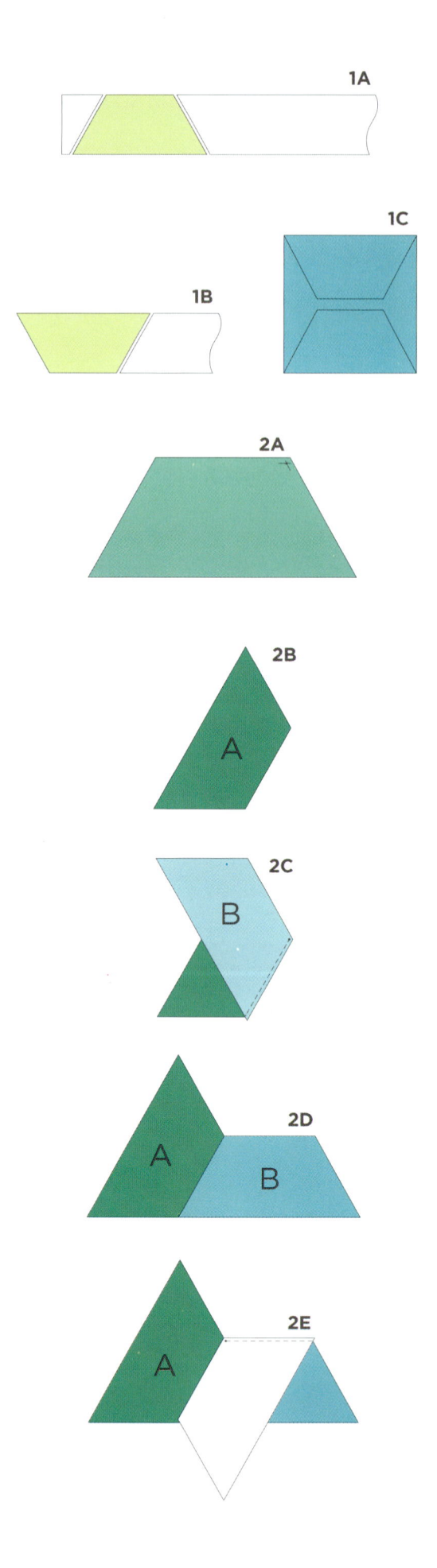

Press towards unit A. **2D**

Lay a background half-hexagon face down atop the sewn unit as shown, lining up the top edges of the background and unit B half-hexagons. The marked point should lay directly atop the seam you just sewed. In the previous manner, start sewing at the marked point, carefully backstitch, then sew along the matched edges as shown. **2E**

Open and press unit B.

Turn the sewn unit over. Fold unit B in half, smooth out and line up the edges of unit A and the background half-hexagon. Start sewing at the marked point, carefully backstitch, then sew along the matched edges of unit A and the background half-hexagon. **2F**

Open and press. **Make 40** triangle blocks. **2G**

Triangle Block Size:
14¾" unfinished triangle, 14¼" finished triangle

3 arrange, sew, & trim

Refer to the diagram **3A** as needed to lay out your triangle blocks in **5 rows of 8**. The triangle blocks in each row will alternate points from top to bottom and the background sections of the triangle blocks should meet to form whirligig shapes. **Hint:** As you sew your triangle blocks, be sure to line up the tip of each triangle block with the long edge of the previous block. This will ensure you have a ¼" seam allowance at each of your top and bottom points. You will have small tips sticking past the edges of your rows, which you can leave or trim if preferred.

Nest the seams and sew the rows together to complete the quilt center. **3A**

After the center of your quilt top is complete, measure ¼" toward the outside edge from the center and vertical point of each triangle along the left and right edges. Trim your triangle blocks along each side of your quilt. **3B**

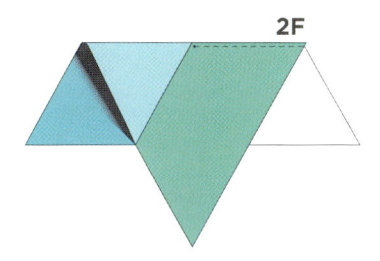

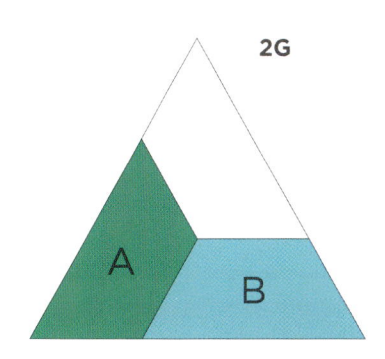

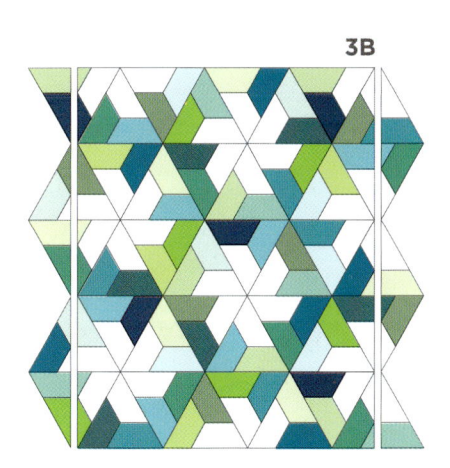

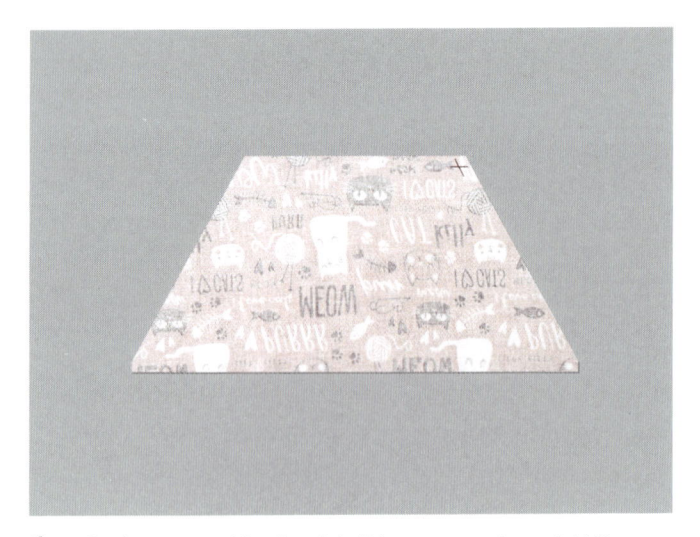

1. On the reverse side of each half-hexagon, mark a point ¼" from the top and right sides using a disappearing fabric pen or pencil.

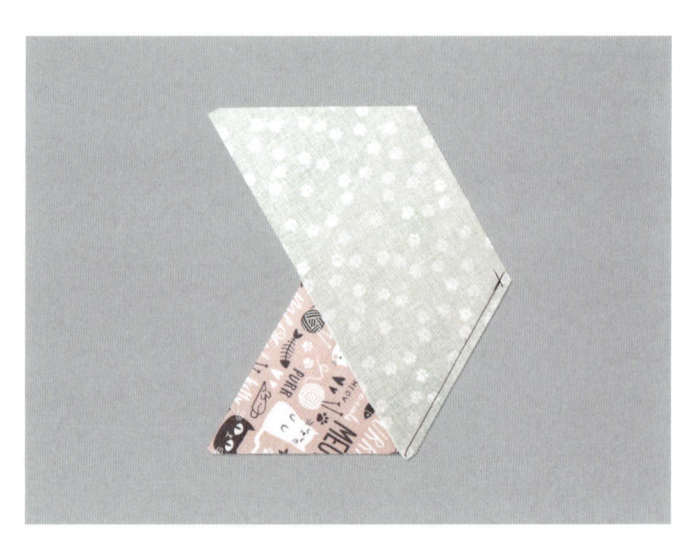

2. Lay a contrasting print half-hexagon face down atop unit A as shown. We'll call this unit B for clarity. Line up the right edges. Start your needle at the marked point and sew the units together along the right edges using a ¼" seam allowance, backstitching at the beginning.

3. Press towards unit A.

4. Lay a background half-hexagon face down atop the sewn unit as shown, lining up the top edges of the background and unit B half-hexagons. Start sewing at the marked point, backstitch, then sew along the matched edges.

5. Turn the sewn unit over. Fold unit B in half, and line up the edges of unit A and the background half-hexagon. Start sewing at the marked point, backstitch, then sew along the matched edges.

6. Open and press. Make 40 triangle blocks.

4 inner border

Cut (6) 2½" strips across the width of the background fabric. Sew the strips together to form 1 long strip. Trim the borders from this strip. Refer to Borders (pg. 238) in the Construction Basics to measure, cut, and attach the borders. The approximate lengths of the strips are 61¾" for the sides and 54½" for the top and bottom.

5 outer border

Cut (7) 5" strips across the width of the outer border fabric. Sew the strips together to form 1 long strip. Trim the borders from this strip. Refer to Borders (pg. 238) in the Construction Basics to measure, cut, and attach the borders. The approximate lengths of the strips 65¾" for the sides and 63½" for the top and bottom.

6 quilt & bind

Layer the quilt with batting and backing, then quilt. See Construction Basics (pg. 238) to finish your quilt.

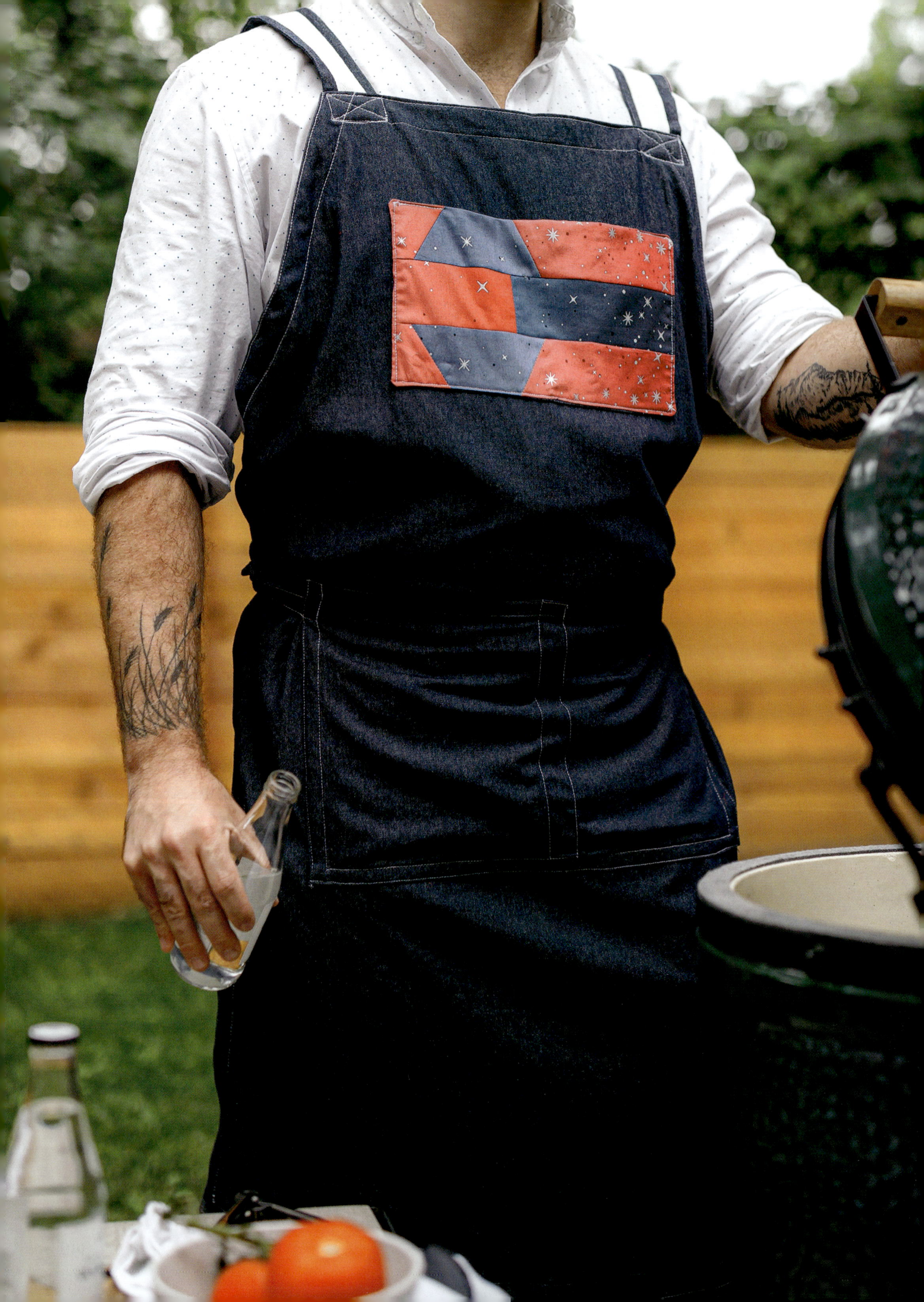

Half-Hexi Denim Apron

materials

APRON SIZE
fits most

BLOCK SIZE
6½" x 11" unfinished, 6" x 10½" finished

PROJECT SUPPLIES
2 yards denim fabric
(2) 10" print squares

OTHER SUPPLIES
Missouri Star Small Half-Hexagon Template for 5" Charm Packs & 2.5" Jelly Rolls
4 yards of 1" cotton twill tape

SAMPLE PROJECT
Indigo Denim by Robert Kaufman Fabrics for Robert Kaufman

1 cut

Select (1) 10" print square to form the wrench and 1 square for the background of the block.

- From the 10" square for the wrench, cut (2) 2½" strips across the width of the square.
  - From 1 strip, subcut (1) 2½" x 7½" rectangle.
  - From the remaining strip, subcut 2 half-hexagons using the template.

- From the square you chose for the background, cut (4) 2½" strips across the width of the square.
  - From 3 strips, subcut a **total of (3)** 2½" x 7½" rectangles. Stack 2 rectangles right sides together. Use the template to trim 1 end of the stacked rectangles. **1A**
  - From the remaining strip, subcut 2 half-hexagons using the template.

Fold the denim fabric in half *lengthwise* and press. Cut (2) 2½" strips along the *length* of the folded fabric to yield a **total of (4)** 2½" x 72" strips for the straps.

- Cut (1) 46" strip across the **width** of the remaining fabric that is still folded. Measure 18" from the folded edge of the strip and mark a cutting line. Cut along your marked line to yield 1 folded 36" x 46" apron body rectangle.

- Cut (1) 12" strip across the **width** of the remaining fabric. Unfold and subcut (1) 12" x 20" skirt pocket rectangle from the strip.

- Cut (1) 6½" strip across the **width** of the remaining fabric. Unfold and subcut (1) 6½" x 11" pocket rectangle from the strip. Subcut (2) 3" strips across the **width** of the remainder of the strip. Subcut (1) 3" x 12" pocket loop rectangle from 1 strip and (1) 3" x 18" waist loop from the other.

From the twill tape, cut (2) 72" lengths.

2 block construction

Layout the pieces you cut from the print squares in 3 rows as shown. Sew the pieces together to form the rows. Press. **2A**

Line up the straight edge of the rows and then sew them together. Press. Trim to 6½" x 11". **2B 2C**

Block Size: 6½" x 11" unfinished, 6" x 10½" finished

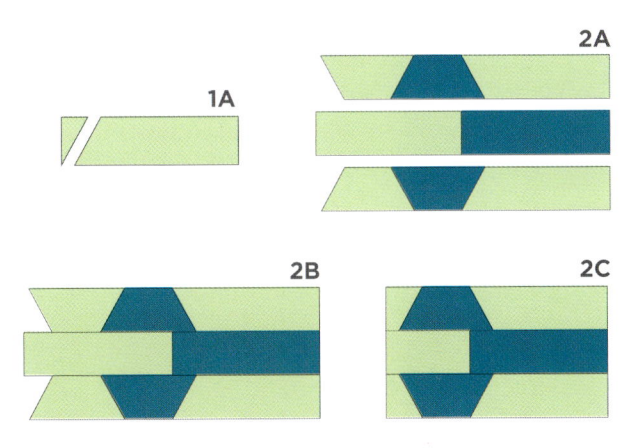

3 create the pockets

Place the block you just created on top of the 6½" x 11" pocket rectangle, right sides facing. Leave about 3" open for turning on the bottom edge and sew around the perimeter. **3A**

Clip the corners to reduce the bulk and then turn right side out. Press. Start and stop ¼" from the ends and topstitch ¼" from the top edge. Set the wrench pocket aside for now. **3B**

Fold the 2 short sides of the skirt pocket over 1" towards the wrong side of the fabric and press. Open the folds and tuck the raw edges of the pocket into the crease and press again. In the same manner, fold the top and bottom edges of the pocket and press. Topstitch along the top of the pocket ⅛" from the folded edge and again ⅛" from the hemmed edge, backstitching at each end. **3C**

Fold the skirt pocket in half widthwise with right sides facing. Press to crease. Set aside for now.

4 create the loops

Fold each loop rectangle in half lengthwise. Press to crease. Open and fold the 2 long edges of the rectangle to meet in the crease. Press. Topstitch along both edges. Cut each loop in half to yield (2) ¾" x 6" pocket loops and (2) ¾" x 9" waist loops. Set aside for now. **4A 4B**

5 create the straps

Place (2) 2½" x 72" strips together, right sides facing. Sew along the 2 long edges. **5A**

Turn right side out and press.

Tip: Use a dowel to push the fabric right side out.

Center (1) 72" length of twill tape on the strap and topstitch it in place along both sides. **Make 2** straps. **5B**

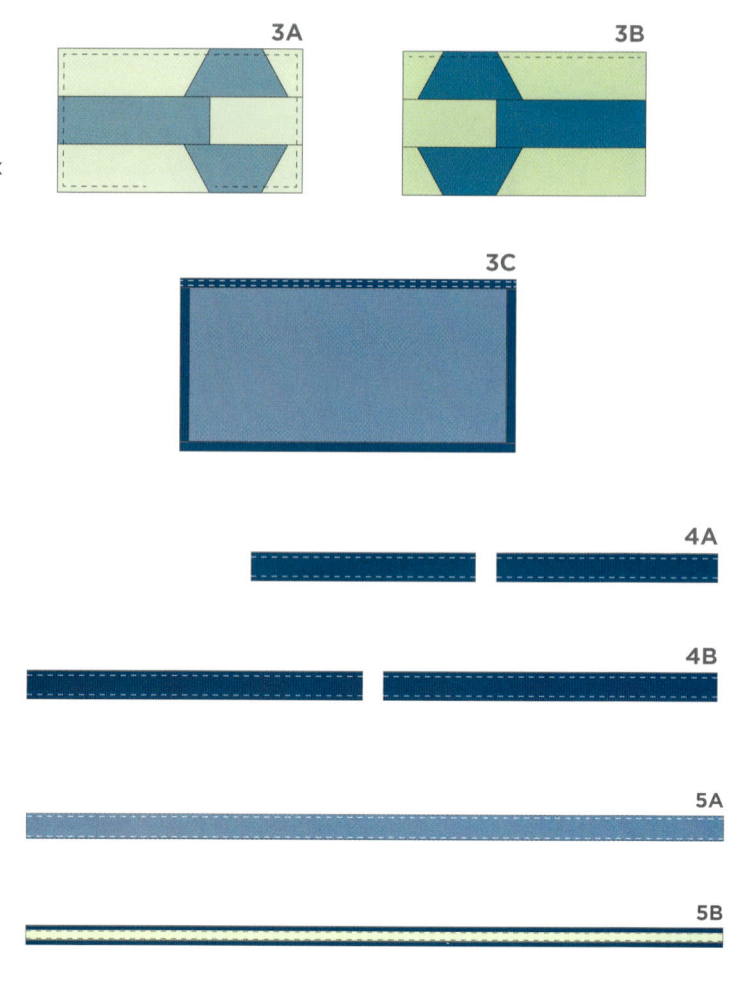

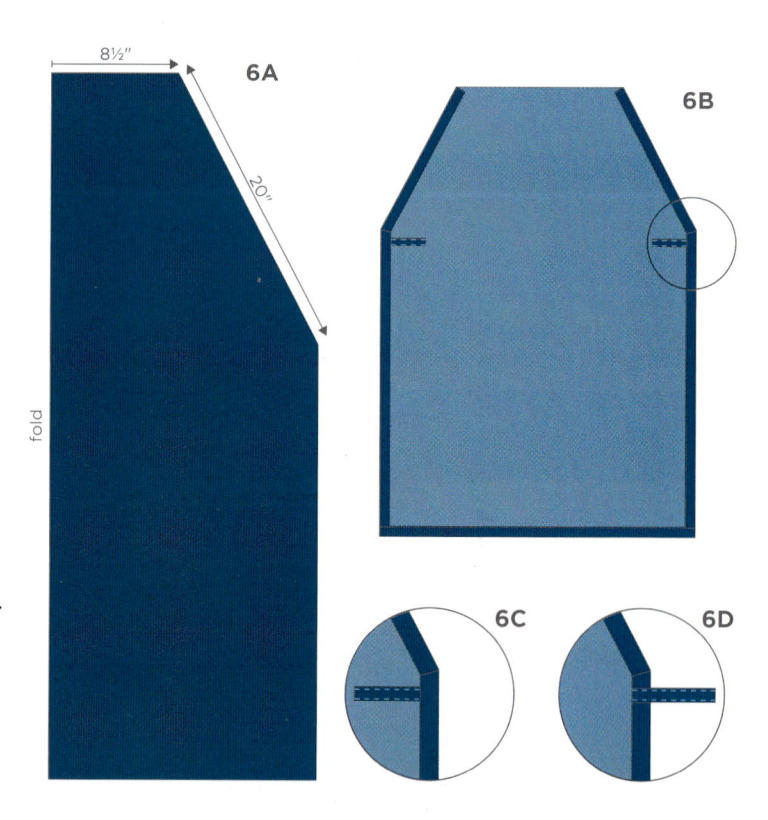

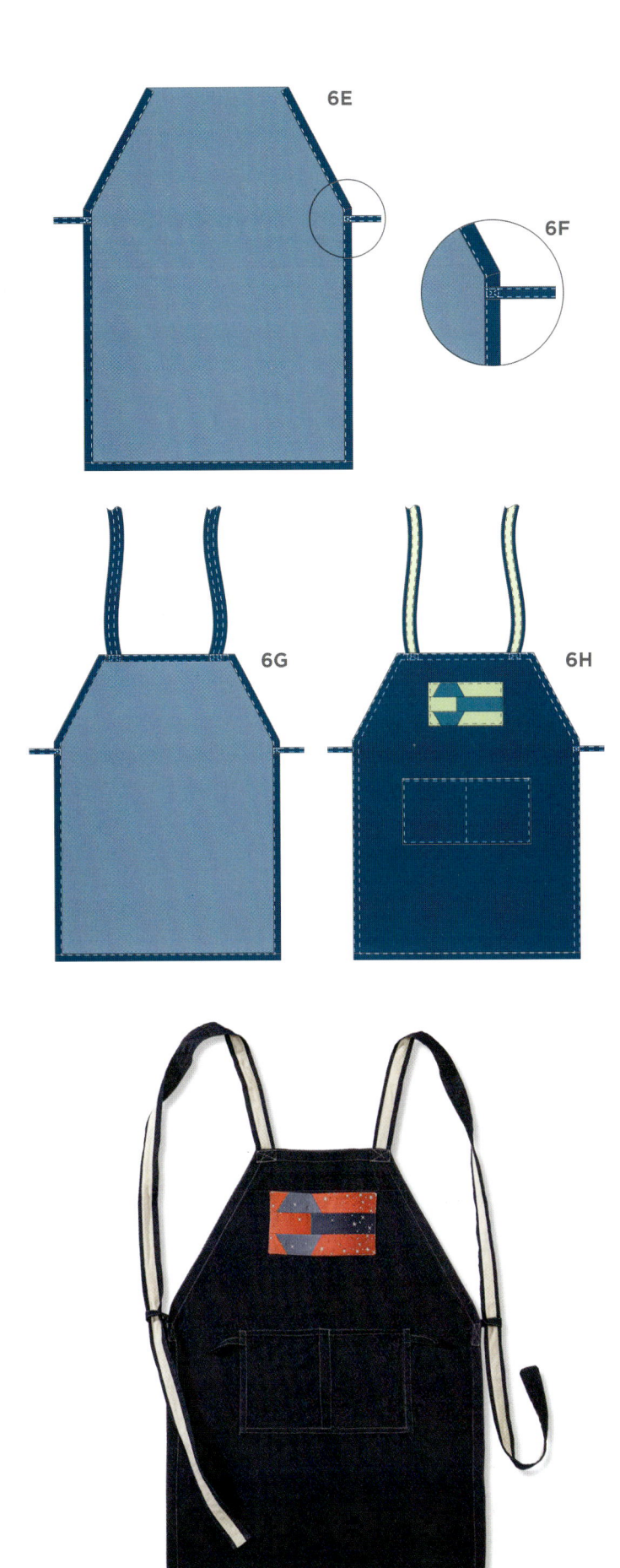

6 finish the apron

If needed, refold the 36" x 46" apron body rectangle in half lengthwise. Measure 8½" from the fold along the top edge and mark. Place the end of your ruler at this mark and pivot it from this point until the 20" mark on your ruler touches the edge of the apron body. Mark along the edge of your ruler, if necessary, and then cut along the drawn line. **6A**

Fold the angled edges of the apron body 2" towards the wrong side of the fabric. Press. Open the fold and tuck the raw edge of the fabric into the crease and press again. Repeat along the long sides of the apron and the bottom edge. Insert a ¾" x 9" waist loop that is folded in half into the folded hem just below the angled sides of the apron as shown. **6B 6C**

Fold the strap over the hem and pin in place. Repeat on the opposite side. **6D**

Topstitch along the bottom and sides. Stitch a box with an "x" in it at the waist loops. **6E 6F**

Fold the top edge of the apron body 2" towards the wrong side of the fabric. Press. Open the fold and tuck the raw edge of the fabric into the crease and press again. Insert the straps into the folded hem at each end of the top edge, similar to how you inserted the waist loops. Topstitch along the top edge of the apron and pause to attach the straps with a box and an "x" at each strap. Topstitch once more, this time ⅛" from the folded hem. **6G**

Find the center of the wrench pocket. Place the wrench pocket 4" from the top of the apron body with the center of the pocket and the center of the apron body aligned. Backstitch at the beginning and end and topstitch the pocket to the body along the 2 sides and bottom of the pocket, ¼" from each edge. Center the skirt pocket on the apron body, 7" below the bottom of the wrench pocket. Pin in place. Slide waist loops into the 2 sides of the skirt pocket, ½" from the top edge and pin in place. Backstitch at the ends and over both loops and topstitch in place along the 2 sides and the bottom of the pocket. Topstitch down the center crease. **6H**

Tie the straps as desired and you're ready to tackle your next project.

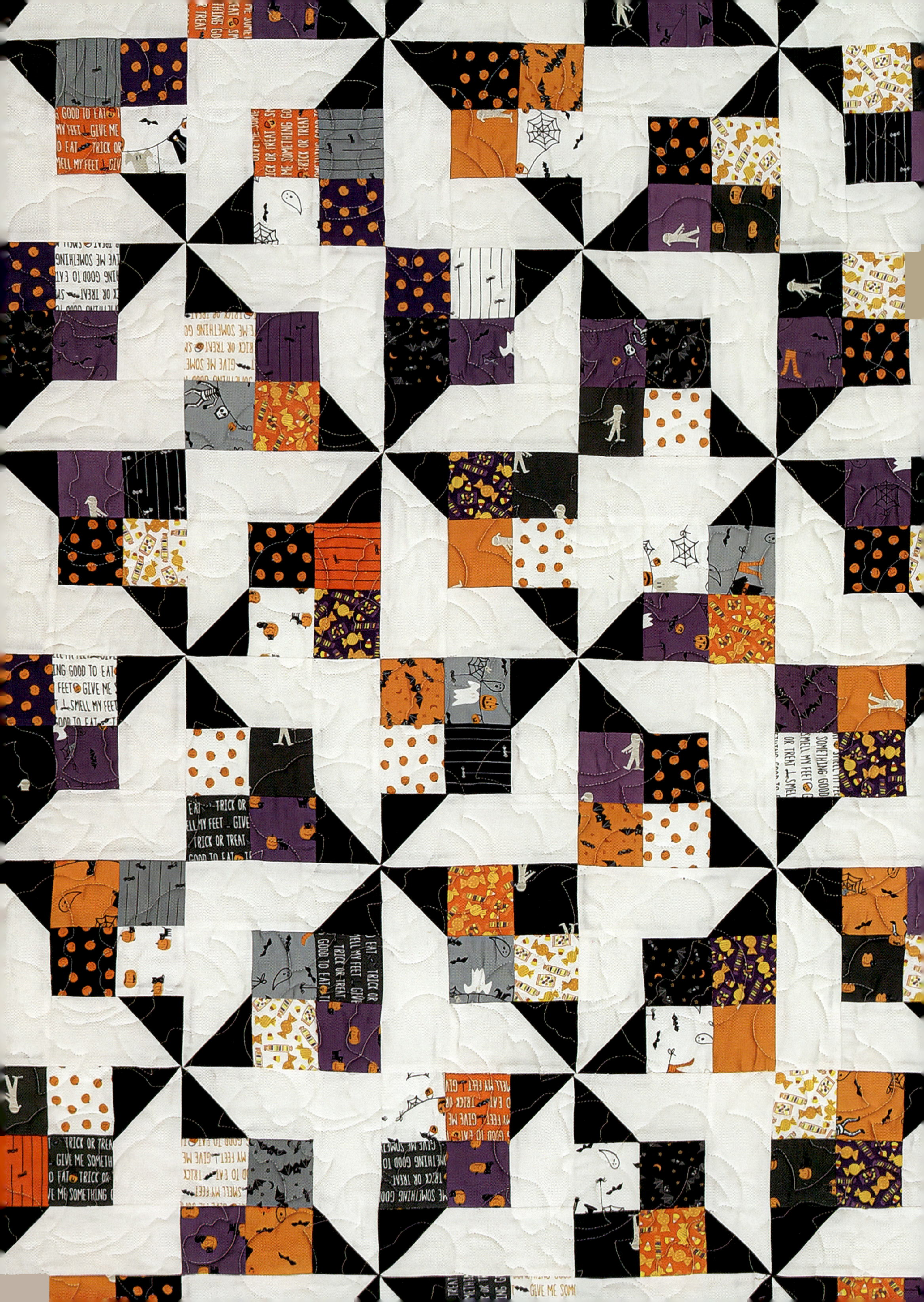

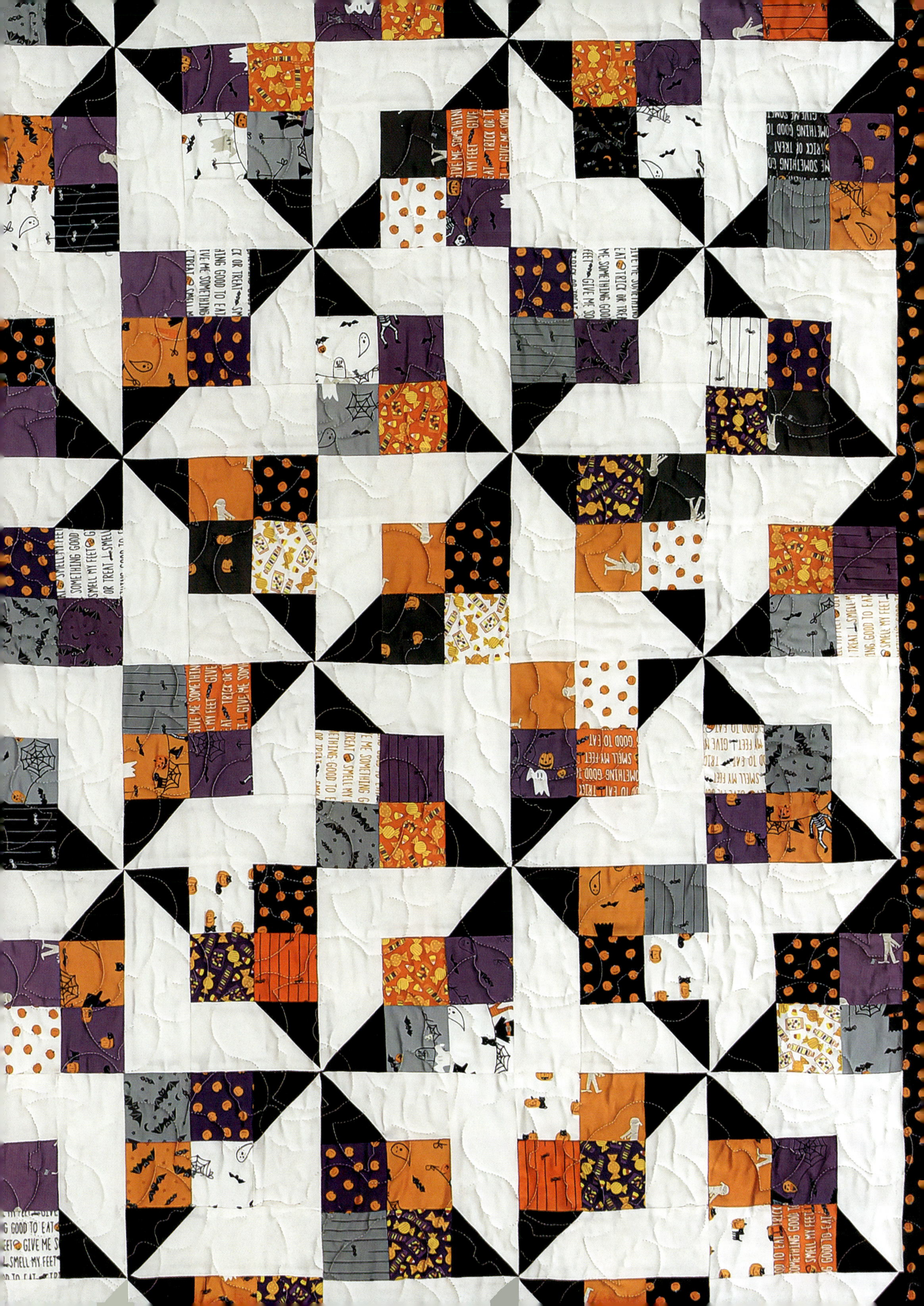

154

Double Square Stars

TRIPLE PLAY

Don't just do a double take on this cute pattern, do a triple take! The double square star is very versatile because it starts with a simple patchwork square, adds a couple snowballed strips, and makes so many interesting secondary patterns when you put the blocks together! Between the three of us, we came up with a few unique designs that all started with the same exact block and ended up with flowers, pinwheels, and more. It's really easy to play with the negative space on this block. Have fun with it!

The way this block begins almost looks like a little square with wings and when you put four of them together, it looks like a full eight-pointed star. But we didn't stop there. This was an easy choice for the Triple Play because there really are so many options. You can invert the fabrics and have the background go darker rather than lighter, you can also see what the negative space does when you turn blocks or move them around. There's so much you can do with these amazing little double square stars. It does more than double duty.

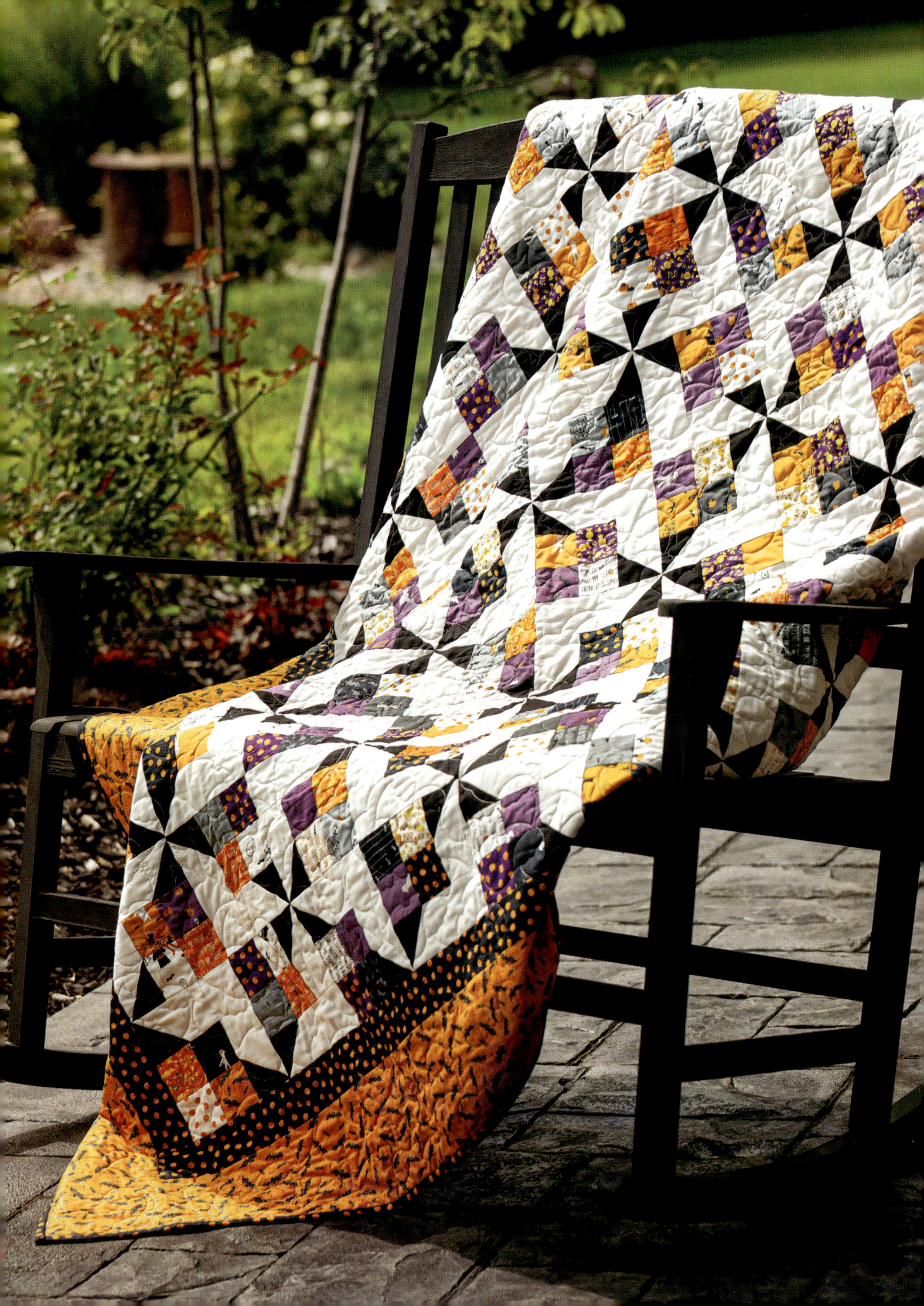

Double Square Star Four-Patch

Jenny's Play

Jenny doubles your fun with a pattern that takes the simple four-patch quilt block and adds sashing for an extra special touch! Rotate a couple of the blocks and you've got an incredible pattern that looks complicated, but couldn't be simpler.

materials

QUILT SIZE
63" x 75"

BLOCK SIZE
12½" unfinished, 12" finished

QUILT TOP
2 packages 5" print squares
¾ yard accent fabric
1¾ yards background fabric

INNER BORDER
½ yard

OUTER BORDER
1¼ yards

BINDING
¾ yard

BACKING
4¾ yards - vertical seam(s) or
    2½ yards 108" wide

SAMPLE QUILT
Ghouls and Goodies by Stacey Iest Hsu for Moda Fabrics

1 cut

From the accent fabric, cut (10) 2½" strips across the width of the fabric. Subcut each strip into (16) 2½" squares for a **total of 160** accent squares.

From the background fabric, cut (24) 2½" strips across the width of the fabric.
- Subcut 14 strips into 2½" x 6½" rectangles. Each strip will yield up to 6 rectangles and a **total of (80)** 2½" x 6½" background rectangles are needed.

- Subcut 10 strips into 2½" x 4½" rectangles. Each strip will yield 8 rectangles and a **total of (80)** 2½" x 4½" background rectangles are needed.

2 snowball rectangles

Fold each 2½" accent square on the diagonal and press a crease. **2A**

Lay a creased 2½" accent square atop a 2½" x 4½" rectangle as shown, right sides facing. Sew along the marked diagonal line and trim the excess fabric ¼" away from the seam to snowball the rectangle. Press. Repeat to snowball a **total of (80)** 2½" x 4½" rectangles. We'll call these short rectangles for clarity. **2B 2C 2D**

Lay a marked 2½" accent square atop a 2½" x 6½" rectangle as shown, right sides facing. Notice the diagonal is the opposite direction from the 2½" x 4½" rectangles. Sew along the creased line and trim the excess ¼" away from the seam to snowball the rectangle. Press. Repeat to snowball a **total of (80)** 2½" x 6½" rectangles. We'll call these long rectangles for clarity. **2E 2F 2G**

Set the snowballed rectangles aside for the moment.

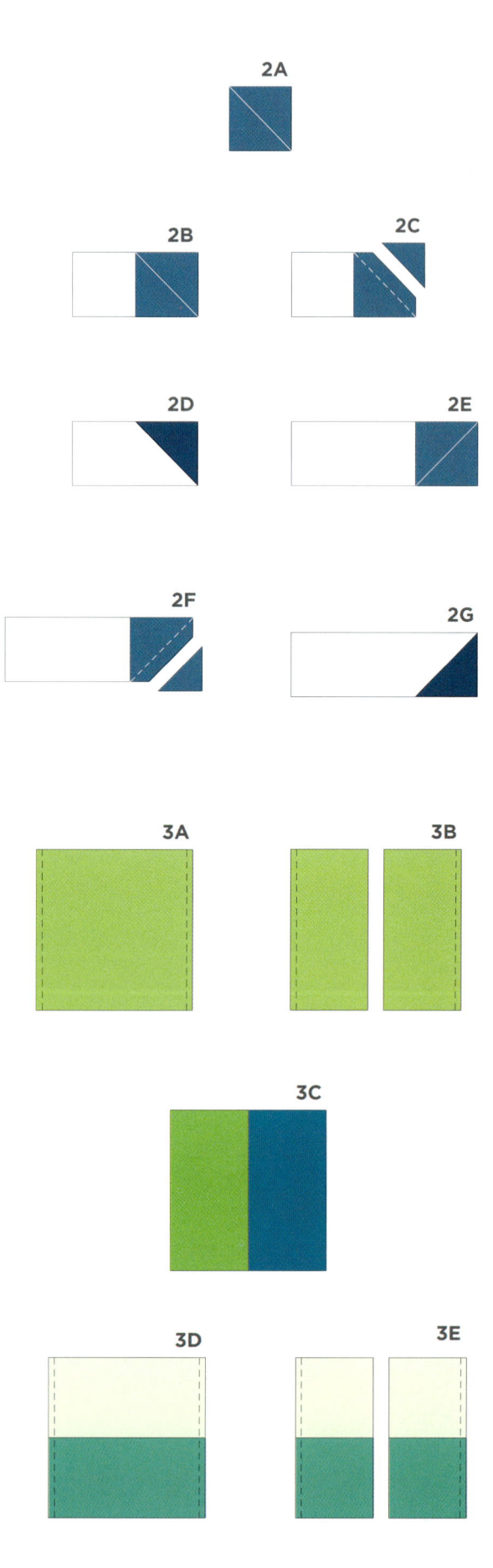

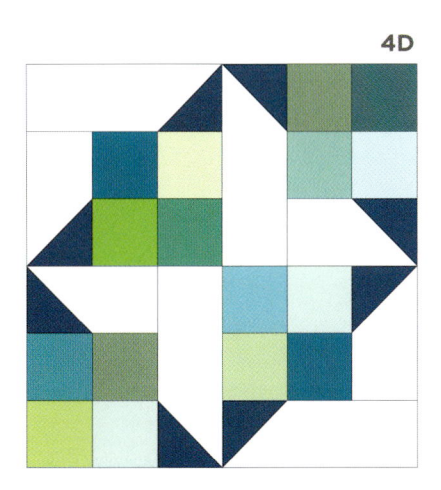

3 make 4-patches

Set (4) 5" print squares aside for another project.

Layer a 5" print square atop a differing 5" print square right sides together. Sew down 2 sides of the stacked squares. **3A**

Measure 2½" from either side and cut the sewn squares in half vertically. **3B**

Open to reveal 2 strip units. Repeat with the remaining 5" print squares. Press. **3C**

Select 2 differing strip units. With seams running horizontally and right sides together, layer 1 unit on top of the other. Sew down the 2 sides of the strip units, perpendicular to the seams. **3D**

Measure 2½" from either side and cut the sewn squares in half vertically. **3E**

Open to reveal (2) 4-patch units. Press. **Make (80)** 4-patch units. **3F**

4 sew rows

Sew a short rectangle to the left side of a 4-patch as shown. Press. **4A**

Sew a long rectangle to the top of the 4-patch/rectangle unit as shown. Press to create a quadrant. **Make 80** quadrants. **4B**

Arrange 4 quadrants in a 4-patch formation as shown. Notice the orientation of the quadrants within the 4-patch. Sew the quadrants together in rows. Press. Nest the seams and sew the rows together. Press to complete the block. **Make 20**. **4C 4D**

Block Size: 12½" unfinished, 12" finished

5 arrange & sew

Refer to the diagram on page 161 as necessary to lay out your units in **5 rows of 4** blocks. Sew the blocks together in rows. Press. Nest the seams and sew the rows together. Press to complete the center of the quilt.

1. Lay a marked 2½" accent square atop a 2½" x 4½" rectangle as shown, right sides facing. Sew along the marked diagonal line and trim the excess fabric ¼" away from the seam to snowball the rectangle. Press. Repeat to snowball a total of (80) 2½" x 4½" rectangles.

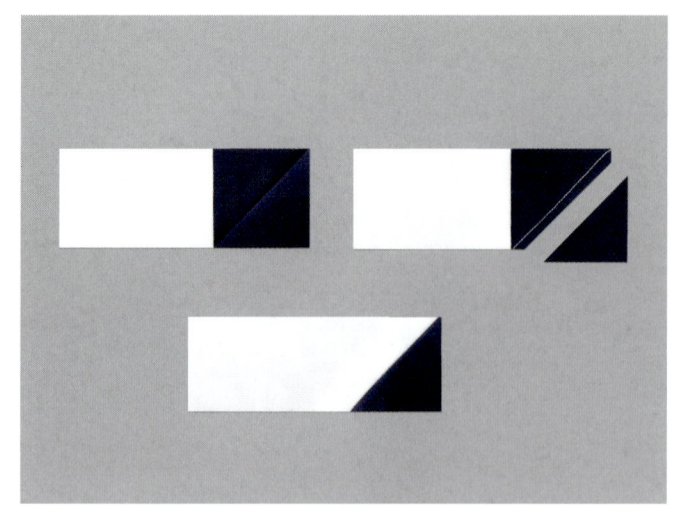

2. Lay a marked 2½" accent square atop a 2½" x 6½" rectangle as shown, right sides facing. Sew along the marked diagonal line and trim the excess ¼" away from the seam to snowball the rectangle. Press. Repeat to snowball a total of (80) 2½" x 6½" rectangles.

3. Layer a 5" print square atop a differing 5" print square right sides together. Sew down 2 sides. Cut the sewn squares in half vertically. Open to reveal 2 strip units. Repeat with the remaining 5" print squares. Press toward the darker fabric.

4. Select 2 differing strip units and layer 1 unit on top of the other with the seams lying horizontally. Sew down the 2 sides perpendicular to the seams. Cut the sewn squares in half vertically. Open to reveal (2) 4-patch units. Press. Make (80) 4-patch units.

5. Sew a short rectangle to the left side of a 4-patch as shown. Press towards the rectangle. Sew a long rectangle to the top of the 4-patch/rectangle unit as shown. Press towards the long rectangle to create a quadrant. Make 80 quadrants.

6. Arrange 4 quadrants in a 4-patch formation as shown. Sew the quadrants together in rows. Press the seams in opposite directions. Nest the seams and sew the rows together. Press to complete the block.

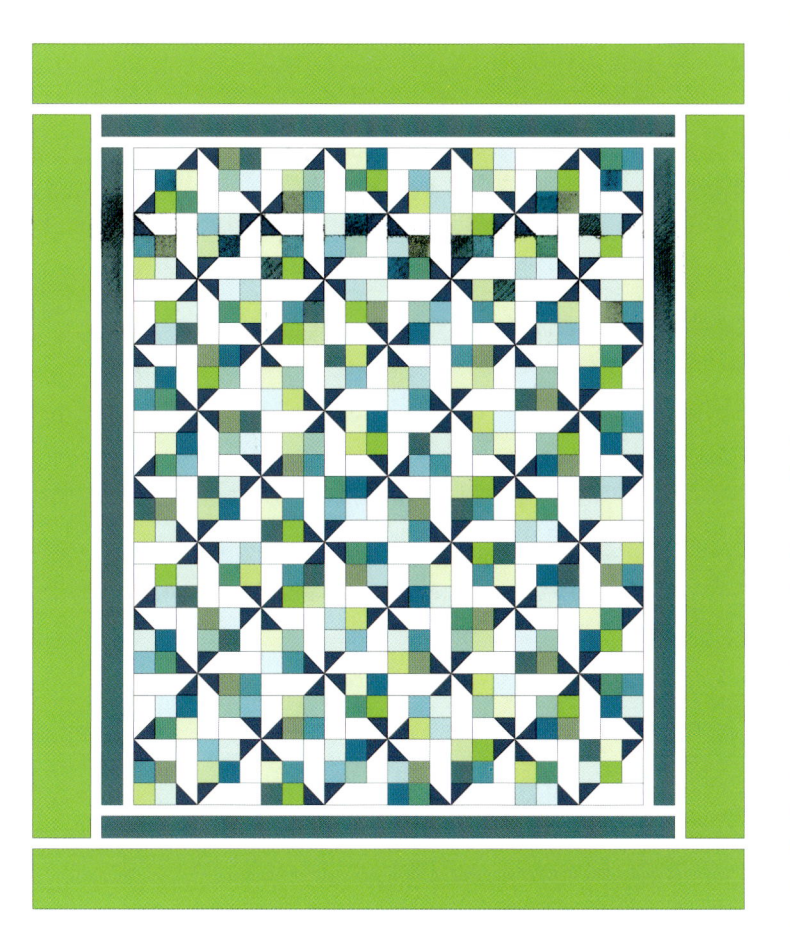

6 inner border

Cut (6) 2½" strips across the width of the inner border fabric. Sew the strips together to form 1 long strip. Trim the borders from this strip. Refer to Borders (pg. 238) in the Construction Basics to measure, cut, and attach the borders. The approximate lengths of the strips are 60½" for the sides and 52½" for the top and bottom.

7 outer border

Cut (7) 6" strips across the width of the outer border fabric. Sew the strips together to form 1 long strip. Trim the borders from this strip. Refer to Borders (pg. 238) in the Construction Basics to measure, cut, and attach the borders. The approximate lengths of the strips are 64½" for the sides and 63½" for the top and bottom.

8 quilt & bind

Layer the quilt with batting and backing, then quilt. After the quilting is complete, see Construction Basics (pg. 238) to finish your quilt.

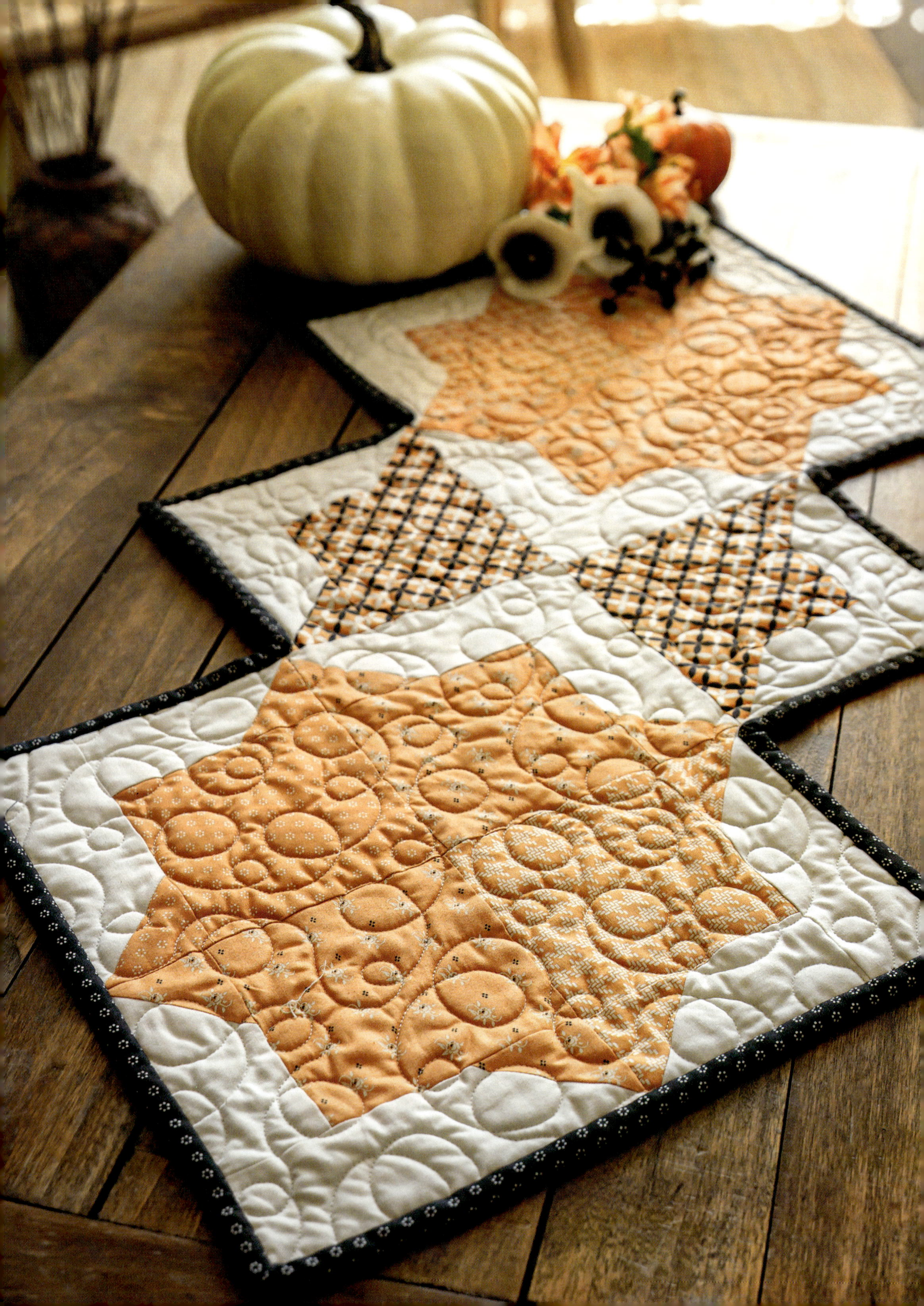

Double Square Star Table Runner
Natalie's Play

Do a double take when you stitch up this easy Double Square Star table runner from Natalie. Created with a unique pointed shape, as if three squares are overlapped on each other, when it's all finished, we think you're going to positively flip!

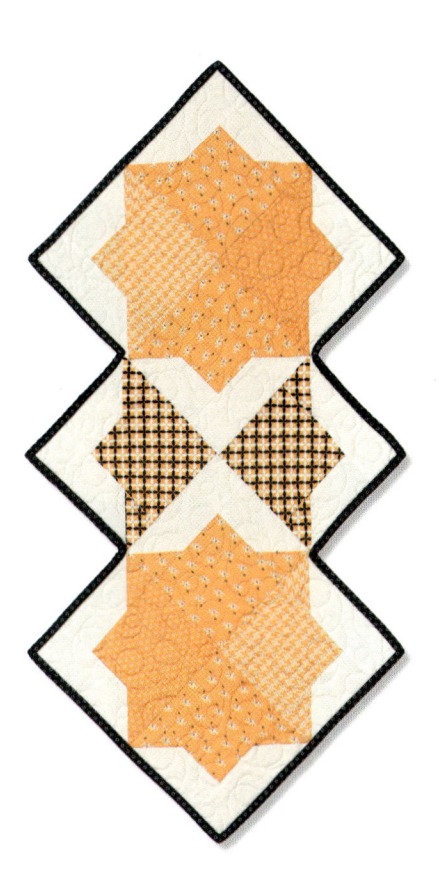

materials

TABLE RUNNER SIZE
37" x 18½"

BLOCK SIZE
13½" unfinished, 13" finished

PROJECT TOP
5 sets of 3 matching 5" print squares
4 packages 5" background squares
¼ yard background fabric

BINDING
¼ yard

BACKING
¾ yard

SAMPLE PROJECT
All Hallow's Eve by Fig Tree & Co.
(Joanna Figueroa) for Moda Fabrics

1 sort & cut

Sort the 5" squares into 5 sets of 3 matching squares.

From each set of 3 squares, cut (1) 5" square in half vertically and horizontally. Each 5" square will yield (4) 2½" squares and a **total of 20** are needed. Keep the matching prints together.

From the background fabric, cut (3) 2½" strips across the width of the fabric. Subcut:

- 1 strip into (8) 2½" x 5" rectangles.

- 1 strip into (6) 2½" x 7" rectangles.

- 1 strip into (2) 2½" x 5" rectangles and (4) 2½" x 7" rectangles. Add these to the previously cut rectangles for a **total of (10)** 2½" x 5" rectangles and a **total of (10)** 2½" x 7" rectangles.

2 block construction

Select a 5" square and 2 matching 2½" squares. Fold each 2½" print square on the diagonal and press a crease. **2A**

Lay a creased 2½" print square atop a 2½" x 5" rectangle as shown, right sides facing. Sew along the creased line and trim the excess fabric ¼" away from the seam. Press. We'll call these short rectangles for clarity. **2B 2C**

Lay a marked 2½" print square atop a 2½" x 7" rectangle as shown, right sides facing. Notice the diagonal is the opposite direction from the 2½" x 5" rectangle. Sew along the marked diagonal line and trim the excess fabric ¼" away from the seam. Press. We'll call these long rectangles for clarity. **2D 2E**

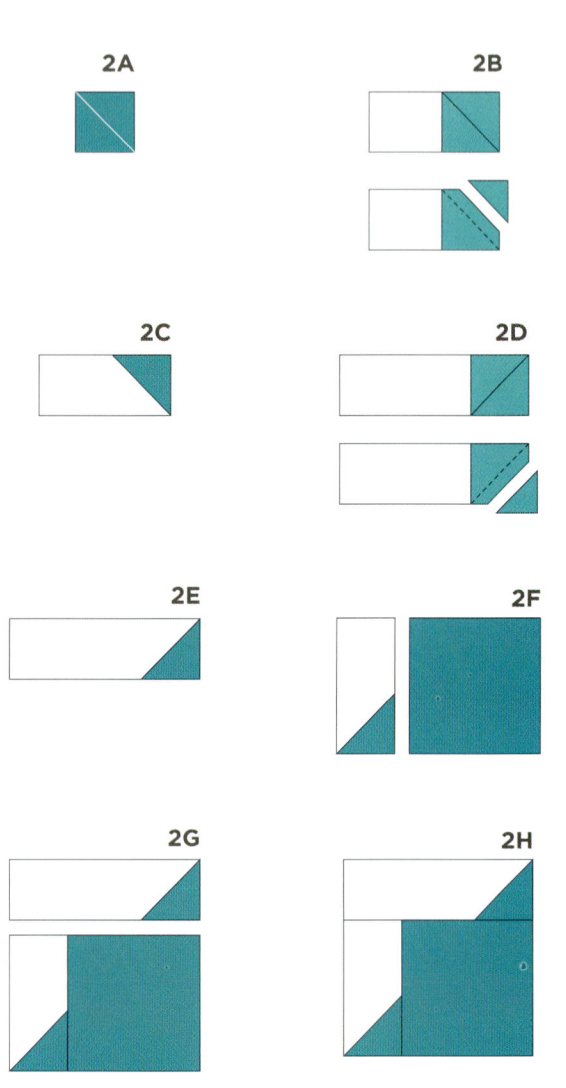

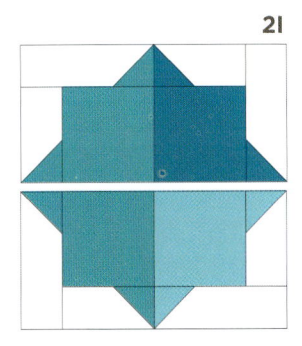

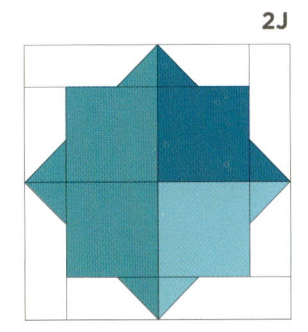

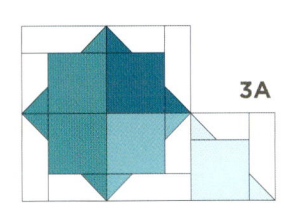

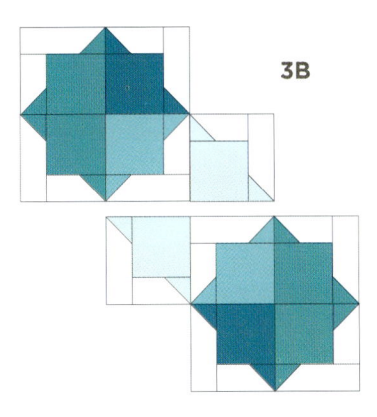

Add the shorter rectangle to the left side of the 5″ square as shown. Press. **2F**

Add the longer rectangle to the top of the sewn unit as shown. Press to complete the block. **Make 10**. **2G 2H**

Arrange 4 units in a 4-patch formation as shown. Notice the squares should all meet in the center. Sew the units together in rows. Press. Nest the seams and sew the rows together. Press to complete the block. **Make 2**. **2I 2J**

Block Size: 13½″ unfinished, 13″ finished

3 arrange & sew

Sew 1 unit to the right side of 1 block as shown, aligning the bottom edges. Press towards the left. **Make 2**. **3A**

Rotate 1 unit 180° and sew the 2 halves together as shown, nesting the seams between the blocks and the smaller units and matching points. Press to complete the project top. **3B**

4 quilt

Layer the table runner with batting and backing, then quilt. See Contruction Basics (pg. 238) to finish your project.

1. Lay a creased 2½" print square atop a 2½" x 5" rectangle as shown, right sides facing. Sew along the marked diagonal line and trim the excess fabric ¼" away from the seam. Press towards the print corner. We'll call these short rectangles for clarity.

2. Lay a marked 2½" print square atop a 2½" x 7" rectangle as shown, right sides facing. Sew along the marked diagonal line and trim the excess fabric ¼" away from the seam. Press towards the print corner. We'll call these long rectangles for clarity.

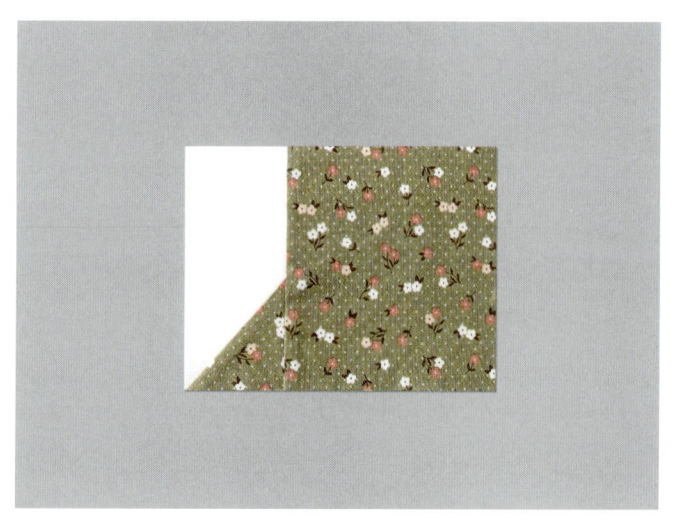

3. Add the short rectangle to the left side of the 5" square as shown. Press towards the square.

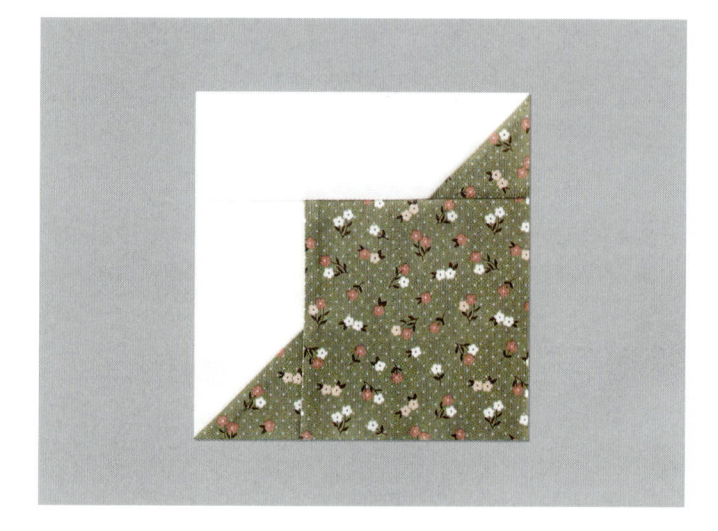

4. Add the long rectangle to the top of the sewn unit as shown. Press towards the rectangle to complete the unit. Make 10.

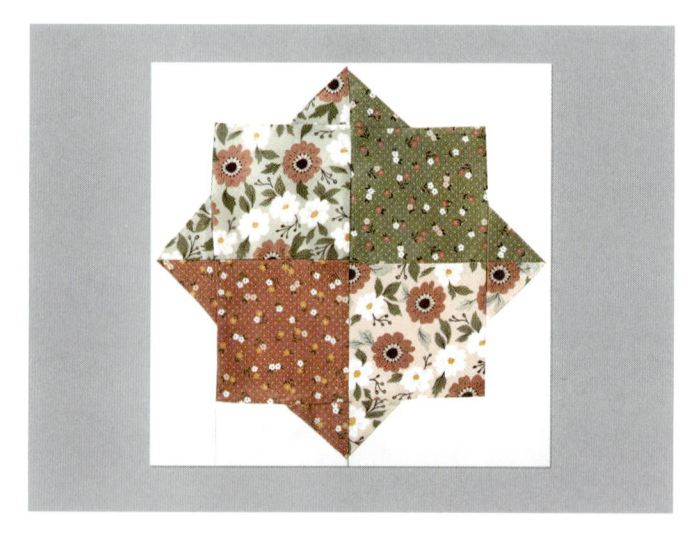

5. Arrange 4 units in a 4-patch formation as shown. Notice the squares should all meet in the center. Sew the units together in rows. Press the seams of the rows in opposite directions. Nest the seams and sew the rows together. Press to complete the block. Make 2.

5 binding

Add binding to complete the table runner. See Construction Basics (pg. 238) for basic binding instructions, including joining the strips for binding.

To bind the inner points of the project, first sew a row of stay stitching slightly less than ¼" from the edge of each inner point. At each inside corner, clip a small V into the angle being sure to not clip the seam just made. **5A**

Start your binding on a long edge. As you come to each inside corner, pause your sewing and draw a ¼" line from the raw edge of your binding strip that is even with both edges of the point. The drawn lines will create a pivot point for your needle. **5B**

Attach the binding into the inside point, stopping with the needle down at the pivot point. The point clipped previously will allow you to now pull the edges of the quilt so that they are straight in front and behind your presser foot and align the quilt edge with the edge of your presser foot. Continue sewing away from the inner point.

Refer to Construction Basics (pg. 238) for finishing instructions for your binding.

Note: If needed, you can clip a small V in the excess binding of the corner to reduce the bulk. Cut close to, but do not clip, your seam.

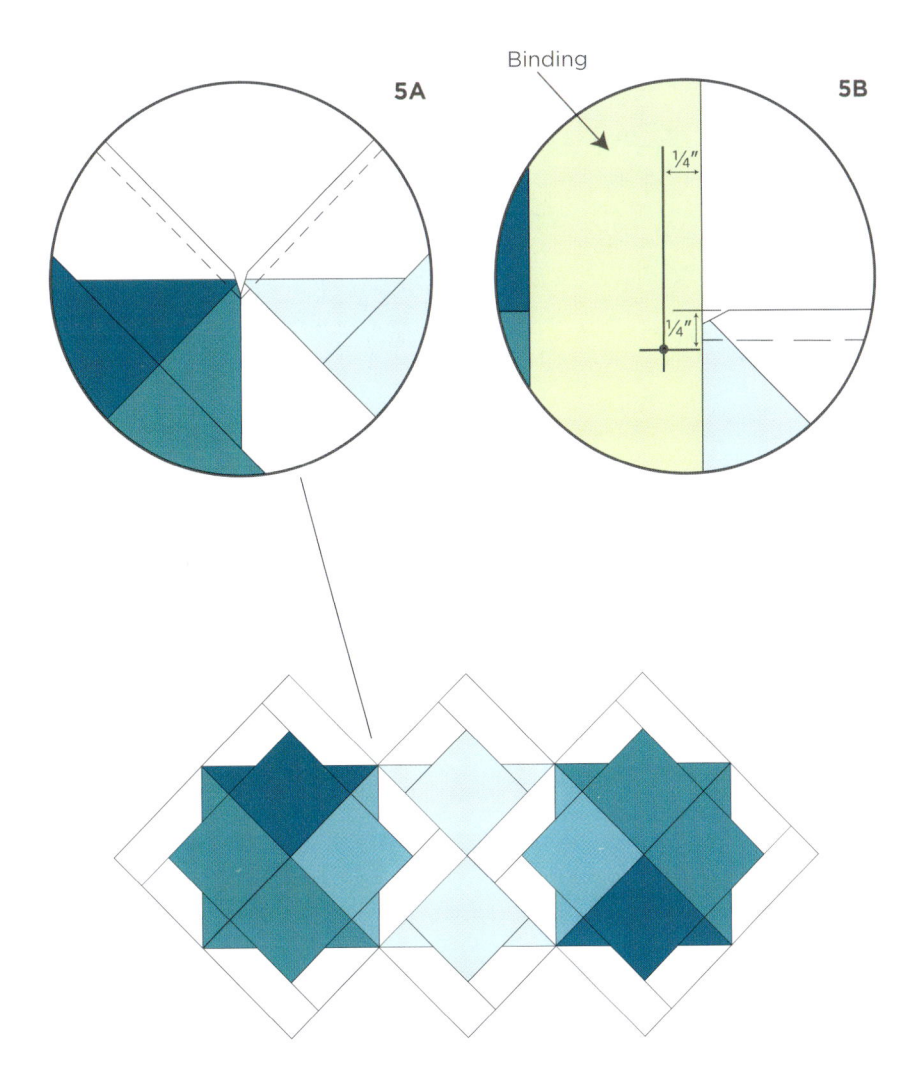

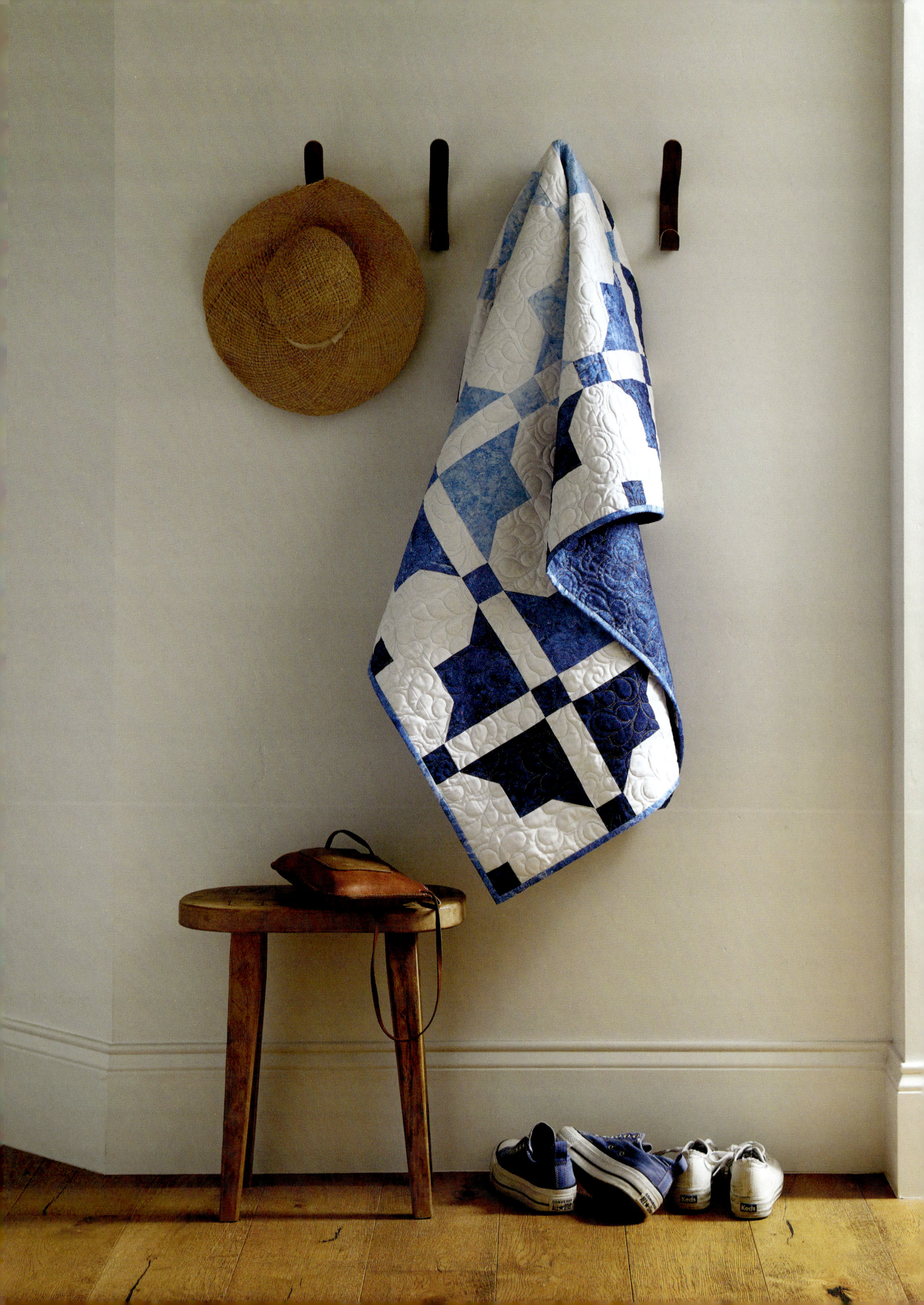
CONVERSE
ALL★STAR
Keds
Keds

Sashed Double Square Star
Misty's Play

In most quilts, sashing seems like an afterthought, but in this snazzy little pattern, Misty makes it the star of the show! Sashing helps this block truly shine as it causes the secondary design to really pop. You'll be amazed at how easy it is to create this stunning quilt.

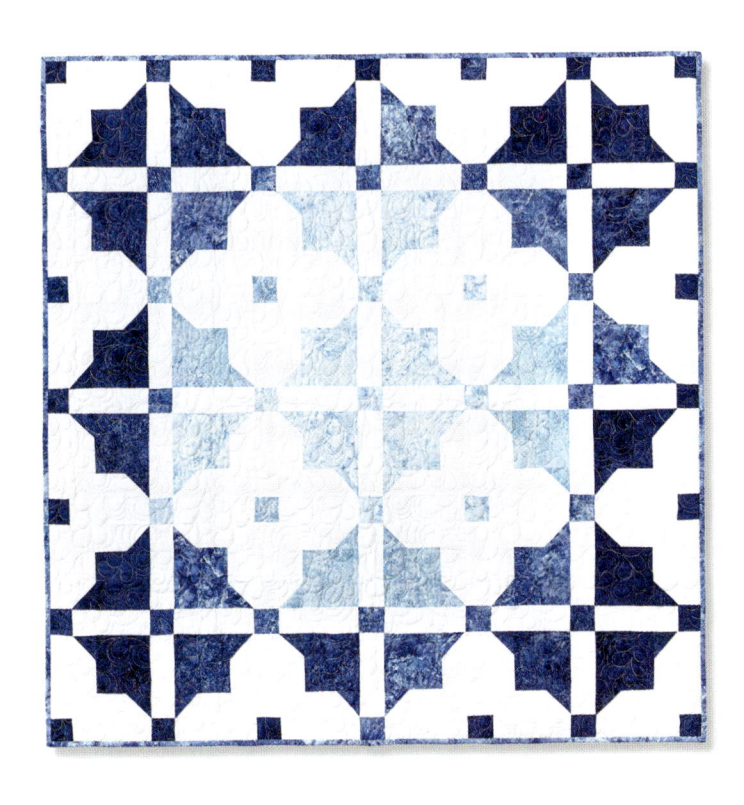

materials

QUILT SIZE
53" x 53"

BLOCK SIZE
15½" unfinished, 15" finished

QUILT TOP
2 packages 5" print squares
2 yards background fabric

BINDING
½ yard

BACKING
3½ yards - vertical seam(s)

SAMPLE QUILT
Stonehenge Gradations Bright - Indigo
by Linda Ludovico for Northcott

1 sort

Sort the 5" squares so there are 2 squares of the same color/print together. You will need 36 pairs of matching squares. Set the remaining squares aside for another project.

2 cut

From each pair of matching squares, cut (1) 5" square in half vertically and horizontally to yield 2½" squares. Each 5" square will yield (4) 2½" squares. Set 2 of the 2½" squares aside for the cornerstones. Keep the 2 remaining 2½" squares and the uncut 5" square of matching fabric together.

From the background fabric, cut (25) 2½" strips across the width of the fabric.
- From 5 of the strips, subcut a **total of (36)** 2½" x 5" rectangles.

- From 20 of the strips, subcut a **total of (120)** 2½" x 7" rectangles—36 for the blocks and 84 for the sashing.

3 block construction

Select a matching set of (2) 2½" squares and (1) 5" square. Mark a line once corner to corner on the reverse side of each 2½" square. **3A**

Place a marked square on the right end of a 2½" x 5" background rectangle, right sides facing, as shown. Sew on the marked line and trim the excess fabric ¼" away from your sewing line. **3B**

Open and press. We'll refer to this as the short rectangle for clarity. **3C**

Place the other marked square on the right end of a 2½" x 7" background rectangle, right sides facing, as shown. Sew on the creased line and trim the excess fabric ¼" away from your sewing line. **3D** Open and press. We'll refer to this as the long rectangle for clarity. **3E**

Sew the short rectangle to the top edge of the 5" print square as shown. Press towards the square. **3F**

Sew the long rectangle to the left side of the unit, as shown. Press towards the square. **Make 36** corner units. **3G**

Note: If you would like your quilt to look like our sample quilt, you may like to lay out the entire quilt before moving onto the next step.

Select 4 corner units, (1) 2½" cornerstone square, and (4) 2½" x 7" background rectangles. Lay the pieces out in 3 rows of 3 as shown. Sew the pieces together to form rows. Press each row towards the background rectangles. Nest the seams and sew the rows together. Press. **Make 9**. **3H 3I**

Block Size: 15½" unfinished, 15" finished

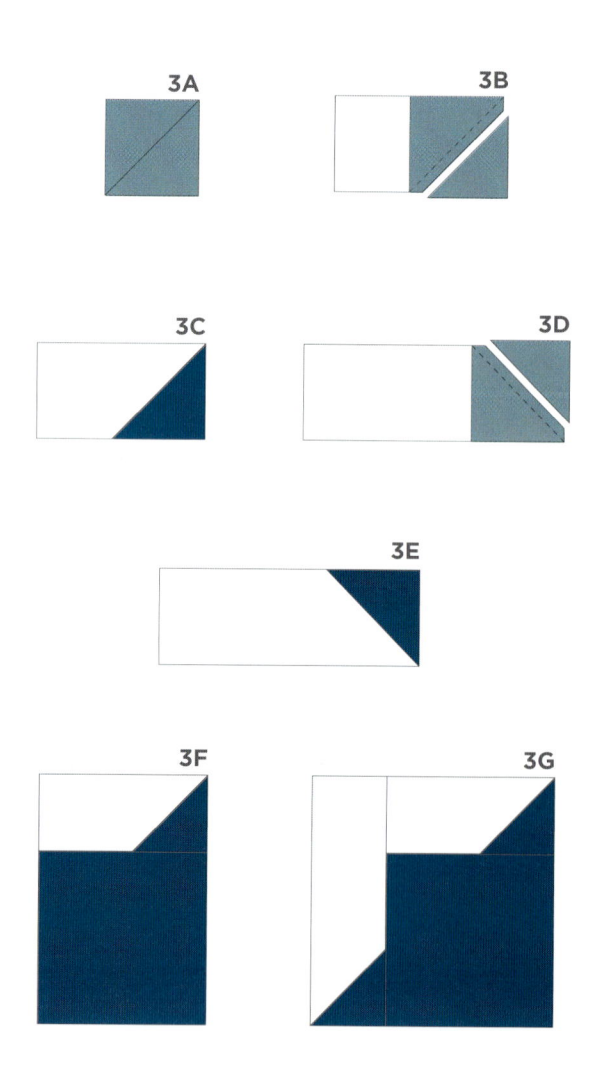

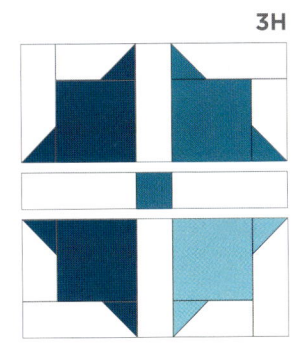

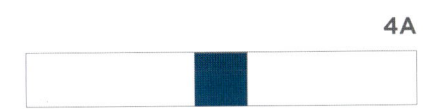

4 make vertical sashing strips

Arrange (2) 2½" x 7" background rectangles and (1) 2½" cornerstone as shown. Sew the units together and press towards the background rectangles. **Make 12**. **4A**

5 make horiztonal sashing strips

Select (7) 2½" cornerstone squares and (6) 2½" x 7" background rectangles as shown. Sew the units together and press towards the background rectangles. **Make 4** horizontal sashing strips. **5A**

6 arrange & sew

Refer to the diagram on page 173 to lay out the blocks in **3 rows of 3**. Place a vertical sashing strip in between each block and on both ends. Sew the blocks and vertical sashing strips together to form the 3 rows. Press. Place a horizontal sashing strip in between each row and on the top and bottom. Sew the rows and horizontal sashing strips together. Press.

7 quilt & bind

Layer the quilt with batting and backing, then quilt. See Construction Basics (pg. 238) to finish your quilt.

1. Fold 2 matching 2½" print squares once on the diagonal. Place 1 creased square on the end of a 2½" x 5" background rectangle. Sew on the creased line and then trim away the excess fabric. Press towards the darker fabric.

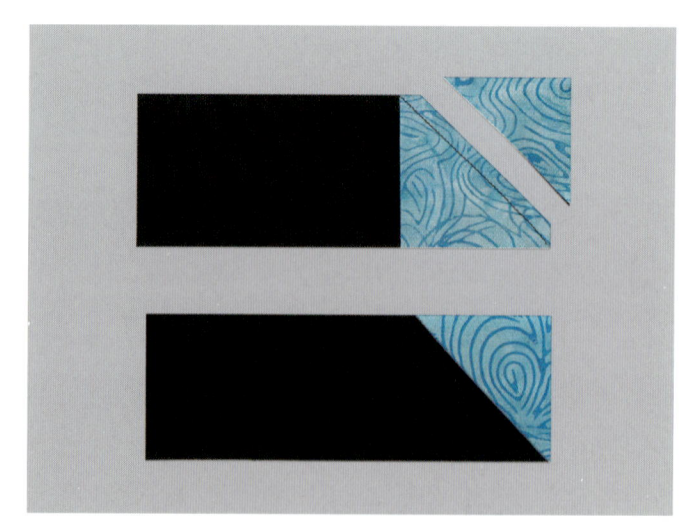

2. Place the other marked square on the end of a 2½" x 7" background rectangle as shown. Sew on the creased line and then trim away the excess fabric. Press towards the darker fabric.

3. Sew the short rectangle to the top edge of a matching 5" print square, oriented as shown. Press towards the square.

4. Sew the long rectangle to the left edge of the unit, oriented as shown. Press towards the square. Make 4 units.

5. Arrange the 4 units, (4) 2½" x 7" background rectangles, and (1) 2½" cornerstone square in 3 rows of 3 as shown. Sew the units together to form rows. Press the seams towards the background rectangles.

6. Nest the seams and sew the rows together to form the block. Press. Make 9 blocks.

173

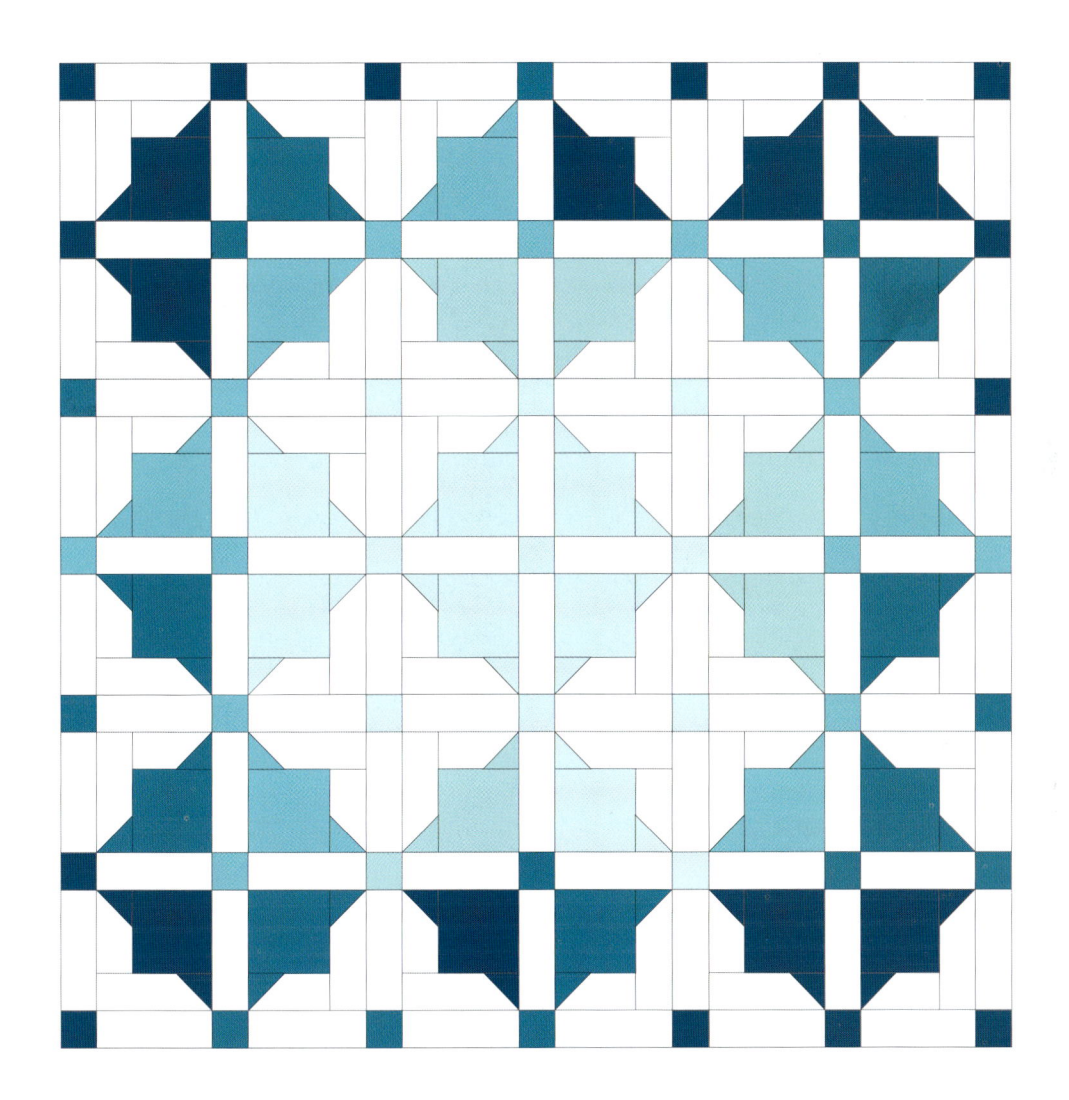

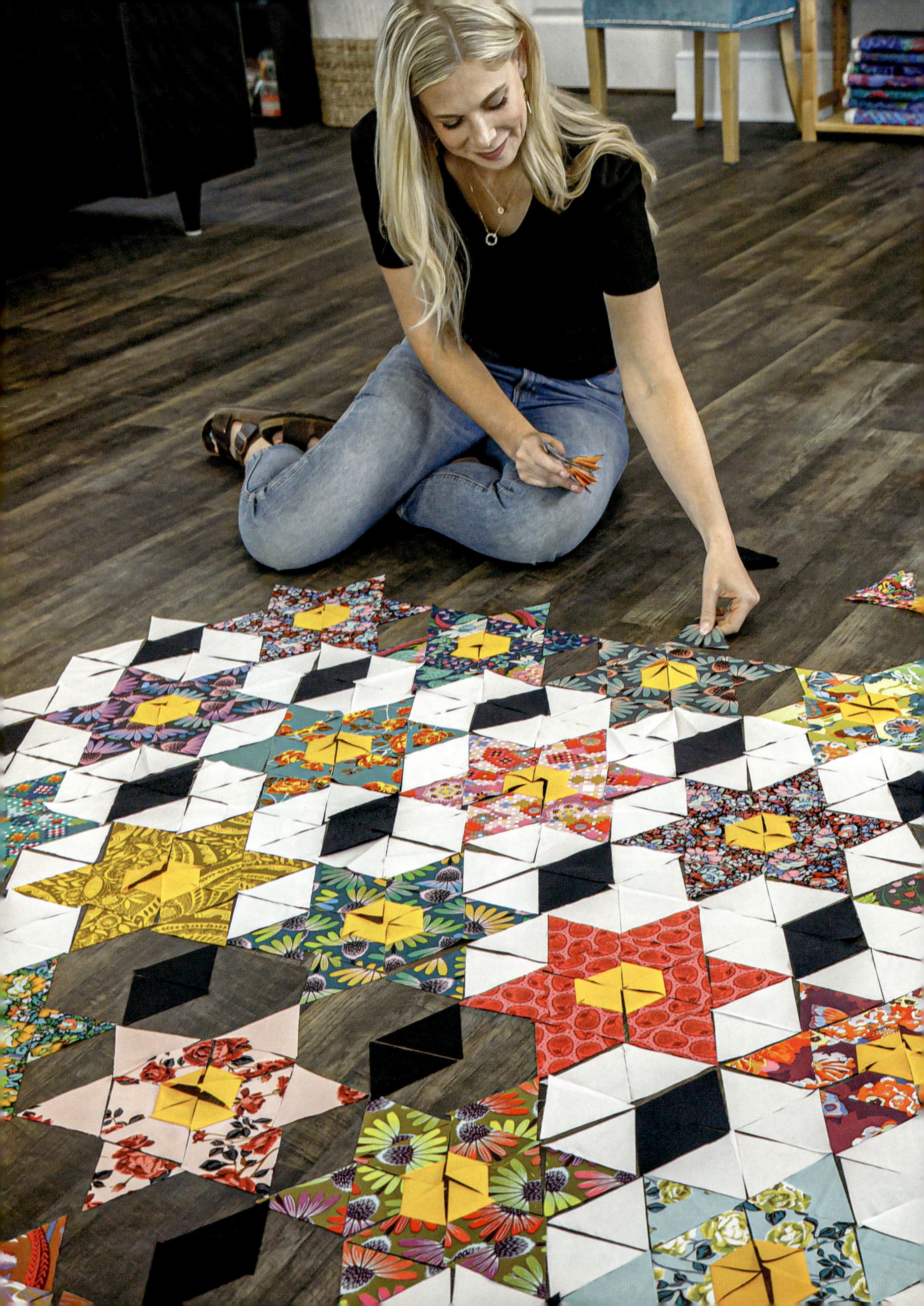

Misty Doan

Imperfection is Beautiful

Misty is Jenny Doan's daughter-in-law. She's married to Jenny's son, Jake, who is the sixth of seven children. They've been married now for over 15 years and have three awesome children. Misty grew up immersed in sewing and quilting and when she became a part of the Doan family, she fit right in. Her love of quilting comes from her grandmother, Sandi. Misty says, "For as long as I can remember, I've been surrounded by sewing and quilting. My mom is an avid crafter and was often found sewing on a project while I was growing up. She passed that on to me. I still love anything crafty. But, my love of quilting began with my Grandma Sandi. She was an accomplished seamstress and fabulous quilter. I'd often spend time with her while she was working. When she got sick with cancer, she lost some of the use of her hand and I had the privilege of helping her cut and sew when she couldn't." Misty continues, "I saw so much about the creative journey and commitment in her life. She's always going to be the most important quilter in my life."

"I love to sew, but what I really love is people. I think every single one of us has something special to offer."

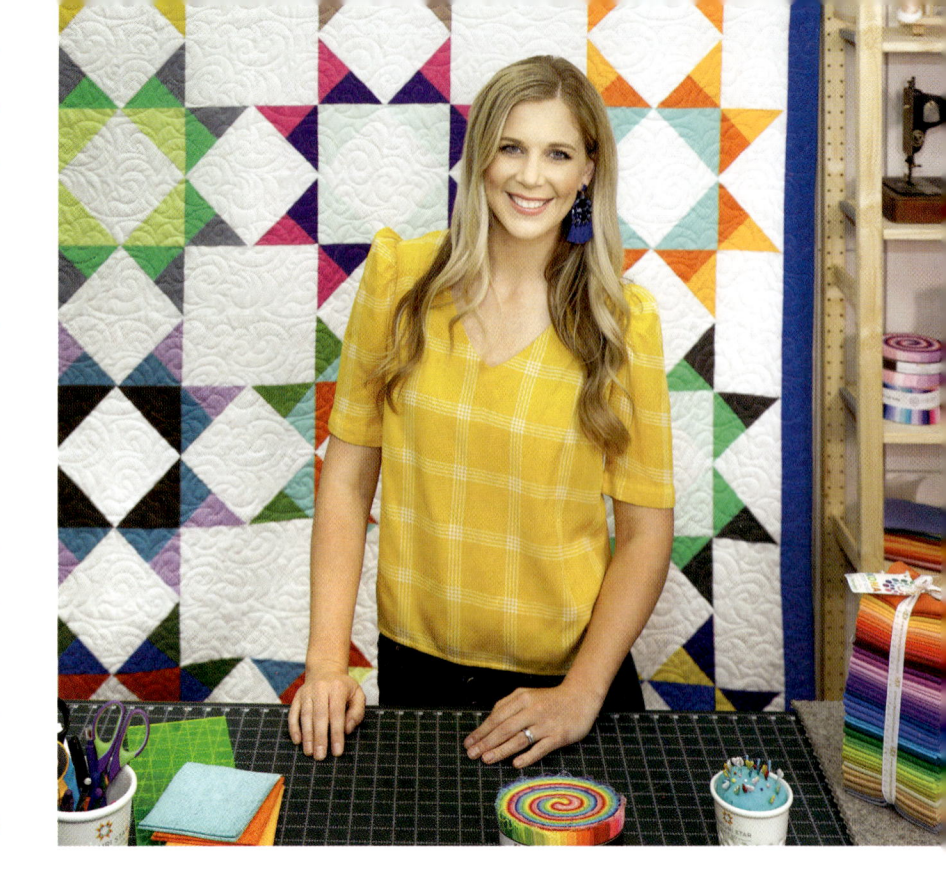

For Misty, quilting is all about the love. She's not naturally outgoing, but that doesn't stop her from making it a priority to reach out to others. She says, "I've always had a great group of friends that I could be myself around, but it took a long time for me to feel comfortable putting myself out there. Hosting the live show and teaching each week was so nerve wracking for me early on, but I'm so thankful to now feel like I'm spending time with my best quilty friends each week. Thank you for being so kind and supportive!" She also wants you to know, "I love to sew, but what I really love is people. That's what motivates me every day. I love being able to make something special and unique for people that I care about. And now, I love being able to connect with people all over the world through a shared hobby. I think every single one of us has something special to offer." Misty has found a way to associate with quilters all around the world through her weekly quilting and sewing tutorials every Tuesday morning and it brings her great joy.

Misty pictured with her grandmother, Sandi

> "All of us have a desire to be creative. It's a moment to play and find childlike wonder."

As we spoke with Misty about how she expresses her creativity, it soon became clear that she is all about enjoying the process. When asked, what's your favorite thing about quilting? She responded, "It is really forgiving. It's a beautiful creative process. In the end you get this beautiful finished project and those imperfections are what makes it human." Truly, the idea that quilting isn't about perfection has become a motto for Jenny, Natalie, and Misty. They are very realistic about their expectations for a finished product and that's a big part of what makes their Triple Play tutorials relatable and fun. After all, if it isn't fun, you aren't doing it right! Misty adds, "It brings me joy and takes me back to what really matters. All of us have a desire to be creative. It's a moment to play and find childlike wonder."

Starting to design a quilt is a natural process that can't be forced for Misty, but she finds ways to ease herself into a mindset where inspiration can take place. She says, "Inspiration is funny because sometimes I have to really work to find it, but often it can strike when you least expect it! Sometimes ideas just seem to blossom out of thin air. I'll see a pattern or shape in tile or carpet and think, could that be a quilt? But most often, I'm designing with someone or something specific in mind and that guides me along the way." Limitations to a design or a pattern are necessary and she embraces the challenge. Misty says, "It's all over the map. Sometimes I have an idea that I just want to try. Sometimes I'm inspired by the fabric and I want to create something that goes along with that. Often we have fabric before we have a design." She begins simply by "blocking out time that is just design and sew time.

Allowing myself that chunk of time. Sometimes it's super productive and sometimes it's not. That's part of the creative process. We're not machines." Sitting down to sew may have varying results, but the important thing to remember is, we'll eventually get there. It's a journey that's meant to be enjoyed, not an end result that needs to be forced. As Misty likes to say, "Don't be afraid to try, try again and remember that all good things take time."

Making mistakes is one of the most effective ways to learn something new and Misty would be the first to tell you that she is constantly seeking to give herself the grace to allow mistakes to happen. She explains, "I am really critical of myself and most of my life I have been. Those mistakes are learning opportunities and they make our quilts and ourselves unique. If it bothers me enough to see it, I'll fix it. The farther I get in the quilting journey, the less those mistakes bother me." But part of that grace is also knowing when to rest. After a tough day with too many encounters with the seam ripper, it's okay to set everything aside and relax. She says, "If I'm trying to make something and I hit a wall three times, I'm done for the day. I just take a breather and come back the next day." Three times sounds like a good compromise to us! Then it's time for one of Misty's favorite things in the world and that's her husband's delicious bread. She'll tell you that bread speaks to her heart. "Bread! Bagels. Sourdough. Croissants. Give me all the carbs. Jake and I often joke that bread is my love language."

"Don't be afraid to try, try again and remember that all good things take time ... That's a part of the creative process. We're not machines."

Out of all the Triple Play projects Misty has created so far, her favorites are based around the Drunkard's Path and Flying Geese blocks. She says, "I love the Drunkard's Path template. I have always been afraid of curves and I thoroughly enjoyed making that quilt and I loved how it turned out." Her lovely Morning Glory quilt takes those classic Drunkard's Path curves and puts them to good use as flower petals by combining two of them with two charm squares. Then, when they are assembled in quadrants of four, they make large-scale flowers. Her other favorite is the Gaggle of Geese quilt because she designed it together with her husband. She says, "Jake has an incredible amount of quilt knowledge because he filmed tutorials for years and years. It's so fun to bounce ideas off of him. He got really into that quilt." And the result is fabulous! It combines three different sizes of flying geese for a fresh, modern look. The rainbow of colors travels in a circular pattern on the quilt, and the geese also travel in a circular motion. It's a wonderful reminder of the cycle of creation and that what may seem like the end simply leads to another beginning.

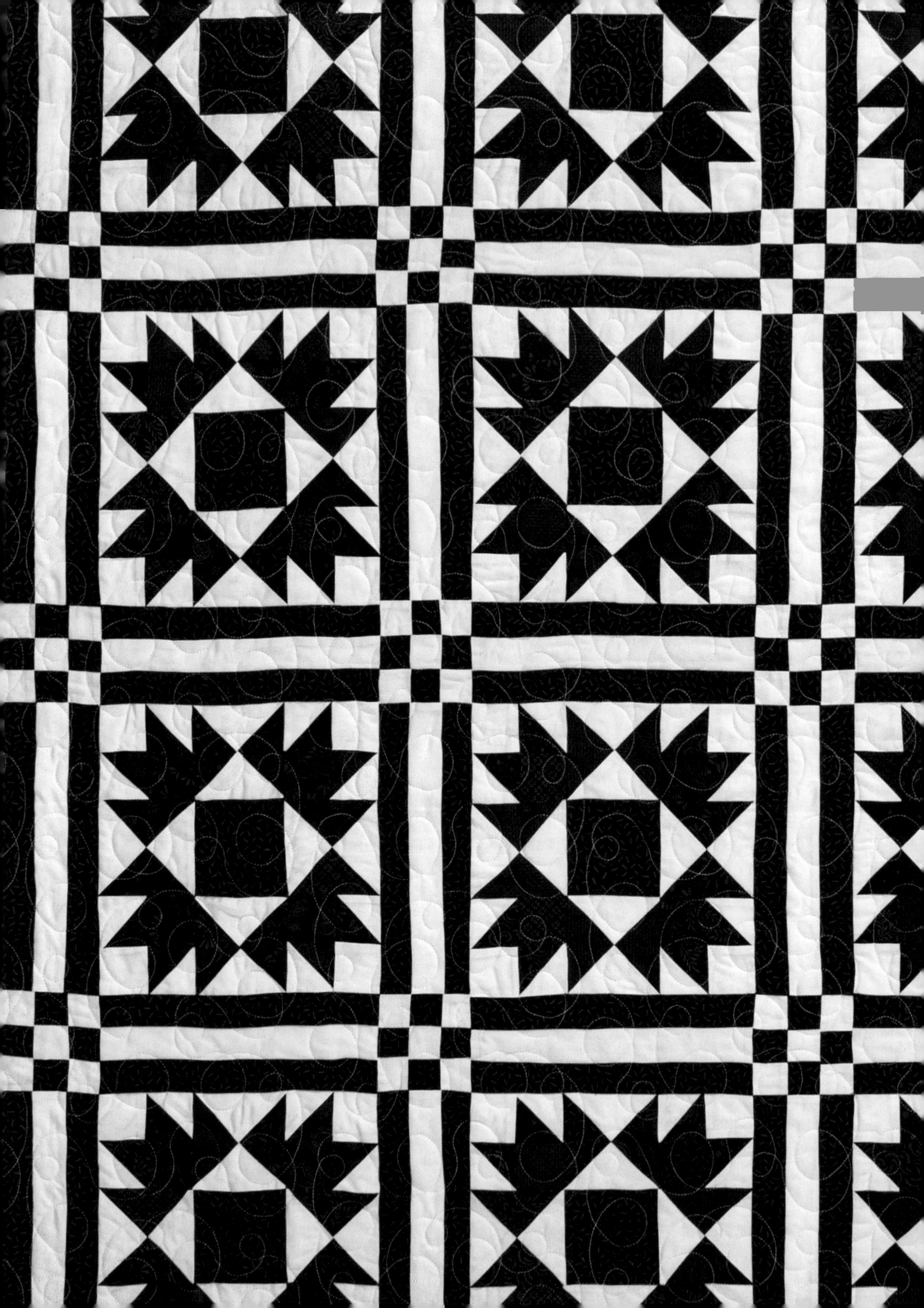

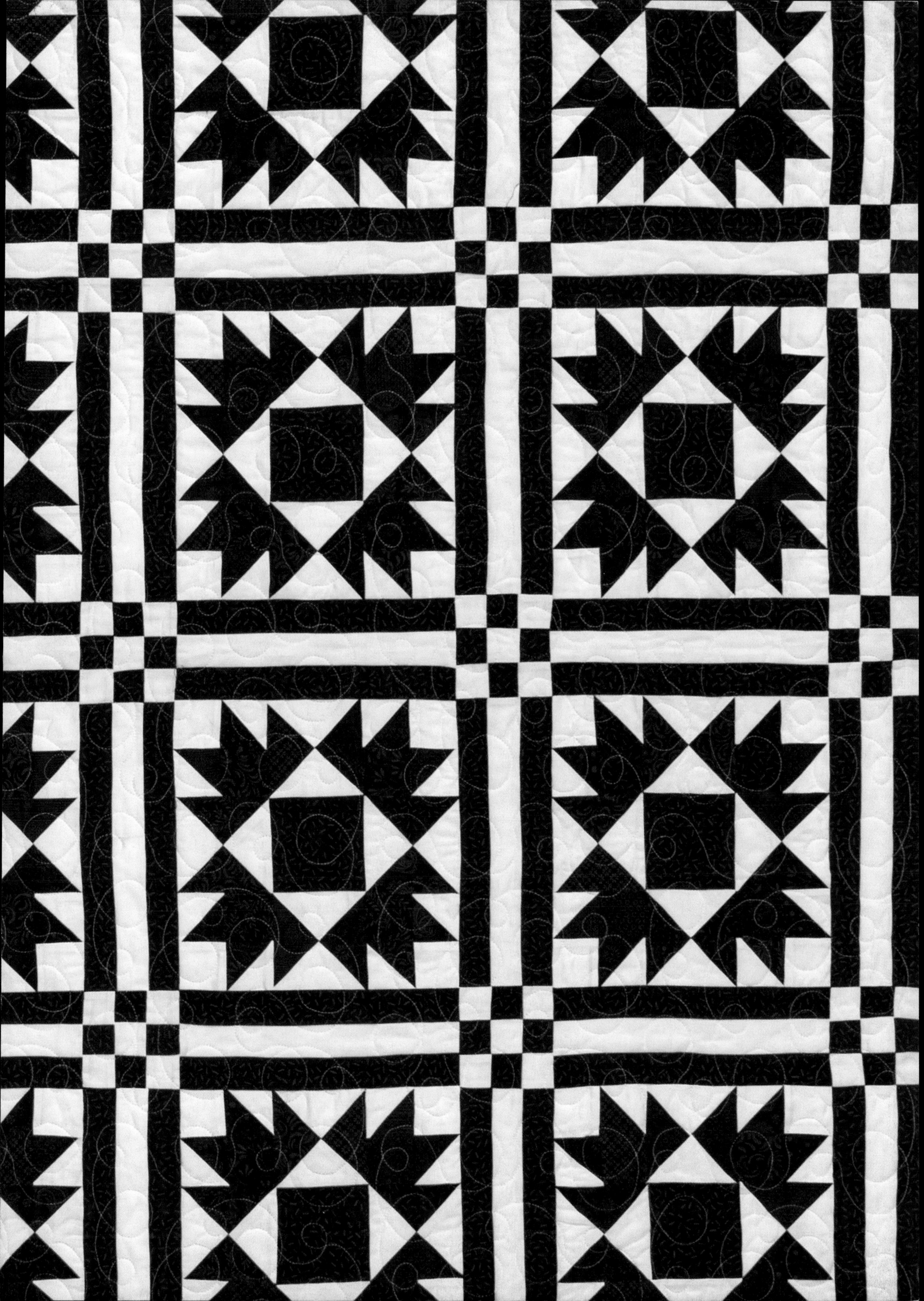

182

Ohio Star

TRIPLE PLAY

This classic eight-pointed star block has a long history that we absolutely love. And with just a couple of small tweaks, it becomes completely fresh and new. We'll never tire of Ohio stars. When you break it down, this complex looking star is only four hourglass blocks surrounding a center square. That's it? Really, that's it. But we pushed it even further for our Triple Play tutorial.

The Ohio star is created in a traditional nine-patch setting, but there's so much you can do within those nine simple squares. How about snowballing those corner background squares? Or adding four-patch blocks instead? Or even trying half-square triangles in unexpected ways? By turning and flipping the hourglass blocks, you'll also get some gorgeous variations. The result will have you saying, "Oh my stars!"

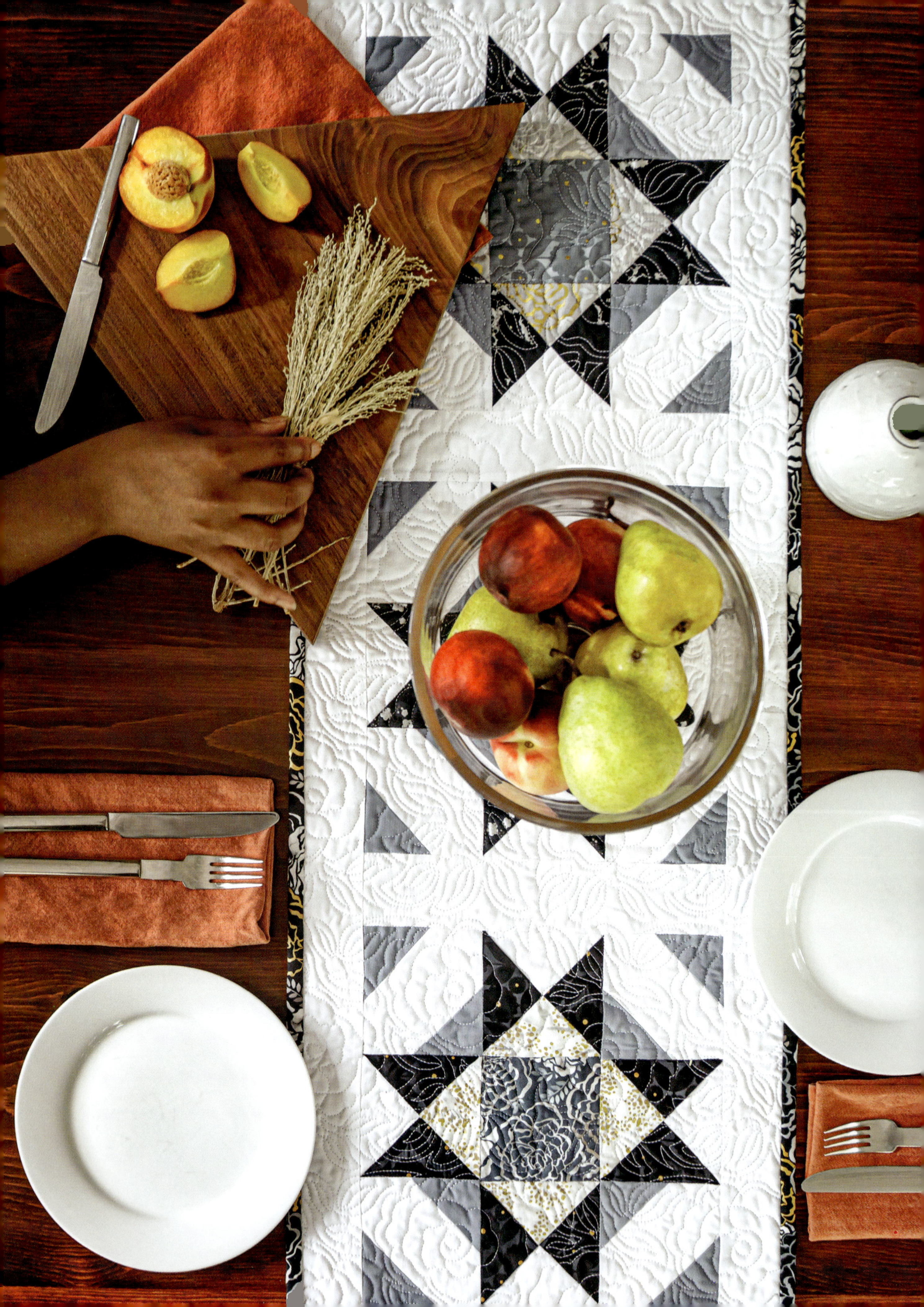

Ohio Star Celebration Table Runner

Jenny's Play

Steeped in rich history, the Ohio Star quilt block celebrates the legacy of Civil War heroes and it remains a popular pattern today. Recreate this classic block with Jenny and watch as she adds snowballed corners and cornerstones to create a lovely secondary pattern.

materials

PROJECT SIZE
39½" x 14½"

BLOCK SIZE
11" unfinished, 10½" finished

PROJECT TOP
1 package of 5" print squares
¼ accent fabric
¾ yard background fabric - includes sashing and inner border

BINDING
½ yard

BACKING
¾ yard - cut lengthwise and sewn with vertical seam(s)

OTHER
Clearly Perfect Slotted Trimmer B - optional

SAMPLE PROJECT
Silverstone by Wishwell for Robert Kaufman

1 cut

From the accent fabric, cut (2) 2½" strips across the width of the fabric. Subcut a **total of (24)** 2½" squares.

From the background fabric:
- Cut (1) 5" strip across the width of the fabric. Subcut a **total of (3)** 5" background squares, then trim the remainder of the strip to 4". Subcut (2) 4" squares.
- Cut (1) 4" strip across the width of the fabric. Subcut (10) 4" squares and add them to those previously cut for a **total of (12)** 4" squares.

Set the remainder of the fabric aside for the sashing and border.

2 sort

Note: As you sort, stack the squares for each section and label each stack. We will reserve the remainder of the cutting for each section.

For the hourglass units, stack 3 pairs of matching dark print squares, 3 light print squares, and the (3) 5" background squares.

For the snowballed corners, stack the 24 accent squares and (12) 4" background squares.

For block construction, select 3 medium print squares for the star centers. Set the remaining print squares aside for another project.

3 make hourglass units

Pick up the stack of squares for the hourglass units. Draw a line once on the diagonal on the reverse side of each light print square and background square in the stack. **3A**

Select 1 pair of matching dark squares from your stack. Lay a background square atop a dark print square, right sides facing. Sew ¼" on both sides of the drawn line. Cut the square in half on the drawn line. Open to reveal 2 dark print/background half-square triangles. Press the seams toward the darker print. **3B**

Repeat with the light print square and the matching dark print square to **make 2** dark print/light print half-square triangles. **3C**

Draw a line once on the diagonal on the reverse side of the dark print/background half-square triangles. **3D**

Place the marked half-square triangle atop a dark print/light print half-square triangle, right sides facing, and dark prints touching either background or light print. Sew ¼" on either side of the drawn line. Cut the sewn units in half on the drawn line. **3E**

Each pair of dark print/background and dark print/light print half-square triangles yields 2 hourglass units. Repeat with the other half-square triangles to make a set of 4 matching hourglass units.

Note: When trimming, be careful to retain the corner points as you trim both sides of a corner. If you are using the slotted trimmer, trim each unit to 4", then open and press the seam allowance to 1 side.

If you are not using the slotted trimmer, open each unit and press the seam allowances to 1 side. Measure each unit 2" from the center point and trim to 4" square.

Repeat with the selected print and background pairs make a **total of 3** sets of 4 hourglass units. **3F**

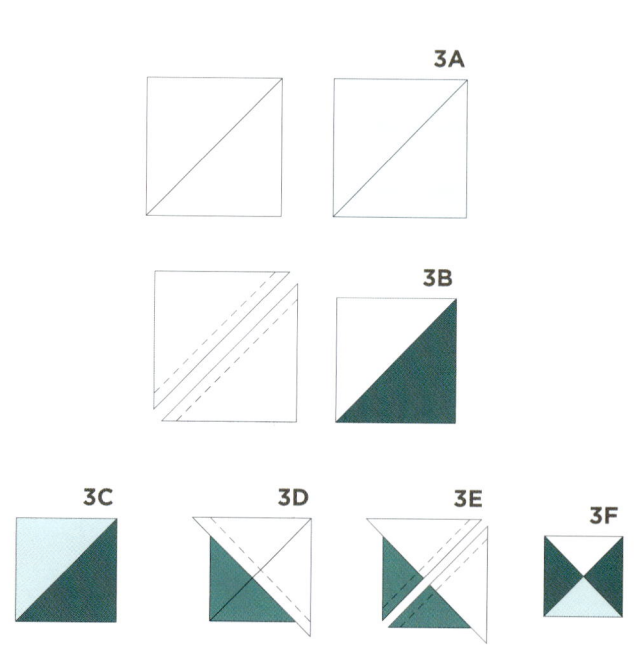

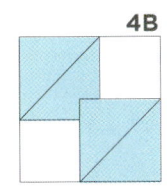

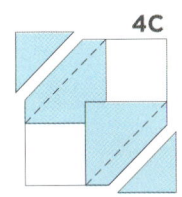

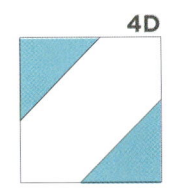

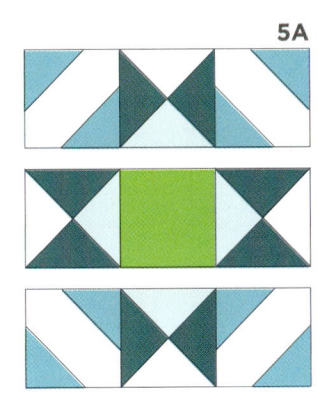

4 snowball corners

Pick up the stack of squares for the snowballed corners. Mark a line once on the diagonal on the reverse side of each accent square. **4A**

Place a marked square on 2 opposite corners of a background square, right sides facing. Sew on the marked lines. Trim the excess fabric ¼" away from the sewn seams. **4B 4C**

Press. **Make 12** snowballed units. **4D**

5 block construction

Pick up the 3 print squares selected for block construction and trim each square to 4".

Select (1) 4" print square, 1 set of hourglass units, and 4 snowballed units. Arrange the units in 3 rows of 3 as shown. Sew the units together in rows and press in opposite directions. Nest the seams and sew the rows together. Press. **Make 3** blocks. **5A 5B**

Block Size: 11" unfinished, 10½" finished

6 make sashing strips

From the background fabric, cut (4) 2½" strips across the width of the fabric. Set 2 strips aside for the border. From the remaining strips, subcut a **total of (4)** 2½" x 11" sashing rectangles.

7 arrange & sew

Refer to the diagram on page 189 to lay out the blocks in **1 row of 3**. Place a sashing rectangle in between the blocks. Sew the blocks and sashing rectangles together to form the row. Press.

1. Layer a background square with a dark print square, right sides facing. Sew ¼″ on both sides of the drawn line. Cut the square in half on the drawn line. Open to reveal 2 dark print/background half-square triangles. Press.

2. Repeat with a light print square and the matching dark print square to make 2 dark print/light print half-square triangles.

3. Place the marked background/dark print half-square triangle atop a dark print/light print half-square triangle, right sides facing, and dark prints opposite of one another. Sew ¼″ on either side of the drawn line, then cut on the drawn line. Open and press. Trim to 4″ square.

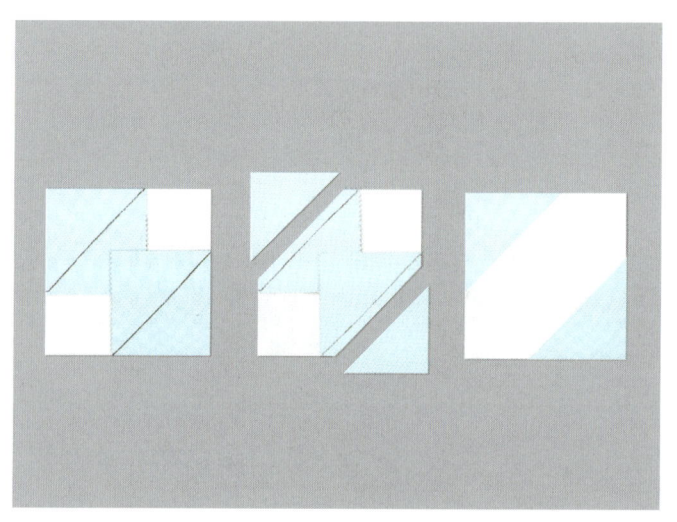

4. Place a marked square on 2 opposite corners of a background square, right sides facing. Sew on the marked lines. Trim the excess fabric ¼″ away from the sewn seams. Press. Make 12.

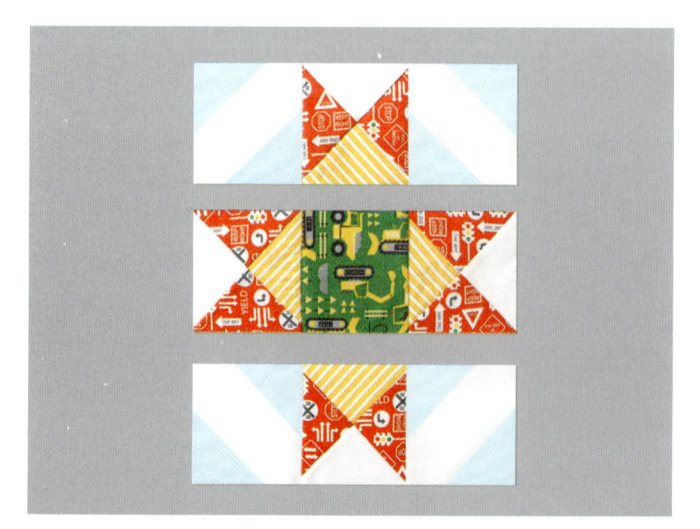

5. Select (1) 4″ print square, 1 set of hourglass units, and 1 set of 4 snowballed units. Arrange the units in a 9-patch formation, as shown. Sew the units together in 3 rows and press each row towards the hourglass units.

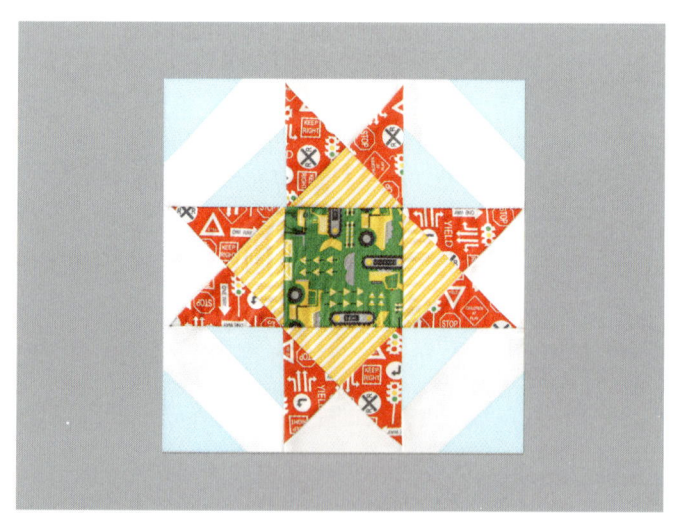

6. Nest the seams and sew the rows together to complete the block. Press 1 direction. Make 3 blocks.

8 border

Refer to Borders (pg. 238) in the Construction Basics to measure, cut, and attach the border. The remaining 2½" x 11" sashing rectangles are used for the border on the ends and are attached first. The long side borders will be trimmed from the 2½" strips set aside previously and are approximately 40".

9 quilt & bind

Layer the project top with batting and backing, then quilt. See Construction Basics (pg. 238) to finish your table runner.

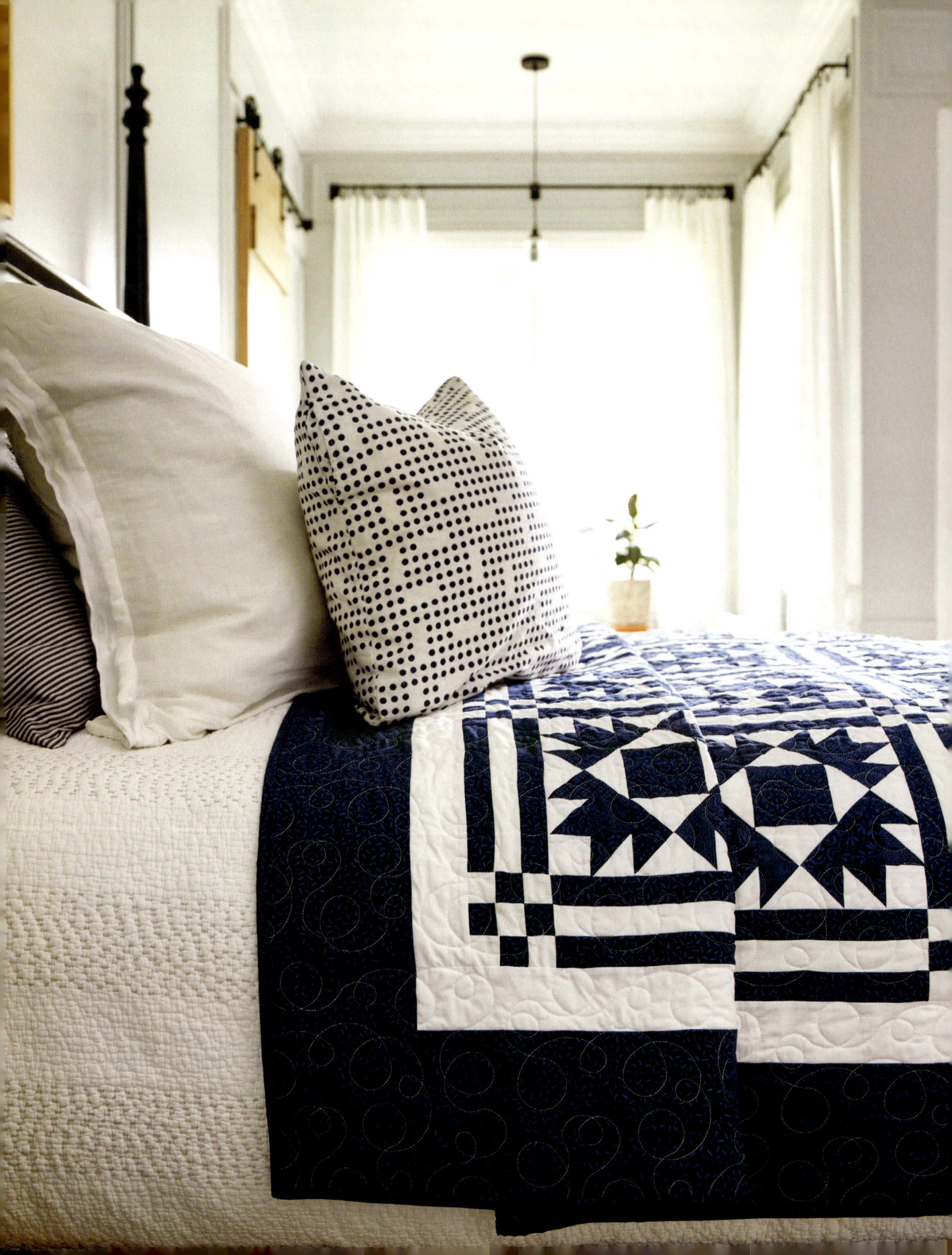

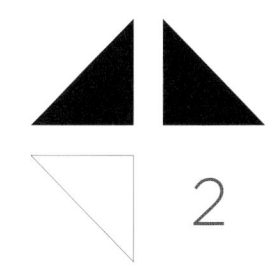

Blue Ribbon Ohio Star
Natalie's Play

Two-color quilts are so fresh and cheerful and this embellished Ohio Star quilt by Natalie in blue and white is no exception! Accented with tiny 9-patch squares and triple sashing, we think it would win a blue ribbon at the fair.

materials

QUILT SIZE
66" x 78"

BLOCK SIZE
9½" unfinished, 9" finished

QUILT TOP
2 packages 5" navy print squares
2 packages 5" background squares
2¾ yards navy print - includes sashing and outer border
1½ yards background fabric
 - includes sashing and inner border

BINDING
¾ yard

BACKING
5 yards - vertical seam(s) or
 2½ yards 108" wide

OTHER
Clearly Perfect Slotted Trimmers A & B
 - optional

SAMPLE QUILT
Wilmington Essentials - In the Navy
by Wilmington Prints

1 cut

Trim (20) 5" navy print squares to 3½". Set these aside for the block centers.

Set (4) 5" navy print squares and (24) 5" background squares aside for another project.

From the navy print yardage, cut:
- (4) 2" strips across the width of the fabric. Subcut a **total of 80** for the corner units.

- (28) 1½" strips across the width of the fabric. Set these aside for the sashing and cornerstones. Set the remaining fabric aside for the outer border.

From the background fabric, cut:
- (4) 2" strips across the width of the fabric. Subcut a **total of 80** for the corner units.

- (18) 1½" strips across the width of the fabric. Set these aside for the sashing and 9-patches. Set the remaining fabric aside for the inner border.

2 make hourglass units

Mark a line from corner to corner once on the diagonal on the reverse side of (40) 5" background squares. **2A**

Place a marked background square atop a 5" navy print square with right sides facing. Sew on both sides of the marked line using a ¼" seam allowance. Cut on the marked line. Open to reveal 2 half-square triangles and press. **2B**

On the reverse side of 1 half-square triangle, mark a diagonal line corner to corner perpendicular to the seam. **2C**

Lay the marked half-square triangle on top of the other half-square triangle, right sides facing and background sides touching print sides. Sew on both sides of the diagonal line with a ¼" seam allowance. Cut on the marked line. **2D**

Note: When trimming, be careful to retain the corner points as you trim both sides of a corner.

If you are using the slotted trimmer, trim each unit to 3½", then open and press. If you are not using the slotted trimmer, open each hourglass unit and press the seam allowances to 1 side. Measure each unit 1¾" from the center point and trim to 3½" square. **2E**

Repeat with the remaining 39 marked background squares and 39 navy print squares to make a **total of 80** hourglass units.

3 make corner units

Draw a line from corner to corner twice on the diagonal on the reverse side of (20) 5" background squares. **3A**

Layer a marked background square atop a 5" navy print square with right sides facing. Sew on both sides of each line using a ¼" seam allowance. Cut each set of sewn squares in half vertically and horizontally, then cut on the drawn lines. Square each half-square triangle unit to 2". Open each and press. Each set of sewn squares will yield 8 half-square triangles and a **total of 160** are needed. **3B**

Pick up the 2" navy print squares and 2" background squares set aside earlier. Arrange 2 half-square triangles, 1 navy print square, and 1 background square in a 4-patch formation, as shown. Sew the units together in 2 rows. Press. **3C**

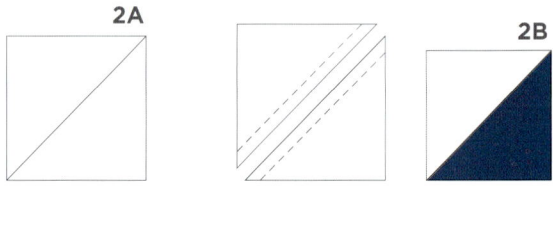

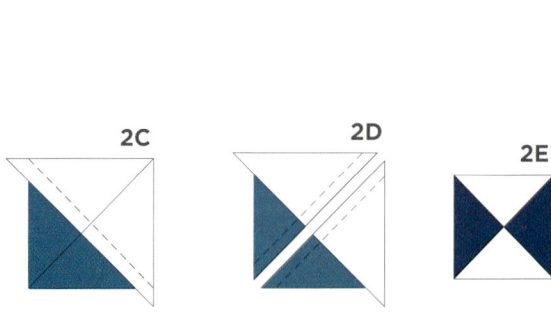

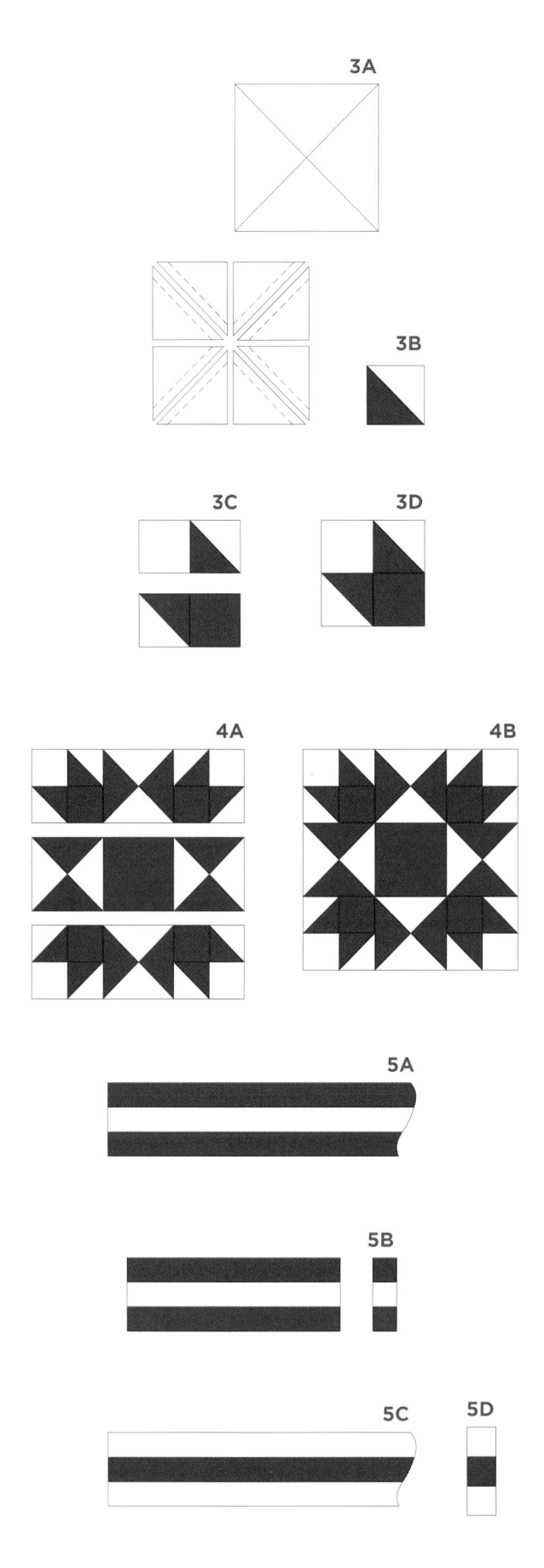

Nest the seams and sew the rows together to make 1 corner unit. Press. Trim to 3½" if needed. **Make 80** corner units. **3D**

4 block construction

Pick up a 3½" navy print square, 4 hourglass units, and 4 corner units. Arrange the units in a 9-patch formation, as shown. Sew the units together in 3 rows and press each row towards the hourglass units. Nest the seams and sew the rows together to complete the block. Press. **Make 20** blocks. **4A 4B**

Block Size: 9½" unfinished, 9" finished

5 sashing & nine-patches

Pick up the 1½" navy print and background strips set aside for sashing. Cut 2 of the navy print strips and 2 of the background strips in half. Set 1 of each of the half strips aside for another project.

Sew a long navy print strip to either side of a long background strip, lengthwise, as shown. Press. **Make 12** long sashing strip sets. **5A**

Repeat to make 1 short sashing strip set using half strips. Each sashing strip set will be 3½" x width of the strip set.

From each of the long sashing strip sets, cut (4) 9½" sashing rectangles and (2) 1½" center units. From the short sashing strip set, cut (1) 9½" sashing rectangle and (6) 1½" center units. Add these to the previously cut pieces for a **total of 49** sashing rectangles and a **total of 30** center units. **5B**

Sew a long background strip to either side of a long navy print strip, lengthwise, as shown. Press. **Make 2** long outer unit strip sets. Repeat to make 1 short outer unit strip set using half strips. **5C**

From the outer unit strip sets, cut 1½" outer units. Each long strip set will yield up to 28 outer units. The remaining outer units can be cut from the short 9-patch strip set and a **total of 60** outer units are needed. **5D**

193

1. Place a marked background square atop a 5″ print square, right sides facing. Sew on both sides of the marked line using a ¼″ seam allowance. Cut on the marked line. Open to reveal 2 half-square triangles and press toward the print fabric.

2. On the reverse side of 1 half-square triangle, mark a diagonal line perpendicular to the seam. Lay the marked half-square triangle on top of another half-square triangle, right sides facing, and background sides touching print sides. Sew on both sides of the diagonal line. Cut on the marked line. Trim to 3½″ square.

3. Layer a marked background square atop a 5″ print square. Sew on both sides of each line. Cut in half vertically and horizontally, then cut on the lines. Square to 2″. Arrange 2 half-square triangles, 1 print square, and 1 background square in 2 rows of 2. Make 80 corner units.

4. Arrange the units in a 9-patch formation, as shown. Sew the units in rows and press. Nest the seams and sew the rows together. Press. Make 20 blocks.

5. Sew a long print strip to either side of a long background strip, as shown. Press. Make 12. Sew a long background strip to either side of a long print strip, as shown. Press. Make 2. Repeat to make 1 more strip set using half strips.

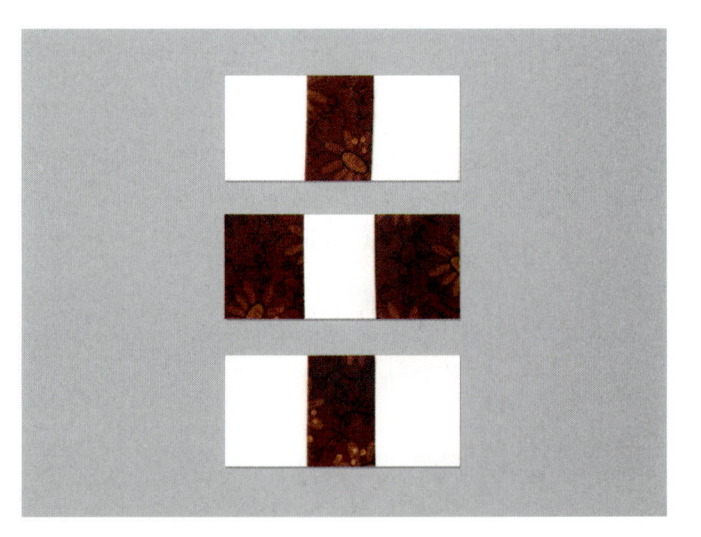

6. Cut 1½″ increments from each strip set. Arrange 2 outer units and 1 center unit in a 9-patch formation as shown. Nest the seams and sew the rows together to complete the 9-patch. Press in 1 direction. Make 30.

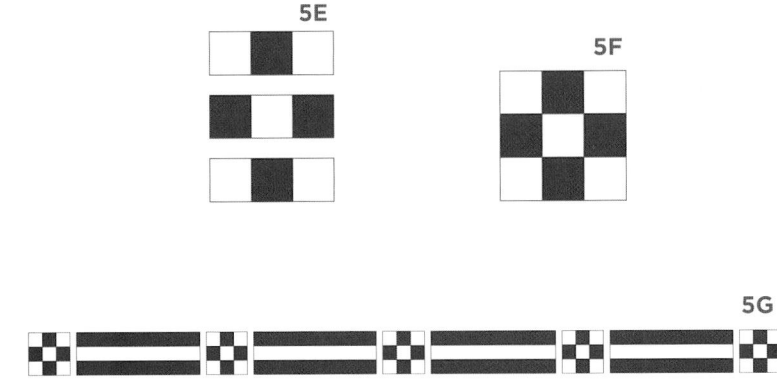

Arrange 2 outer units and 1 center unit in a 9-patch formation as shown. Nest the seams and sew the rows together to complete the 9-patch. Press. **Make 30**. **5E 5F**

Arrange 4 sashing rectangles and (5) 9-patches as shown. Sew the units together in 1 long strip. Press. **Make 6** horizontal sashing strips. **5G**

6 arrange & sew

Refer to the diagram below to lay out the blocks in **5 rows** with each row being made up of **4 blocks**. Place a sashing rectangle in between the blocks and on both ends. Sew the blocks and sashing rectangle together to form the 5 rows. Press. Place a horizontal sashing strip in between each row. Sew the rows and horizontal sashing strips together. Press to complete the quilt top.

7 inner border

From the background fabric, cut (6) 2½" strips across the width of the fabric. Sew the strips together to form 1 long strip. Trim the borders from this strip. Refer to Borders (pg. 238) in the Construction Basics to measure, cut, and attach the borders. The approximate lengths of the strips are 63½" for the sides and 55½" for the top and bottom.

8 outer border

Cut (7) 6" strips across the width of the border fabric. Sew the strips together to form 1 long strip. Trim the borders from this strip. Refer to Borders (pg. 238) in the Construction Basics to measure, cut, and attach the borders. The approximate lengths of the strips are 67½" for the sides and 66½" for the top and bottom.

9 quilt & bind

Layer the quilt with batting and backing, then quilt. See Construction Basics (pg. 238) to finish your quilt.

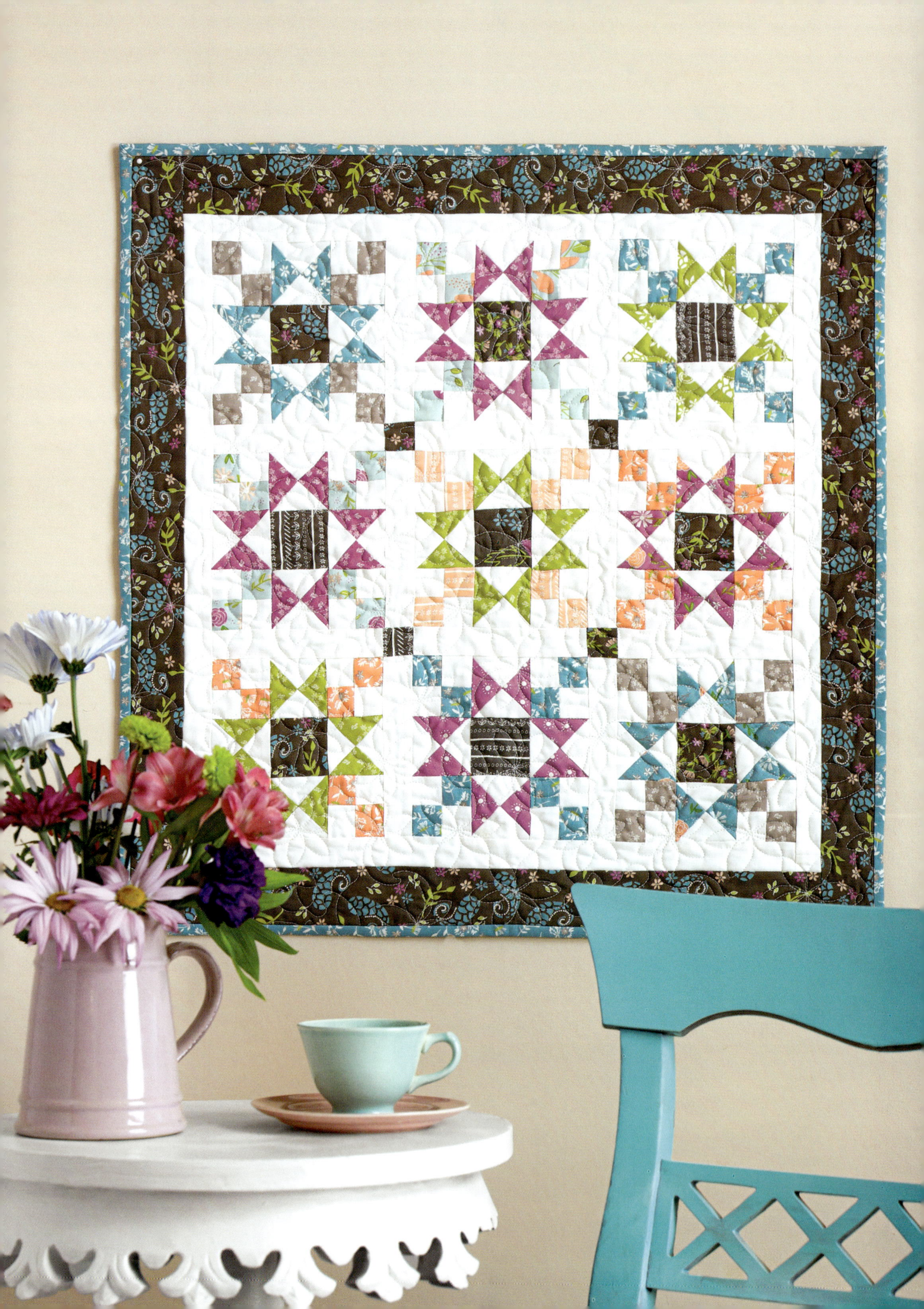

Ohio Starlight Mini
Misty's Play

Stop wishing upon a star and stitch up your very own Ohio Starlight Mini quilt with Misty. It's so cute, it's sure to make your quilty dreams come true. She takes four-patch units and adds them into the corners for a secondary chain pattern you'll adore.

materials

MINI QUILT SIZE
26" x 26"

BLOCK SIZE
6½" unfinished, 6" finished

PROJECT TOP
1 package 5" print squares
¾ yard background fabric
 - includes sashing & inner border

OUTER BORDER
¼ yard

BACKING
1 yard

SAMPLE MINI QUILT
Balboa by Sherri & Chelsi of Quilting Life for Moda Fabrics

1 sort & cut

From the package of print squares, select 3 for the star centers and cornerstones.

- Cut 2 squares in half vertically and horizontally to create (4) 2½" squares from each.

- Cut the remaining square in half once creating (2) 2½" x 5" rectangles.
  - Subcut 1 rectangle into (2) 2½" squares. Set 1 of these squares with the other 2½" squares for a **total of (9)** 2½" squares and set these aside for the star centers.
  - Trim the remaining 2½" square to 1½" square.
  - Trim the remaining 2½" x 5" rectangle to 1½" x 5" and subcut (3) 1½" squares. Add these to the previously cut 1½" square for a **total of (4)** 1½" squares and set these aside for the cornerstones.

From the remaining 5" print squares, select 18 squares for your blocks and set the rest of the squares aside for another project.

From the background fabric, cut (3) 5" strips across the width of the fabric. Subcut 5" squares from the strips. Each strip will yield up to 8 squares and a **total of (18)** 5" background squares are needed. Set the remaining background fabric aside for the sashing and inner border.

2 make hourglass units

Pair a 5" print square with a 5" background square, right sides facing. Sew around the perimeter using a ¼" seam allowance. Cut the sewn square from corner to corner twice on the diagonal to yield 4 half-square triangle units. Open each half-square triangle and press. **2A**

On the reverse side of 1 half-square triangle, mark a diagonal line corner to corner, perpendicular to the seam. **2B**

Lay the marked half-square triangle on top of the other half-square triangle, right sides facing with background triangles touching print triangles. Sew on both sides of the diagonal line with a ¼" seam allowance. Cut on the marked line. **2C**

Note: When trimming, be careful to retain the corner points as you trim both sides of a corner.

If you are using the slotted trimmer, trim each unit to 2½", then open and press the seam allowance to 1 side. If you are not using the slotted trimmer, open each hourglass unit and press. Measure each unit 1¼" from the center point and trim to 2½" square. Press.

Repeat with the remaining half-square triangle units to create a set of 4 matching hourglass units. Keep the matching units together. **2D**

Repeat with the 8 selected print and background pairs to make a **total of 9** sets of 4 hourglass units.

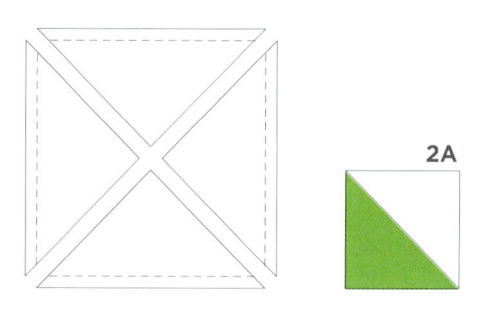

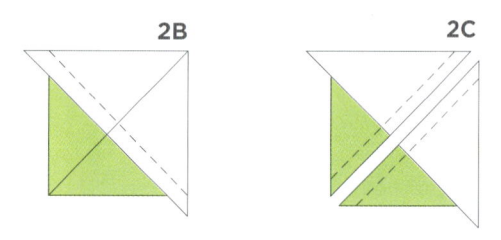

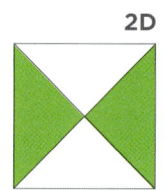

3 make 4-patches

Stack a 5" background square atop a 5" print square, right sides facing, on your cutting surface. Cut (3) 1½" strips across the width of the squares. Take 1 set of strips and sew down 1 long side using a ¼" seam allowance. Repeat with the remaining sets of 1½" strips. Open and press. **3A**

Cut each strip set into 1½" increments. You will need a **total of 8** strip units. **3B**

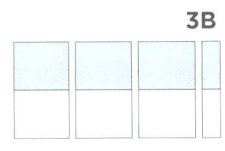

Lay 1 strip unit on top of the other, right sides together, and print sides touching background sides. Sew down 1 side. Open to reveal a 4-patch. Repeat with the remaining strip units to create a set of 4 matching 4-patches. Square each unit to 2½" if needed and keep the matching units together. **3C**

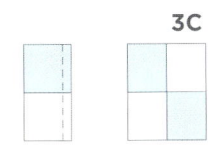

Repeat with 8 additional print and background pairs to make a **total of (9)** 4-patch sets.

4 block construction

Select a 4-patch set, an hourglass set that has a different print than the 4-patches, and a 2½" center square. Arrange the units in a 9-patch formation, as shown. Sew the units together in 3 rows and press each row towards the hourglass units. Nest the seams and sew the rows together to complete the block. Press. **Make 9** blocks. **4A 4B**

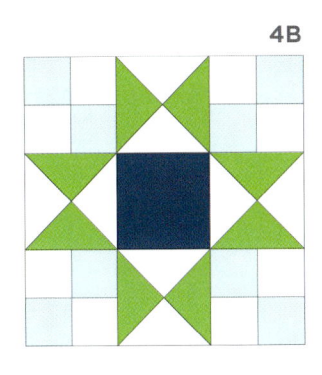

Block Size: 6½" unfinished, 6" finished

5 sashing

From the background fabric, cut (5) 1½" strips across the width of the fabric. Set 3 strips aside for the inner border.*

***Note**: If your background fabric is at least 43" usable width, you will only need (4) 1½" strips total and set 2 aside for sashing.

From the remaining 2 strips, cut (6) 1½" x 6½" rectangles from each for a **total of 12** sashing rectangles.

Arrange 3 rectangles and 2 of the 1½" cornerstones set aside earlier, as shown. Sew the rectangles and cornerstones together in 1 long strip. Press. **Make 2** horizontal sashing strips. **5A**

Set the remaining 6 rectangles aside for vertical sashing rectangles.

1. Pair a 5″ medium print square with a 5″ background square, right sides facing. Sew around the perimeter. Cut the sewn square from corner to corner twice on the diagonal to yield 4 half-square triangle units. Open and press.

2. Lay the marked half-square triangle on top of the other half-square triangle, right sides facing with background triangles touching print triangles. Sew on both sides of the diagonal line. Cut on the marked line. Open and press. Trim to 2½″.

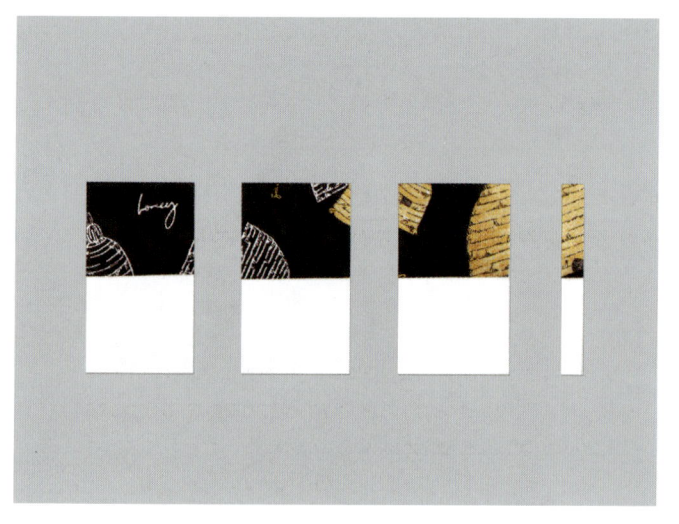

3. Take 1 set of strips and sew down 1 long side using a ¼″ seam allowance. Repeat with the remaining sets of 1½″ strips. Open and press each strip set towards the print. Cut each strip set into 1½″ increments. You will need a total of 8 strip units.

4. Lay 1 strip unit on top of the other, right sides together, and print sides touching background sides. Sew down 1 side. Open to reveal a 4-patch. Repeat to create a set of 4 matching 4-patches. Square each unit to 2½″ and keep the matching units together.

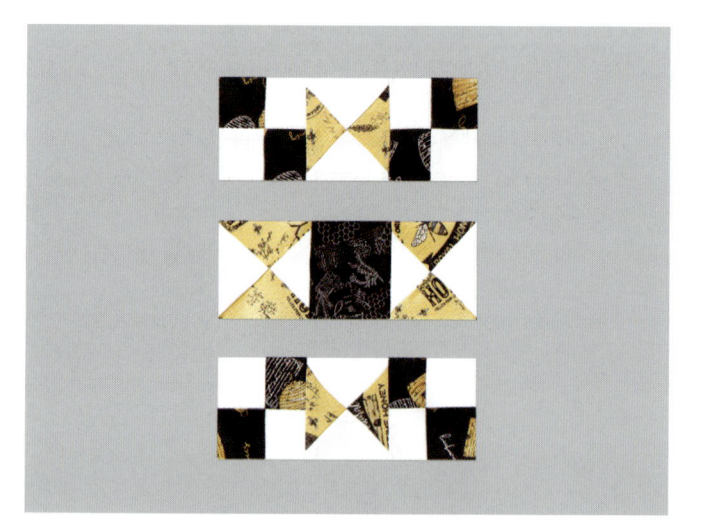

5. Select a 4-patch set, an hourglass set, and a 2½″ center square. Arrange the units in a 9-patch formation, as shown. Sew the units together in 3 rows and press each row towards the hourglass units.

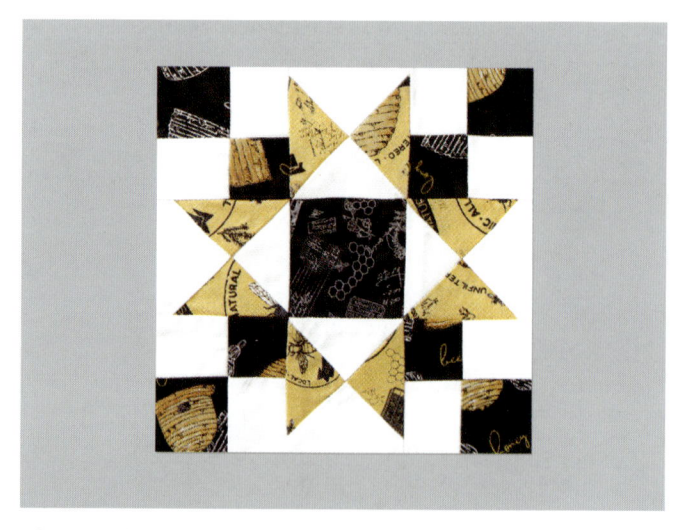

6. Nest the seams and sew the rows together to complete the block. Press. Make 9 blocks.

6 arrange & sew

Refer to the diagram below to lay out the blocks in **3 rows** with each row being made up of **3 blocks**. Place a vertical sashing rectangle in between the blocks. Sew the blocks and vertical sashing rectangles together to form the 3 rows. Press the seams of each row towards the sashing rectangles. Place a horizontal sashing strip in between each row. Sew the rows and horizontal sashing strips together. Press.

7 inner border

Sew the (3) 1½" background strips, set aside earlier, to make 1 long strip.* Trim the borders from this strip.

*****Note**: If you are using 43" background strips, cut (1) 20½" inner border and (1) 22½" inner border from each strip instead of sewing the strips end-to-end.

Refer to Borders (pg. 238) in the Construction Basics to measure, cut, and attach the borders. The strips are approximately 20½" for the sides and approximately 22½" for the top and bottom.

8 outer border

From the border fabric, cut (3) 2½" strips across the width of the fabric. Sew the strips together to form 1 long strip. Trim the borders from this strip. Refer to Borders (pg. 238) in the Construction Basics to measure, cut, and attach the borders. The approximate lengths of the strips are 22½" for the sides and 26½" for the top and bottom.

9 quilt & bind

Layer the project with batting and backing, then quilt. See Construction Basics (pg. 238) to finish your mini quilt.

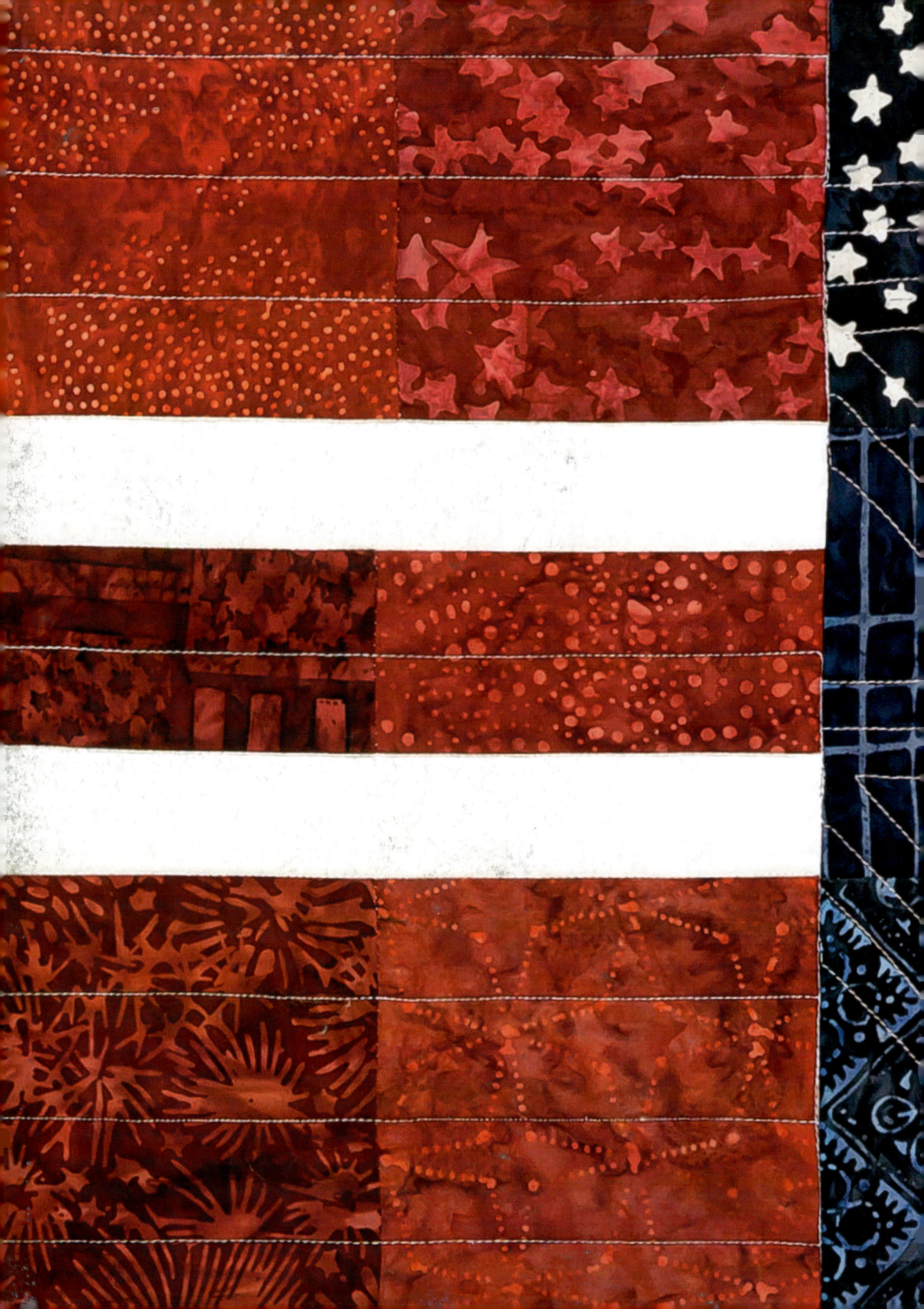

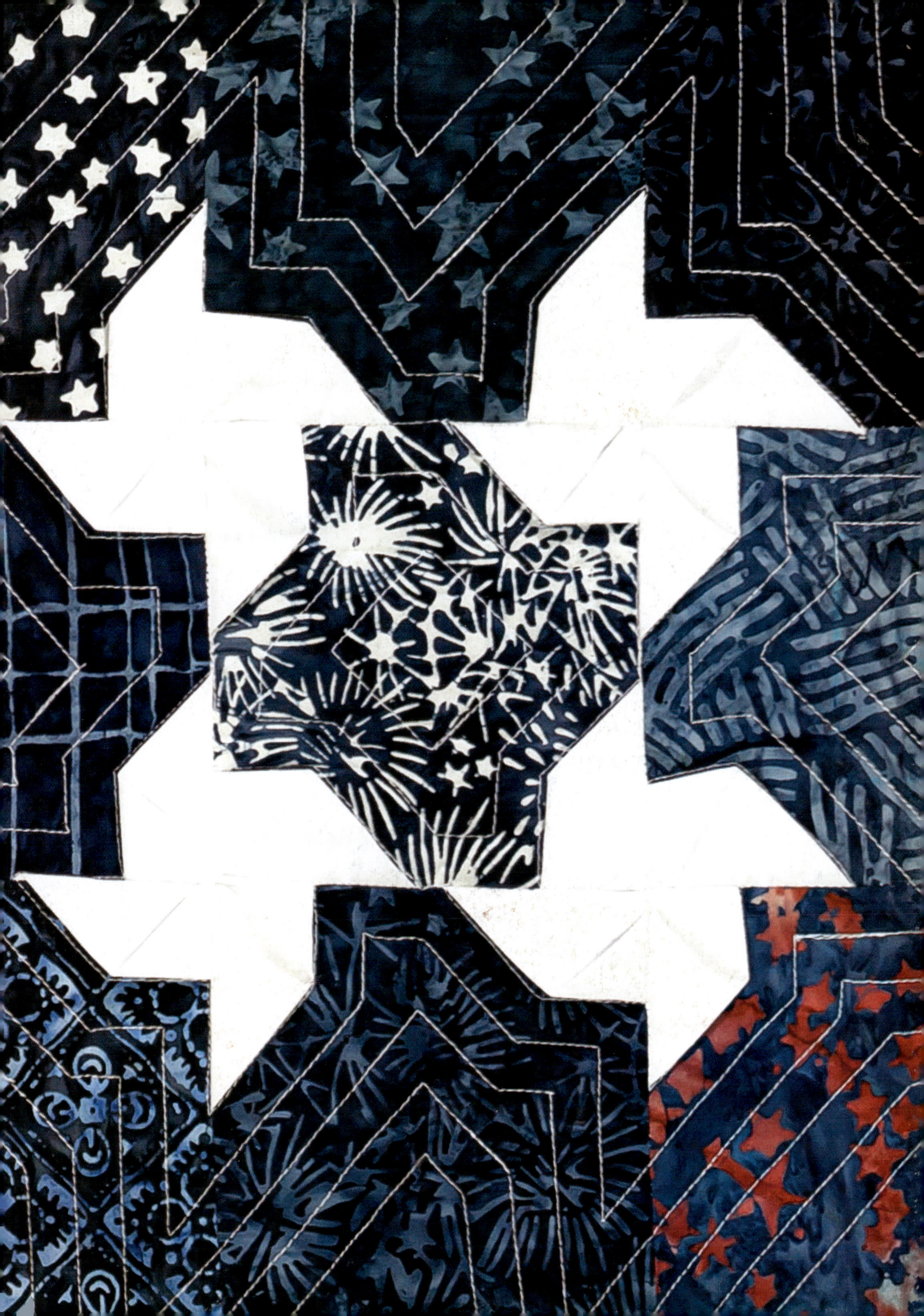

204

3D Pinwheels

TRIPLE PLAY

The pinwheel is a whimsical quilt block we keep coming back to for good reason. Traditionally, they're made with four simple half-square triangles that combine together to create a block with compelling movement. But with the Triple Play tutorial, we took pinwheels even further. The clever 3D pinwheels you'll see in these projects really pop! Originally featured in Block Vol. 6 Issue 2, our special celebration issue, we realized we'd never done a full tutorial on this fabulous technique yet, so we tackled it in the Triple Play.

Creating a 3D pinwheel really couldn't be easier. First, you press a charm square in half diagonally, then fold down one corner and press it as well. The magic happens when you go to stitch this folded square onto a background square. The corner is caught in the seam and stays folded down. By combining four of these folded blocks together, they create a fabulous 3D pinwheel effect. Each of these Triple Play projects is mesmerizing and they all have different applications. Stitch and fold and just wait until you see what happens!

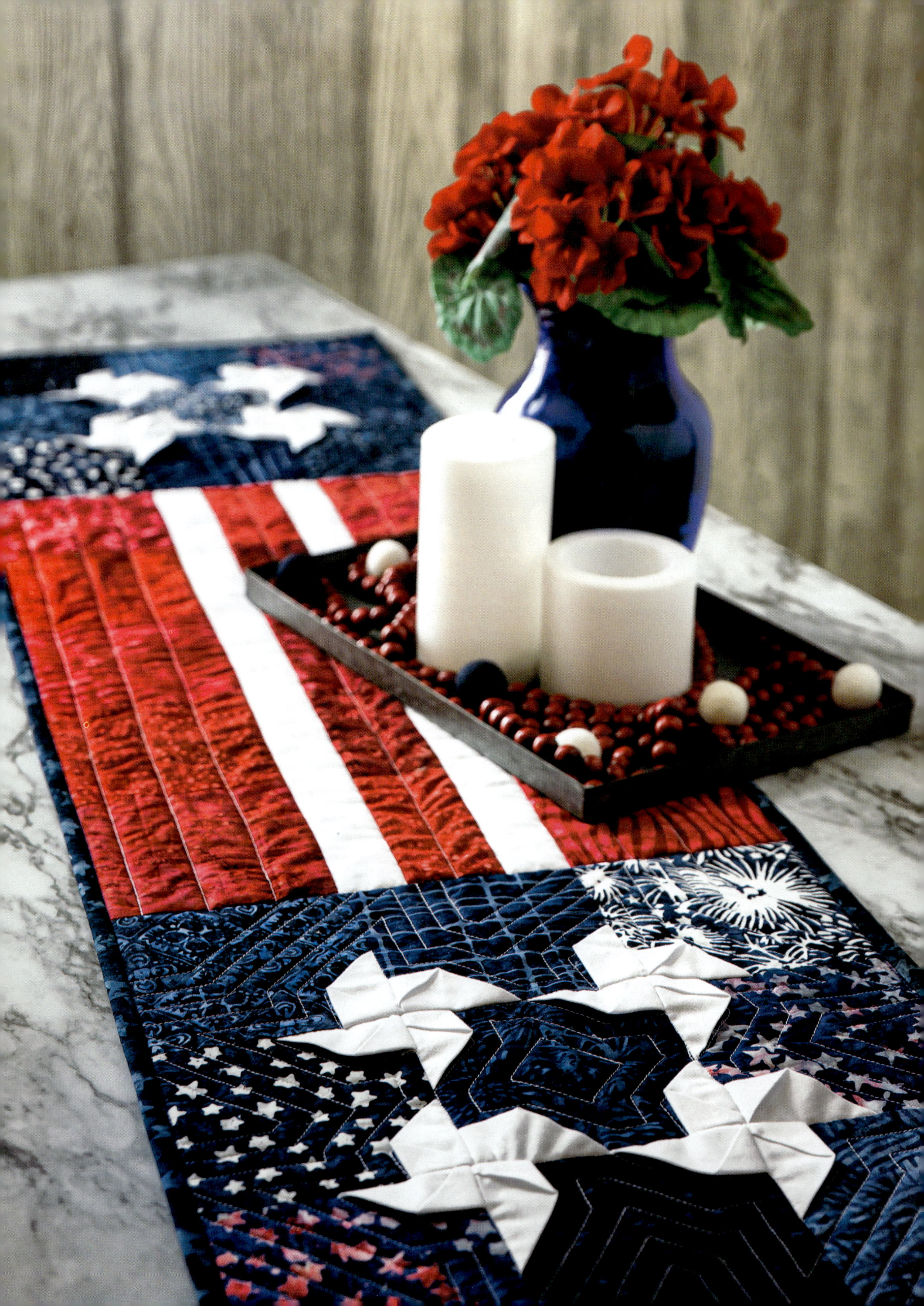

Pinwheel Toss
Jenny's Play

Jenny stitches up a salute to freedom with her red, white, and blue table runner adorned with little white 3D stars for even more appeal. It's adorned with clever 3D pinwheel "stars" for even more appeal. Can't you just picture it at your 4th of July picnic? Toss it on the table and get ready to celebrate!

materials

TABLE RUNNER SIZE
49½" x 13½"

BLOCK SIZE
14" unfinished, 13½" finished

TABLE RUNNER SUPPLIES
1 package 5" print squares*
½ yard white solid fabric

BINDING
½ yard

BACKING
1 yard - cut parallel to the selvages and sewn together along the short ends

SAMPLE PROJECT
Freedom by Tonga Batiks for Timeless Treasures Fabrics

__Note:__ If you want a patriotic table runner like ours, you'll need at least 18 blue squares and 13 red squares in your package of 5" print squares.

207

1 cut & sort

From the white solid fabric, cut:

- (2) 2½" strips across the width of the fabric. Subcut (16) 2½" squares from each strip for a **total of (32)** 2½" white squares.

- (2) 1¾" strips across the width of the fabric. Subcut (1) 1¾" x 23" rectangle from each strip.

Set the remaining white solid fabric aside for another project. Set the rectangles aside for the moment.

Select 18 blue print squares and 13 red print squares from your package of 5" squares. Set the remaining print squares aside for another project. Choose 3 of your selected red print squares and cut them in half lengthwise creating (2) 2½" x 5" rectangles from each square. You will need a **total of 5** red print rectangles. Set the rectangles and remaining red print squares aside for the moment.

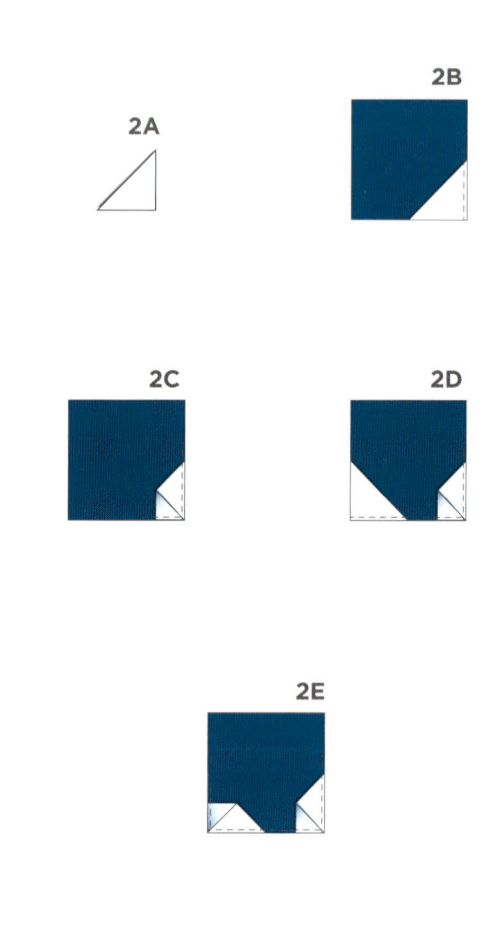

2 make pinwheel units

Fold each 2½" white square from corner to corner once on the diagonal with wrong sides together and press the crease in place. **2A**

Unit A

Place a folded piece onto the bottom right corner of a 5" blue print square. Align the raw edges of the folded piece with the raw edges of the print square. Baste across the right side using an ⅛" seam allowance. (We want this seam allowance to be smaller than usual.) **2B**

Fold the loose corner of the folded piece toward the sewn seam on the right. Pin in place. Baste across the bottom of the square using an ⅛" seam allowance. Repeat the steps to baste the remaining folded pieces to blue print squares. **Make 18**. **2C**

Unit B

To make a Unit B, place a folded piece onto the bottom left corner of a Unit A. Align the raw edges of the folded piece with the raw edges of the blue print square and baste across the bottom using an ⅛" seam allowance. **2D**

Fold the loose corner of the folded piece toward the sewn seam on the bottom. Pin in place. Baste across the left side of the unit using an ⅛" seam allowance. Repeat the steps to baste folded pieces to the units. **Make 10**. **2E**

Unit C

To make the Unit C, select a Unit B. Follow the previous steps to baste folded pieces to the 2 remaining corners. **Make 2**. **2F**

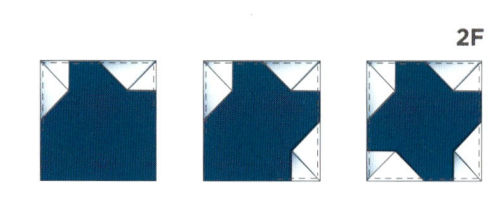

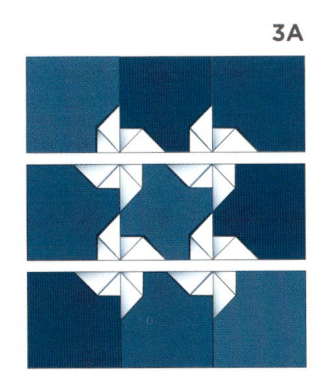

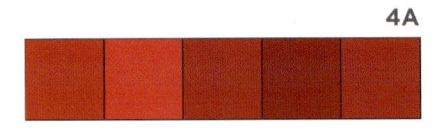

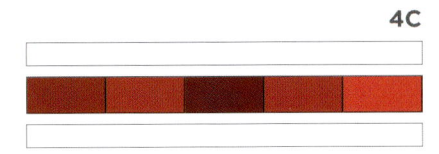

3 make pinwheel blocks

Lay out the units as shown in **3 rows** of **3 units**. Be sure to pay close attention to the orientation of the units. The top row and bottom row will consist of a Unit A, a Unit B, and a Unit A in that order. The middle row will consist of a Unit B, a Unit C, and another Unit B in that order. Using a ¼" seam allowance, sew the units together in 3 rows. Press. Nest the seams and sew the rows together to complete the block. **Make 2**. **3A**

Block Size: 14" unfinished, 13½" finished

4 make stripes

Sew (5) 5" red print squares side-by-side to form a wide stripe. **Make 2** wide stripes. **4A**

Take the (5) 2½" x 5" red print rectangles and sew them end-to-end to create the center stripe. **4B**

Sew a 1¾" x 23" white rectangle to the top and bottom of the center stripe to create a center unit. **4C**

Sew a wide stripe to the top and bottom of the center unit to complete the stripe unit. **4D**

5 arrange & sew

Lay out the table runner as shown in the diagram on page 210. Sew a pinwheel block to either end of the stripe unit.

6 quilt & bind

Layer the table runner with batting and backing, then quilt. **Note:** Be sure to quilt around the pinwheels so that they remain 3-dimensional.

See Construction Basics (pg. 238) for binding instructions.

1. Place a folded piece onto the bottom right corner of a 5" blue print square and align the raw edges. Baste across the right side using an ⅛" seam allowance.

2. Fold the loose corner of the folded piece toward the sewn seam on the right. Pin in place. Baste across the bottom of the square using an ⅛" seam allowance. Make 18.

3. To make a Unit B, place a folded piece onto the bottom left corner of a Unit A. Align the raw edges and baste across the bottom using an ⅛" seam allowance.

4. Fold the loose corner of the folded piece toward the sewn seam on the bottom. Pin in place. Baste across the left side of the unit. Make 10.

5. To make the Unit C, select a Unit B. Follow the previous steps to baste folded pieces to the 2 remaining corners. Make 2.

6. Lay out 4 of Unit A, 4 of Unit B, and 1 Unit C as shown in 3 rows of 3 units. Be sure to pay close attention to the orientation of the units. Sew the units together in 3 rows. Press. Sew the rows together to complete the block. Make 2.

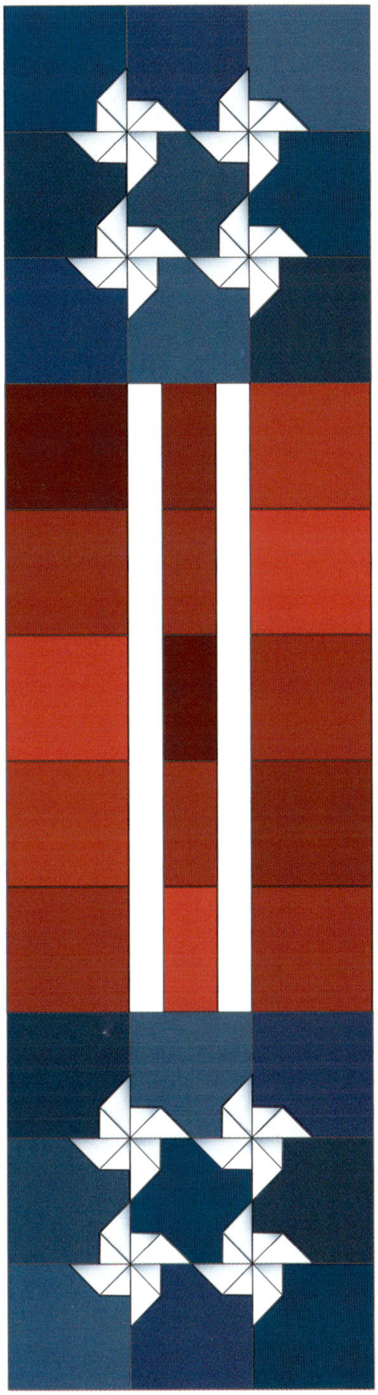

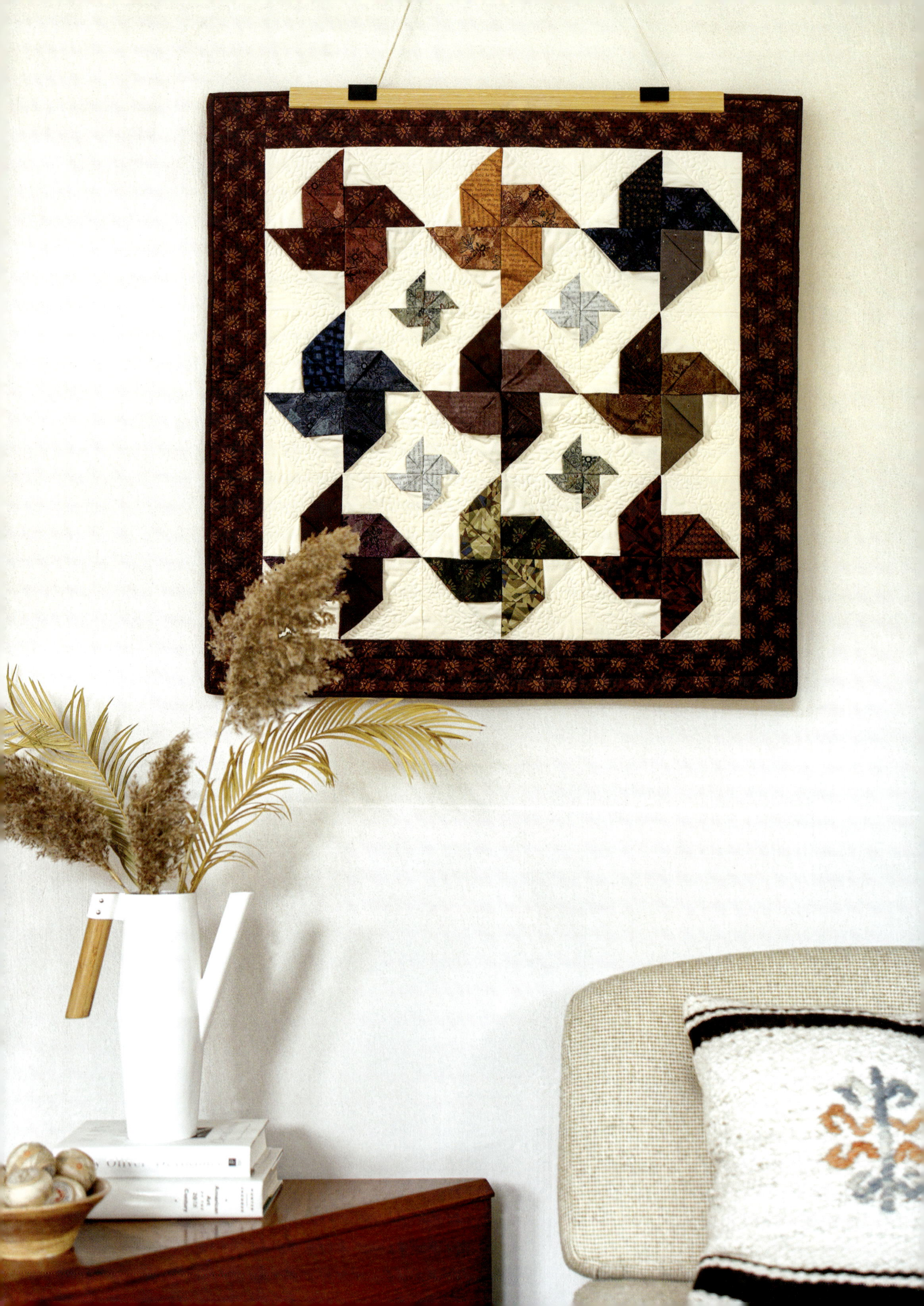

Pinwheel Patch
Natalie's Play

Natalie creates a charming wall hanging with 3D pinwheels in two different sizes to add plenty of cheer to your home decor. Pinwheels add a pop of color to your design. These clever 3D pinwheels are visually and texturally appealing to this darling wall hanging, plus they're so easy to make!

materials

WALL HANGING SIZE
33″ x 33″

BLOCK SIZE
9½″ unfinished, 9″ finished

PROJECT TOP
1 package 5″ print squares
1 package 5″ background squares

BORDER
½ yard

BINDING
½ yard

BACKING
1¼ yards

SAMPLE PROJECT
Scrap Happy by One Sister Designs for Henry Glass

1 sort & cut

Sort your package of 5" print squares into 10 sets of 4 squares of similar colors. Set the 2 remaining print squares along with (6) 5" background squares aside for another project.

Choose 1 set of print squares to use for the small pinwheels. Cut each square of your chosen set in half horizontally and vertically to create (4) 2½" squares for a **total of (16)** 2½" print squares. Set these aside for the moment.

2 make large pinwheel units

Fold a 5" print square from corner to corner once on the diagonal with wrong sides together and press the crease in place. **2A**

Place the folded piece onto the bottom right corner of a 5" background square. Align the raw edges of the folded piece with the raw edges of the background square. Baste across the right side using an ⅛" seam allowance. (We want this seam allowance to be smaller than usual.) **2B**

Fold the loose corner of the folded piece toward the sewn seam on the right. Pin in place. Baste across the bottom of the square using an ⅛" seam allowance. **2C**

Repeat the steps to fold and baste the remaining matching print squares to background squares to **make 36** units. Keep the units in sets of 4 with similar colors.

3 block construction

Select 1 set of large pinwheel units. Arrange the units as shown. Sew the units together in 2 rows. Press. Nest the seams and sew the rows together to complete the block. **Make 9**. **3A**

Block Size: 9½" unfinished, 9" finished

4 add small pinwheel units

Refer to diagram **4A** to assign your blocks to the positions within the project.

Fold a 2½" print square from corner to corner once on the diagonal with wrong sides together and press the crease in place. Place the folded piece onto the bottom right corner of Block A. Align the raw edges of the folded piece with the raw edges of the block and baste across the right side using an ⅛" seam allowance. **4B**

Fold the loose corner of the folded piece toward the sewn seam on the right. Pin in place. Baste across the bottom of the block using an ⅛" seam allowance. **4C**

Refer back to **4A** for placement of the small pinwheel units. Repeat the steps to fold and baste small pinwheel units in the corners of the blocks. Units A, C, G, and I each have 1 small pinwheel unit to a corner of the block. Units B, D, F, and H each have 2 small pinwheel units added. Unit E has a small pinwheel unit added to all 4 corners of the block.

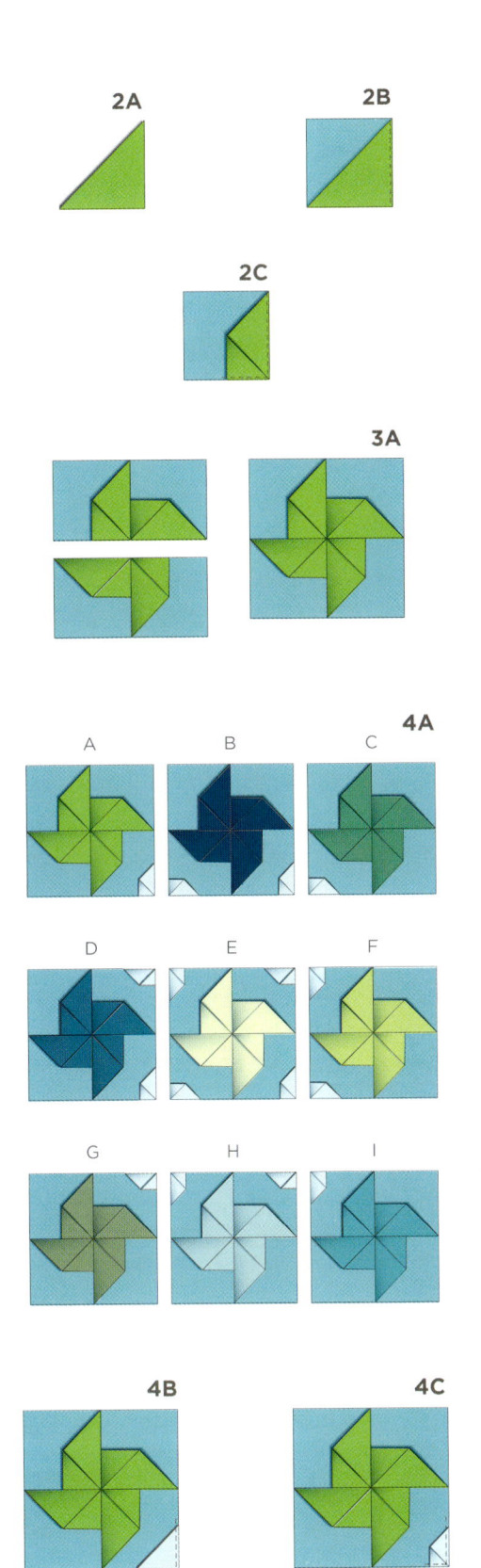

5 arrange & sew

Refer to the diagram on page 217 as needed to lay out the blocks in **3 rows** with each row being made up of **3 blocks**. Be sure to pay close attention to the orientation of the blocks so that the small pinwheel units meet to create small pinwheels. Sew the blocks together in rows. Press. Nest the seams and sew the rows together.

6 border

Cut (4) 3½" strips across the width of the fabric. Sew the strips together to form 1 long strip. Trim the borders from this strip. Refer to Borders (pg. 238) in the Construction Basics to measure, cut and attach the borders. The approximate lengths of the strips are 27½" for the sides and 33½" for the top and bottom.

7 quilt & bind

Layer the wall hanging with batting and backing, then quilt.

Note: You will want to be sure to quilt around the pinwheels so that they remain 3-dimensional.

After quilting is complete, see Construction Basics (pg. 238) for binding instructions.

1. Place the folded piece onto the bottom right corner of a 5" background square, as shown. Baste across the right side using an ⅛" seam allowance.

2. Fold the loose corner of the folded piece toward the sewn seam on the right. Pin in place. Baste across the bottom of the square using an ⅛" seam allowance. Make 36 units.

3. Arrange 4 matching pinwheel units as shown. Sew the units together in 2 rows. Match the seams and sew the rows together to complete the block. Make 9.

4. Place the 2½" folded piece onto the bottom right corner of Block A, as shown. Baste across the right side using an ⅛" seam allowance.

5. Fold the loose corner of the folded piece toward the sewn seam on the right. Pin and baste across the bottom of the block using an ⅛" seam allowance.

217

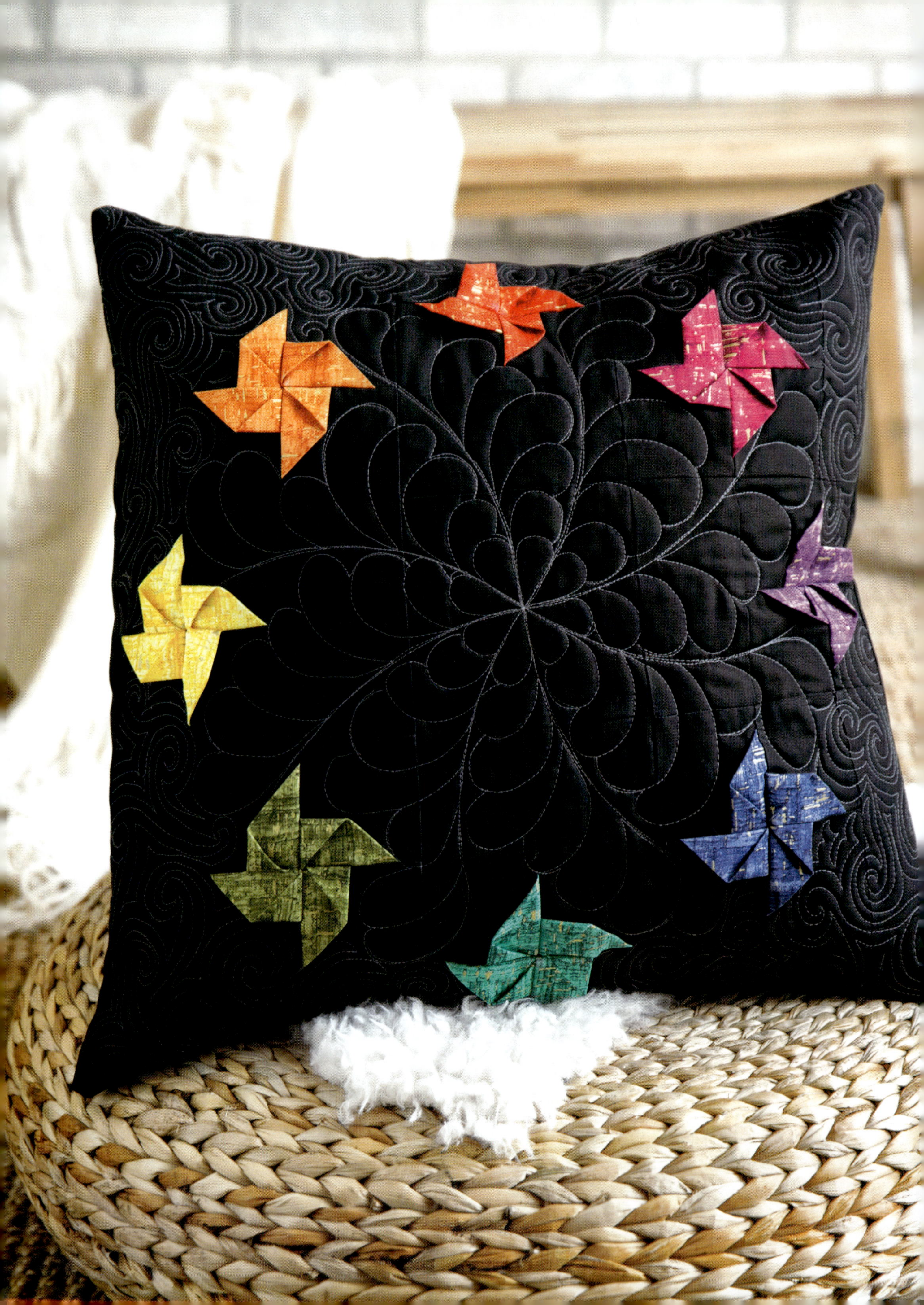

Pinwheel Dance
Misty's Play

Misty makes a pretty pillow for your couch out of a spectrum of colorful 3D pinwheels against a beautiful black background. The result is absolutely stunning! This pretty pillow comes alive with movement and color. It's the perfect accent to an artistic home!

materials

PILLOW SIZE
fits a 20" pillow form

BLOCK SIZE
5½" unfinished, 5" finished

PROJECT SUPPLIES
(8) 5" print squares
1¼ yards background fabric
 - includes pillow back
22½" square of batting

OPTIONAL
¾ yard muslin
Fiberfill

SAMPLE PILLOW
Uncorked Metallic by Another Point of View for Windham Fabrics

1 cut

Cut each 5" print square in half horizontally and vertically to create (4) 2½" squares from each. Set these aside for the moment, keeping matching squares together.

From the background fabric, cut:
- (2) 3" strips across the width of the fabric. Subcut (14) 3" squares from each.

- (1) 14" strip across the width of the fabric. Subcut (2) 14" x 21" rectangles. Set these aside for the pillow back.

- (1) 24½" strip across the width of the fabric. Subcut a 24½" square for the pillow top backing.

From the remaining 24½" piece of background fabric, cut:
- (1) 3" strip across the width of the fabric. Subcut into (4) 3" squares. Add these to the 3" squares cut previously for a **total of (32)** 3" squares.

- (2) 5½" strips across the width of the fabric. Subcut 1 strip into (1) 5½" square and (3) 5½" x 3" rectangles. Subcut the second strip into (5) 5½" x 3" rectangles for a **total of (8)** 5½ x 3" rectangles.

- (1) 8" strip across the width of the fabric. Subcut (4) 8" x 3" rectangles.

2 make the pinwheel blocks

Pick up a set of matching 2½" print squares. Fold each print square from corner to corner once on the diagonal with wrong sides together and press the crease in place. **2A**

Place 1 folded piece onto the bottom right corner of a 3" background square. Align the raw edges of the folded piece with the raw edges of the background square. Baste across the bottom of the square using an ⅛" seam allowance. (We want this seam allowance to be smaller than usual.) **2B**

Fold the loose corner of the folded piece toward the sewn seam on the bottom. Pin in place. Baste the right side of the square using an ⅛" seam allowance. Repeat the steps to fold and sew the remaining print squares to 3" background squares to **make 4** matching quadrants. **2C**

Lay out 4 matching quadrants as shown. Using a ¼" seam allowance, sew the quadrants together in 2 rows. Press. Nest the seams and sew the rows together to complete the block. **Make 8**. **2D 2E**

Block Size: 5½" unfinished, 5" finished

3 arrange & sew

Sew a 5½" x 3" background rectangle to the right side of each block to **make 8** A Units. **3A**

Refer to the diagram on page 223 to assign your blocks to the positions within the pillow top. Sew an 8" x 3" background rectangle to the bottom of the 4 blocks assigned as B Units. **3B**

Referring to the diagram on page 223, lay your pillow top out in 3 rows paying attention to the orientation of each block. Sew a B Unit to both sides of an A Unit for the top and bottom rows. Sew an A Unit to both sides of the 5½" background square for the middle row.

Press. Nest the seams and sew the rows together to complete the pillow top.

4 quilt the pillow top

Layer your pillow top on top of the batting and backing square. Baste and quilt using your favorite methods.

Note: Be sure to quilt around the pinwheels so that they remain 3-dimensional.

After the quilting is complete, square up and trim away all excess batting and backing.

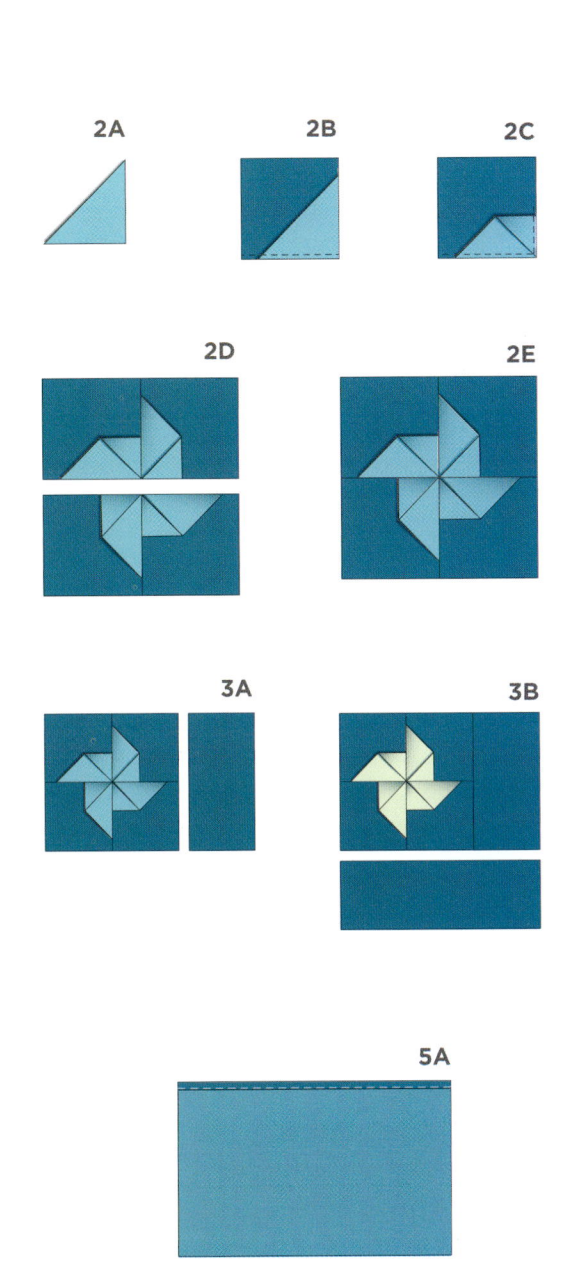

5 make the pillow back

Fold a long edge of a 14" x 21" rectangle over ½" with wrong sides touching. Press. Repeat a second time to enclose the raw edge of the fabric. Topstitch along the folded edge. Repeat to finish 1 long edge of the remaining rectangle to create the 2 pillow back flaps. **5A**

6 finish the pillow

Lay the pillow top with the right side facing up. Lay the 2 pillow back flaps on top, with the right sides facing down, making sure that the pillow back flaps overlap each other by about 4". **6A**

Pin or clip the pillow back flaps to the pillow top. Sew around the perimeter of the pillow using a ½" seam allowance. Finish the edges with a serger or zigzag stitch to prevent fraying.

Clip the corners and turn the pillow right sides out. Insert a pillow form to finish your project.

7 optional pillow insert

Don't have a pillow form handy? Simply cut (2) 21" squares of muslin and sew them together around the perimeter using a ½" seam allowance with right sides facing. Leave an opening about 4-6" wide for turning. Clip the corners and turn right side out. Stuff the pillow with fiberfill and whipstitch the opening closed.

1. Place 1 folded piece onto the bottom right corner of a 3" background square. Align the raw edges. Baste across the bottom of the square using an ⅛" seam allowance.

2. Fold the loose corner of the folded piece toward the sewn seam on the bottom. Pin in place and baste. Make 4 matching quadrants.

3. Lay out 4 matching quadrants as shown. Using a ¼" seam allowance, sew the quadrants together in 2 rows. Press. Nest the seams and sew the rows together to complete the block. Make 8.

4. Sew a 5½" x 3" background rectangle to the right side of each block to make 8 A Units.

5. Refer to the diagram on page 223 to assign your blocks to the positions within the pillow top. Sew an 8" x 3" background rectangle to the bottom of the 4 blocks assigned as B Units.

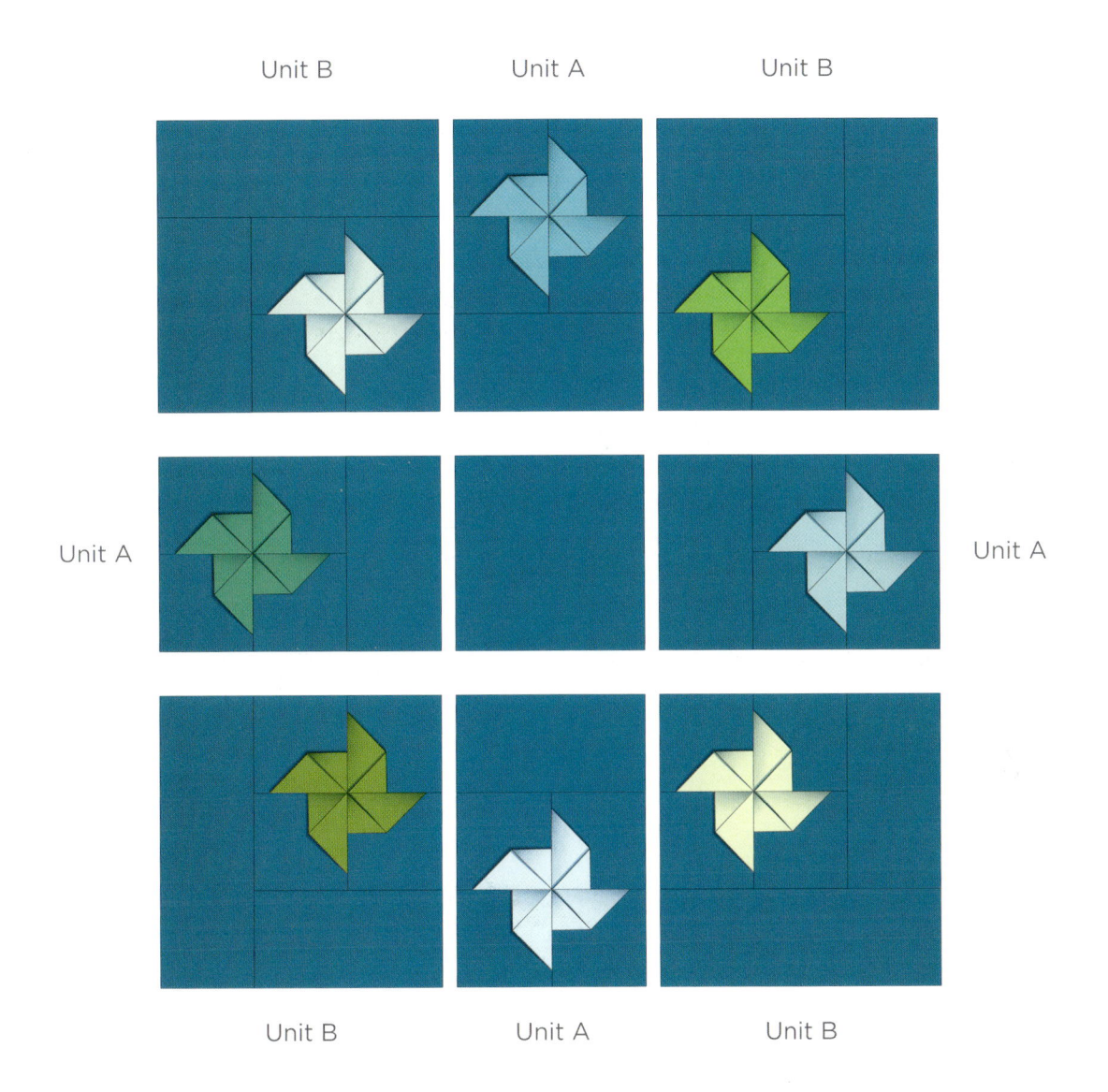

	Unit B	Unit A	Unit B	
Unit A				Unit A
	Unit B	Unit A	Unit B	

223

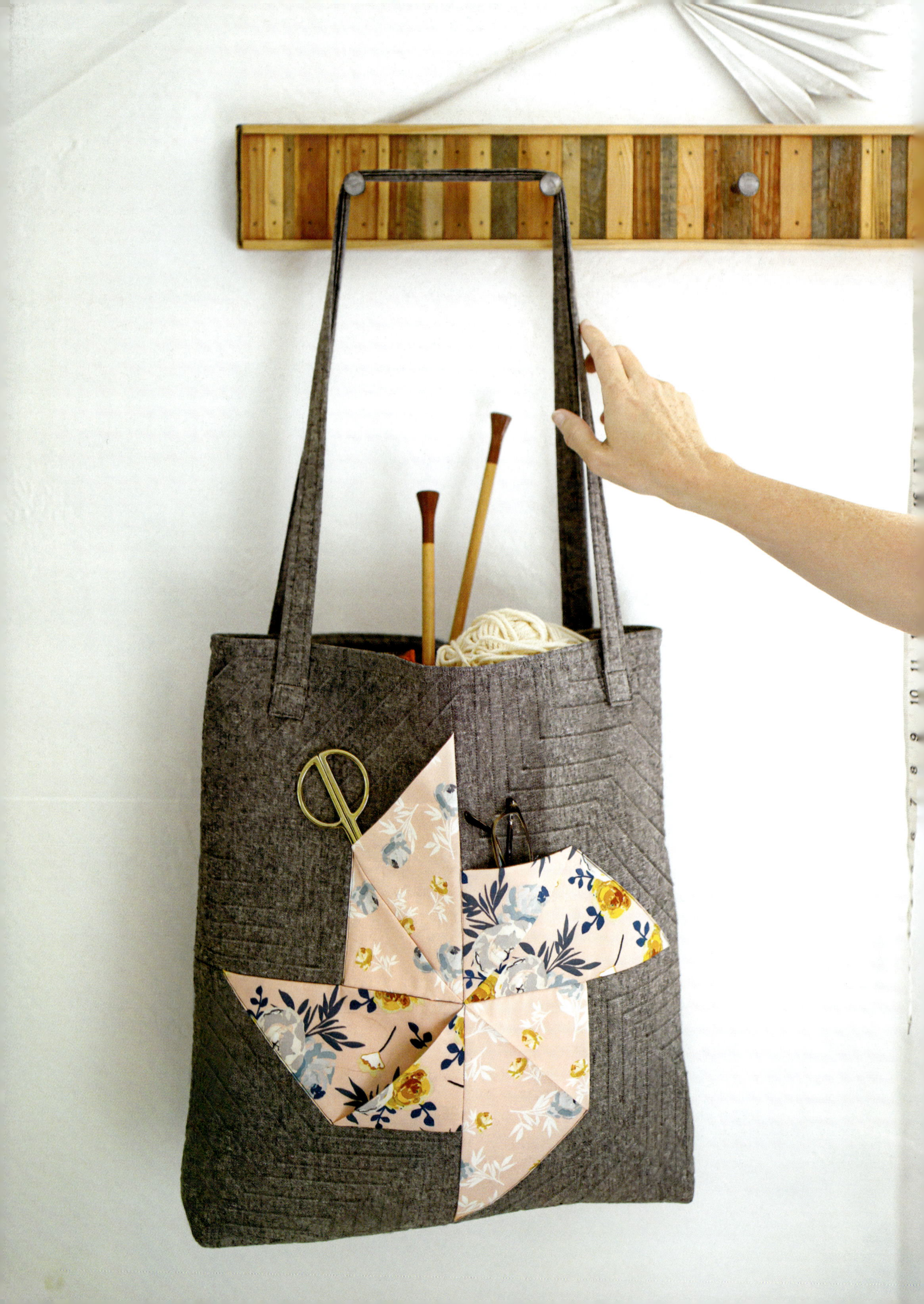

3D Pinwheel Market Tote

materials

BAG SIZE
15½" x 17" x 3"

PROJECT SUPPLIES
(8) 10" print squares
1½ yards of background fabric
In-R-Form Single Sided Fusible Stabilizer
    36" x 58" by Bosal

SAMPLE PROJECT
Blooms and Bobbins by Melissa Mora for Riley Blake

1 cut

Trim each 10" print square to 8".

From the background fabric, cut:
- (1) 19½" strip across the width of the fabric. Subcut (2) 19½" squares.
- (2) 10" strips across the width of the fabric. Subcut (8) 10" squares.
- (2) 4" strips across the width of the fabric. Trim each strip to 39½".

From the foam stabilizer, cut:
- (1) 19½" strip along the **length** of the stabilizer. Subcut (2) 19½" squares.
- (2) ¾" strips along the **length** of the stabilizer. Trim each strip to 37½".

2 make pinwheels

Fold a print square from corner to corner as shown, with wrong sides together, and crease along the fold. **2A**

Fold the bottom left corner to the bottom right as shown and crease the fold. **2B**

Lay the folded piece atop a 10" background square as shown. Pin in place. Baste along the bottom and right sides using an ⅛" seam allowance. Repeat the steps to fold and sew the remaining print squares to 10" background squares. **Make 8**. **2C**

Lay out 4 quadrants for 1 tote side as shown. Using a ¼" seam allowance, sew the quadrants together in 2 rows. Press the seams in opposite directions. Nest the seams and sew the rows together. Press. **Make 2**. **2D 2E**

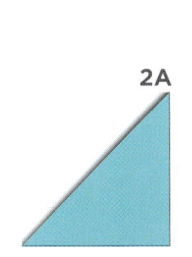

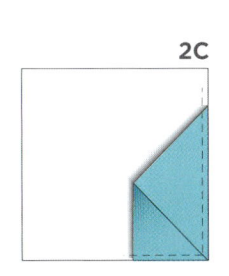

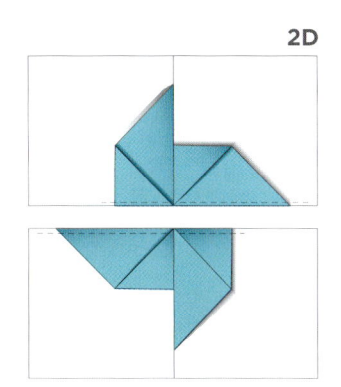

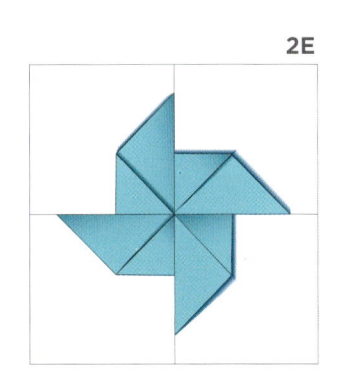

3 quilt

Following the manufacturer's instructions, adhere a foam stabilizer square to the reverse side of each pinwheel.

Quilt along the center seam lines in both directions. Determine which way is up, then quilt along the left side seam of the upper left pinwheel blade, backstitching at both ends. This will create a pocket. Sew along the diagonal seams of each remaining pinwheel blade. This will create a second pocket on the upper right blade. Repeat for the other pinwheel. **3A**

4 make the bag & lining

Lay 1 quilted pinwheel atop the other, right sides together. Make sure both pockets are upright. Sew along 1 side, across the bottom, and up the other side using a ½" seam allowance. **4A**

Open 1 corner of the bag by pulling the sides in opposite directions and making a point with the end seam running vertically down the center. Measure and mark 1½" from the corner point. Line the 45° mark of your ruler with the angled edge of the corner and draw a horizontal line at the mark previously made. Sew along this line to box the corner, backstitching twice at the beginning and end. Repeat to box the other corner. **Note:** You may choose to trim the excess fabric ¼" from the sewn seams. **4B**

In the same manner, sew the (2) 19½" background squares together, right sides facing, along the bottom and 2 sides with a ½" seam allowance. This will be your lining. Repeat the previous directions to box both corners of the lining. **4C 4D**

5 make straps

Press (1) 4" x 39½" background strip in half lengthwise, wrong sides facing. Open and press each long edge to meet the center crease. **5A**

Center a ¾" x 37½" stabilizer strip inside the fold along the center crease. **5B**

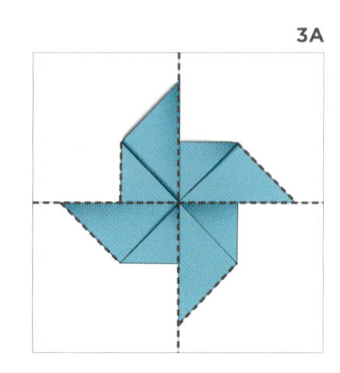

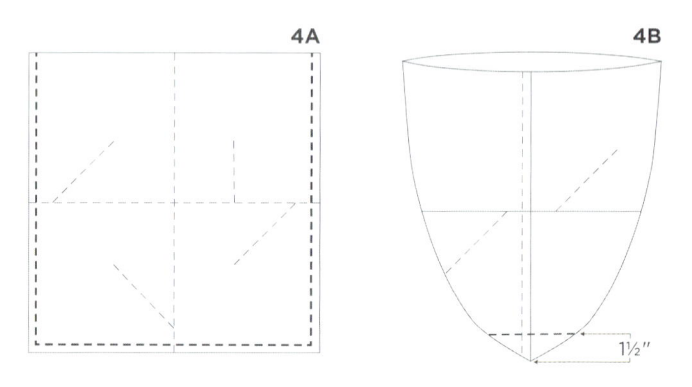

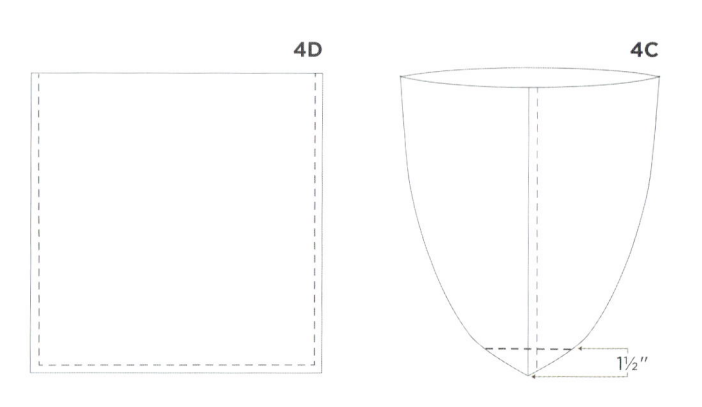

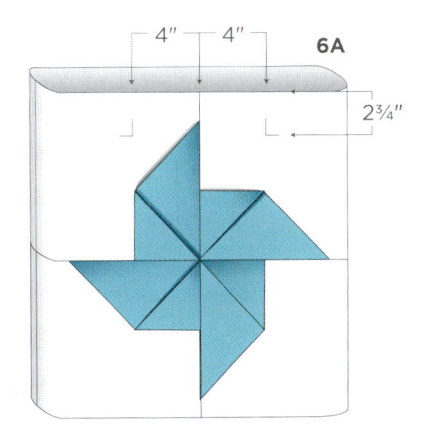

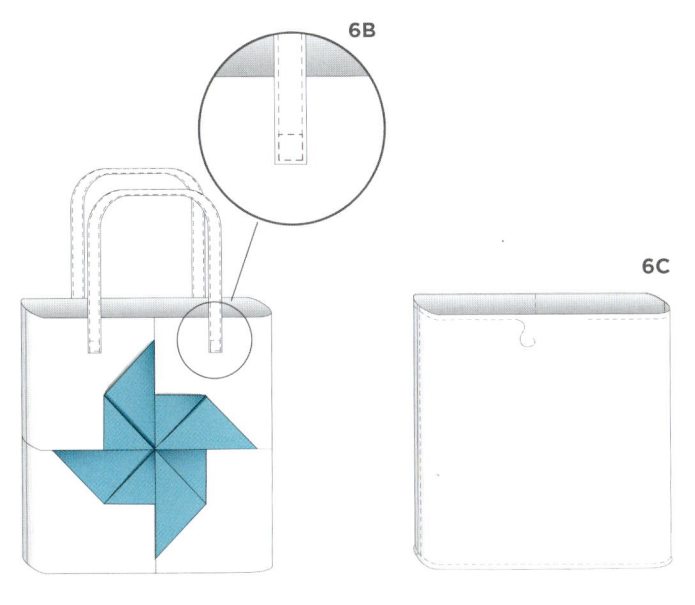

Fold the outer edges back to the center and fold the strip in half around the stabilizer. Topstitch along both long edges, backstitching at both ends. Press. **Make 2**.

Note: There will be 1″ on either end of the straps that will not have the stabilizer. **5C**

6 bag assembly

Turn your pinwheel bag right side out. Measure and mark 4″ from either side of the center seam along the top edge of 1 side. Measure and mark 2¾″ from the top edge. **6A**

Fold 1″ of both ends of 1 strap under and pin to the outside of the marks as shown. Attach 1 end of the strap to the bag by sewing a 1″ square, backstitching at the beginning and end. Repeat for the opposite end of the strap. **6B**

Repeat the steps to measure, mark, and attach the second strap to the other side.

Pin the straps to the outside of the pinwheel bag, away from the top edge. Slide the pinwheel bag into the lining with the right sides facing and match up the top edges. Pin as needed. Sew the bag and lining together along the top edge using a ¼″ seam allowance, leaving a 4″ space for turning. **6C**

Turn the bag right sides out. Turn the edges of the opening in, press, and pin. Topstitch less than ¼″ away from the top edge to enclose the opening, backstitching at both ends. Unpin the straps and you're ready to head to market!

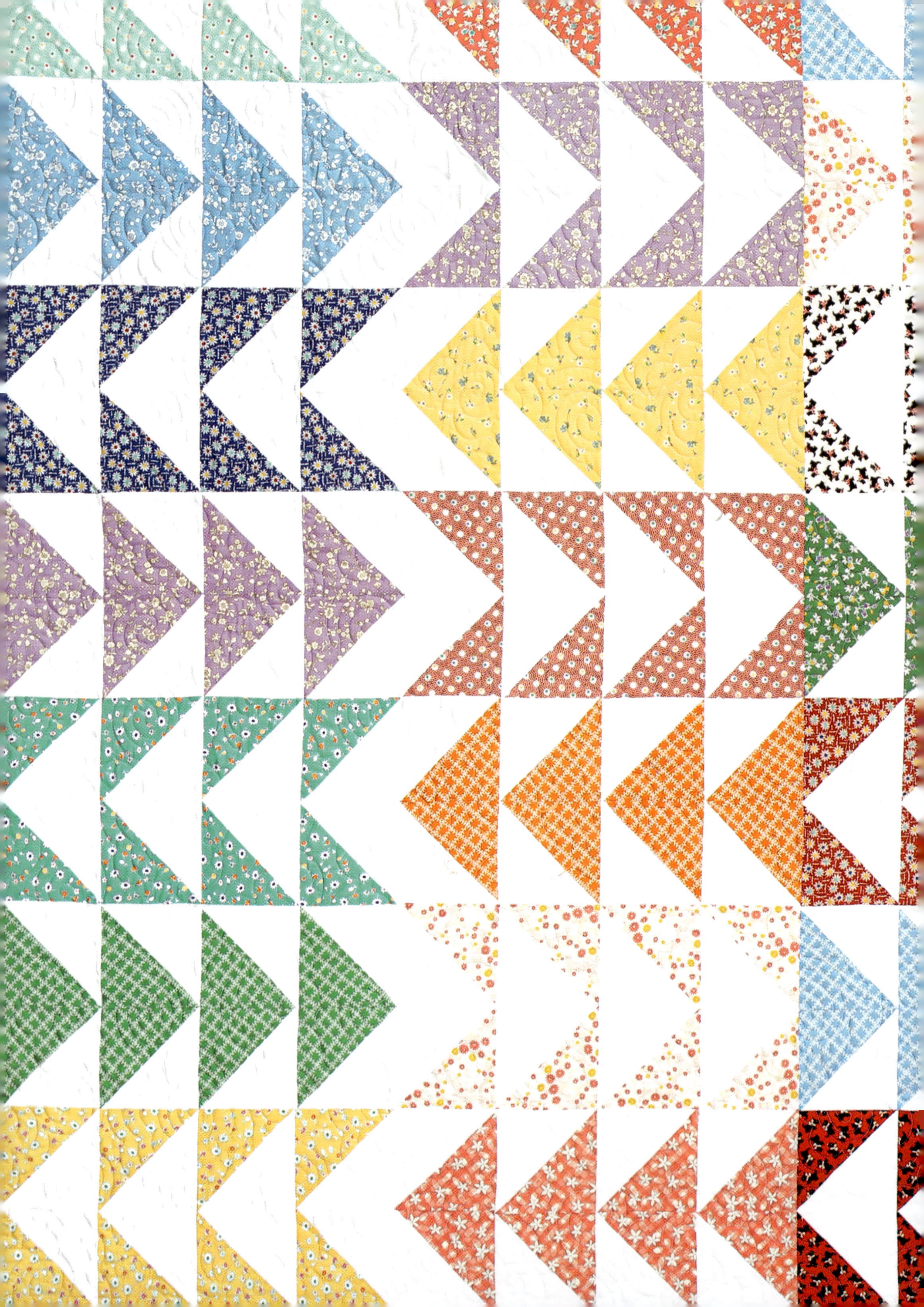

Reference

DOUBLE SQUARE STARS TRIPLE PLAY

156 Double Square Star Four-Path

162 Double Square Star Table Runner

168 Sashed Double Square Star

video tutorial: **msqc.co/doublesquarestar**

DRUNKARD'S PATH TRIPLE PLAY

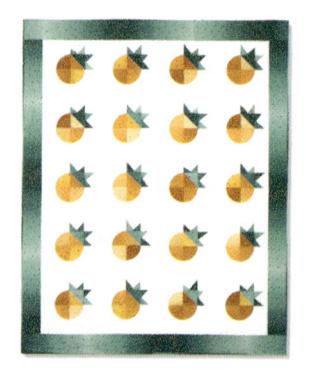

50 Tropical Paradise

56 River Path

62 Morning Glory

video tutorial: **msqc.co/drunkardspath**

FLYING GEESE TRIPLE PLAY

104 Every Which Way But Goose

110 West Wind

116 Gaggle of Geese

122 Finished is Better Than Perfect

video tutorial: msqc.co/flyinggeese

HALF-HEXAGON TRIPLE PLAY

130 Half-Hexagon Boats and Braids

136 Half-Hexi Links

142 Half-Hexi Whirligigs

148 Half-Hexi Denim Apron

video tutorial: msqc.co/halfhexi

OHIO STAR TRIPLE PLAY

184 Ohio Star Celebration Table Runner

190 Blue Ribbon Ohio Star

196 Ohio Starlight Mini

video tutorial: **msqc.co/ohiostar**

3D PINWHEELS TRIPLE PLAY

206 Pinwheel Toss

212 Pinwheel Patch

218 Pinwheel Dance

224 3D Pinwheel Market Tote

video tutorial: **msqc.co/3dpinwheels**

TULIP FIELDS TRIPLE PLAY

72 Tulip Time

78 Tulip Fields

84 Tulip Garden

90 Mini Tulip Crossbody Bag

video tutorial: **msqc.co/tulipfields**

WONKY STARS TRIPLE PLAY

20 Cottage Stars

26 Evening Stars

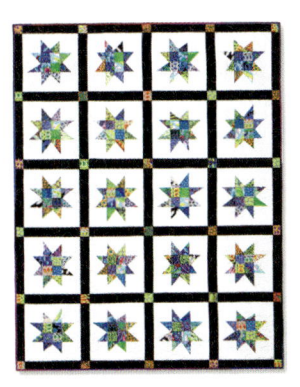

32 Luminary

video tutorial: **msqc.co/wonkystar**

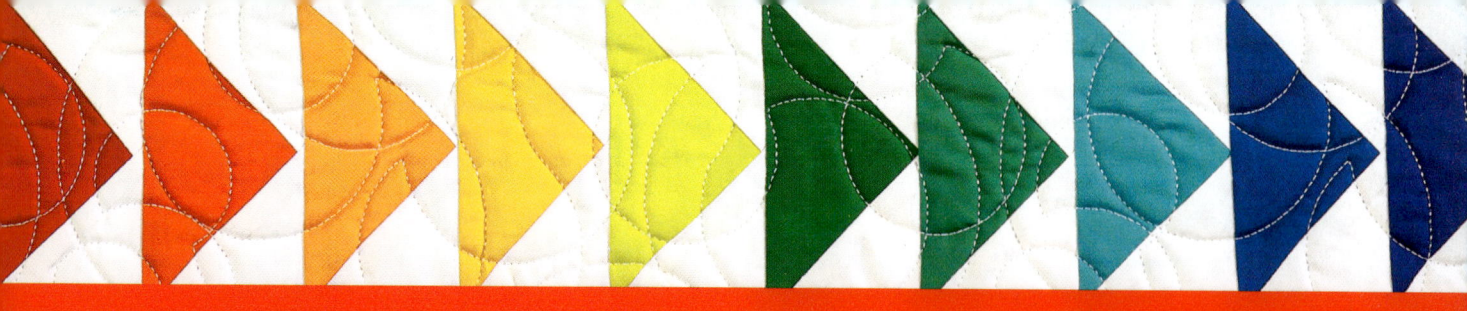

ARTICLES

8   What's a Triple Play?

10   Quilting Guide

14   Precuts

38   **Jenny Doan:** Enjoying the Journey One Stitch at a Time

94   **Natalie Earnheart:** Finding Inspiration in Unlikely Places

174   **Misty Doan:** Imperfection is Beautiful

ACKNOWLEDGEMENTS

From the start, Triple Play has been a family affair. We have so much fun together and I want to, first and foremost, thank my daughter, Natalie Earnheart, and my daughter-in-law, Misty Doan, for all they do. Together we're able to come up with so many new ideas! I also want to thank our Senior Education Manager, Liz Gubernatis, who brings our tutorials to life with her enthusiasm and imagination along with our personal assistant, Cathleen Tripp. She doesn't always want to be thanked, but there it is!

I want to thank our incredible pattern team, Jessica Toye, Kimberly Forman, and Denise Lane, for transforming our designs into clear and precise patterns that you can easily recreate. And then there's the sewing team: Courtenay Hughes, Carol Henderson, and Janice Richardson, who take these designs are recreate them beautifully in Block Magazine. They also provide support for each of us. And we couldn't do it without the Machine Quilting team. They add the perfect finishing touch to all our projects! A big thank you goes to our video team, they are amazing and make sure that we look and sound right, which can be a challenge at times! They catch all our good angles and polish our tutorials to make them the best they can be.

As always, thank you to the tireless Block Magazine team who has worked so hard to put out this beautiful book. Thank you to Christine Ricks, our fearless Creative Director, and the rest of the creative team: Tyler MacBeth, Gunnar Forstrom, Mike Brunner, Lauren Dorton, Jennifer Dowling, Dustin Weant, and Nichole Spravzoff. Their gorgeous photography, designs, and writing make each publication truly shine.

Finally, I want to thank you, all the quilters who have supported Missouri Star over the years and have watched and subscribed to our Triple Play tutorials on YouTube. We couldn't do it without you!

Templates

Missouri Star Templates are available online at msqc.co The printable version can be found here: **MSQC.CO/TRIPLEPLAYTEMPLATES**

Finished is Better than Perfect

All templates are shown at 100% and are reversed for your convenience.

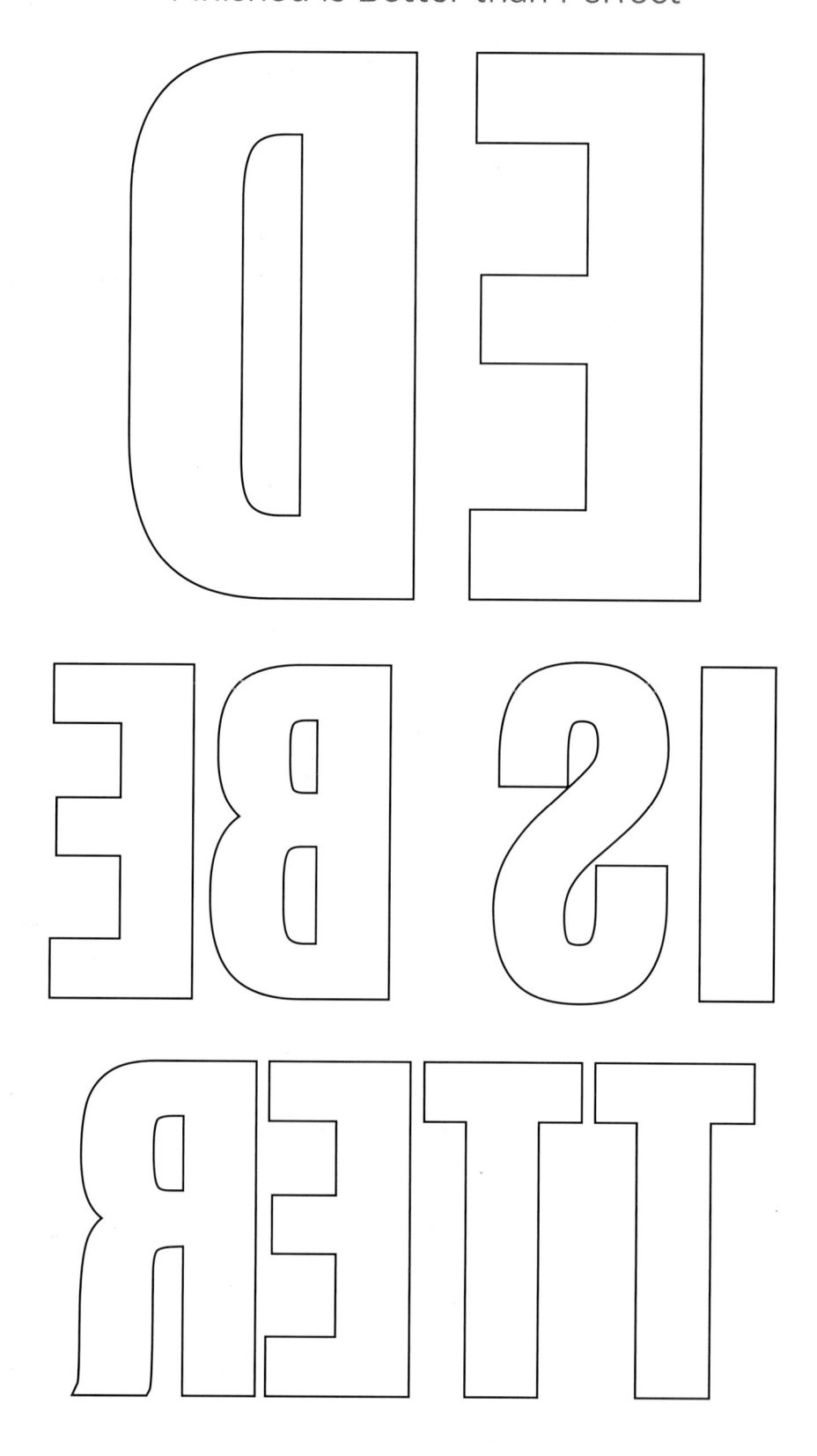

Finished is Better than Perfect

Finished is Better than Perfect

THAN PERFECT!

Construction Basics

General Quilting

- All seams are ¼" unless directions specify differently.
- Cutting instructions are given at the point when cutting is required.
- Precuts are not prewashed, therefore do not prewash other fabrics in the project.
- All strips are cut width of fabric.
- Remove all selvages.

Press Seams

- Use a steam iron on the cotton setting.
- Press the seam just as it was sewn right sides together. This "sets" the seam.
- With dark fabric on top, lift the dark fabric and press back.
- The seam allowance is pressed toward the dark side. Some patterns may direct otherwise for certain situations.
- Follow pressing arrows in the diagrams when indicated.
- Press toward borders. Pieced borders may need otherwise.
- Press diagonal seams open on binding to reduce bulk.

Borders

- Always measure the quilt top 3x before cutting borders.
- Start measuring about 4" in from each side and through the center vertically.
- Take the average of those 3 measurements.
- Cut 2 border strips to that size. Piece strips together if needed.
- Attach 1 to either side of the quilt.
- Position the border fabric on top as you sew. The feed dogs can act like rufflers. Having the border on top will prevent waviness and keep the quilt straight.
- Repeat this process for the top and bottom borders, measuring the width 3 times.
- Include the newly attached side borders in your measurements.
- Press toward the borders.

Binding

find a video tutorial at: www.msqc.co/006

- Use 2½" strips for binding.
- Sew strips end-to-end into 1 long strip with diagonal seams, aka the plus sign method (next). Press the seams open.
- Fold in half lengthwise, wrong sides together, and press.
- The entire length should equal the outside dimension of the quilt plus 15" - 20."

Plus Sign Method

find a video tutorial at: www.msqc.co/001

- Lay 1 strip across the other as if to make a plus sign, right sides together.
- Sew from top inside to bottom outside corners crossing the intersections of fabric as you sew.
- Trim excess to ¼" seam allowance.
- Press seam open.

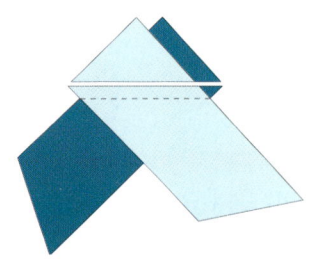

Attach Binding

- Match raw edges of folded binding to the quilt top edge.
- Leave a 10" tail at the beginning.
- Use a ¼" seam allowance.
- Start in the middle of a long straight side.

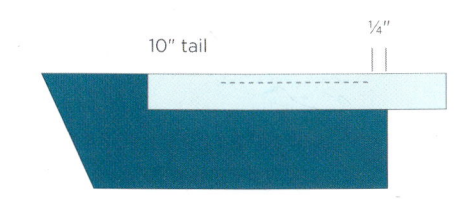

Miter Corners

- Stop sewing ¼" before the corner.
- Move the quilt out from under the presser foot.
- Clip the threads.
- Flip the binding up at a 90° angle to the edge just sewn.
- Fold the binding down along the next side to be sewn, aligning raw edges.
- The fold will lie along the edge just completed.
- Begin sewing on the fold.

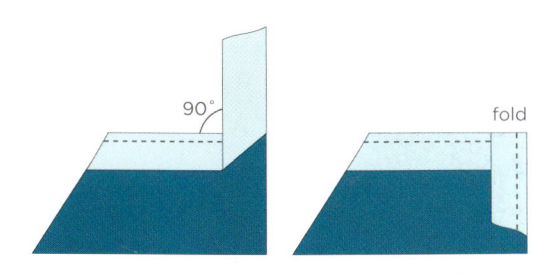

Close Binding

MSQC recommends The Binding Tool from TQM Products to finish binding perfectly every time.

- Stop sewing when you have 12" left to reach the start.
- Where the binding tails come together, trim the excess leaving only 2½" of overlap.
- It helps to pin or clip the quilt together at the 2 points where the binding starts and stops. This takes the pressure off of the binding tails while you work.
- Use the plus sign method to sew the 2 binding ends together, except this time when making the plus sign, match the edges. Using a pencil, mark your sewing line because you won't be able to see where the corners intersect. Sew across.

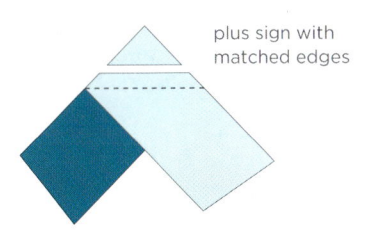

- Trim off the excess; press the seam open.
- Fold in half wrong sides together, and align all raw edges to the quilt top.
- Sew this last binding section to the quilt. Press.
- Turn the folded edge of the binding around to the back of the quilt and tack into place with an invisible stitch or machine stitch if you wish.